THEORETICAL ISSUES
IN NATURAL LANGUAGE PROCESSING

Yorick Wilks
Editor

 LAWRENCE ERLBAUM ASSOCIATES, PUBLISHERS
1989   Hillsdale, New Jersey   Hove and London

Lawrence Erlbaum Associates, Inc., Publishers
365 Broadway
Hillsdale, New Jersey 07642

Library of Congress Cataloging-in-Publication Data

Theoretical issues in natural language processing / Yorick Wilks,
    editor.
        p.   cm.
Includes bibliographic references.
ISBN 0-8058-0183-9. -- ISBN 0-8058-0184-7 (pbk.)
1. Natural language processing (Computer science) I. Wilks,
Yorick, 1939-   .
QA76.9.N38T44   1989
006.3'5--dc20   89-23407
                                                          CIP

PRINTED IN THE UNITED STATES OF AMERICA
10 9 8 7 6 5 4 3 2 1

Table of Contents

Chapter 3: Connectionist and other parallel approaches to natural language processing

Chapter 4: Discourse theory, goals, and speech acts

Chapter 5: Why has theoretical NLP made so little progress?

Chapter 6: Formal versus common sense semantics

Chapter 9: Natural language generation

CONTRIBUTORS

Robert A. Amsler,
Bell Communications Research, Morristown, NJ 70960

Douglas Appelt,
SRI International, Menlo Park, CA 94025

Larry Birnbaum,
Yale University, New Haven, CT 06520

Branimir K. Boguraev,
University of Cambridge, Cambridge CB2 3QG, England

Eugene Charniak,
Brown University, Providence, RI 02912

Garrison W. Cottrell,
University of California at San Diego, La Jolla, CA 92093

Deborah A. Dahl,
Burroughs Co., Paoli, PA 19301

Lynn Fainsilber,
University of Washington, Seattle, WA 98195

Brian Falkenhainer,
Xerox Palo Alto Research Center, Palo Alto, CA 94304

Gerald Gazdar,
University of Sussex, Brighton, England

Dedre Gentner,
University of Illinois, Champaign, IL 61820

Bradley A. Goodman,
BBN Laboratories Inc., Cambridge, MA 02238

Jerry R. Hobbs,
SRI International, Menlo Park, CA 94025

David Israel,
SRI International, Menlo Park, CA 94025

Aravind K. Joshi,
University of Pennsylvania, Philadelphia, PA 19104

Judy Kegl,
Swarthmore College, Swarthmore, PA 19081

Amichai Kronfeld,
SRI International, Menlo Park, CA 94025

Wendy G. Lehnert,
University of Massachusetts, Amherst, MA 01003

James L. McClelland,
Carnegie-Mellon University, Pittsburgh, PA 15213

David D. McDonald,
University of Massachusetts at Amherst, MA 01003

Andrew Ortony,
University of Illinois, Urbana-Champaign, IL 61801

C. Raymond Perrault,
SRI International, Menlo Park, CA 94025

Edwin Plantinga,
University of Toronto, Toronto, Ontario, Canada M5S 1A4,
and Redeemer College, Ancaster, Ontario Canada L9G 3N6

Steve Pulman,
University of Cambridge, Cambridge CB2 3QG, England

Janice Skorstad,
University of Illinois at Urbana-Champaign, IL 61801

Norman K. Sondheimer,
University of Southern California, Marina del Rey, CA
90292

Karen Sparck Jones,
University of Cambridge, Cambridge CB2 3QG, England

Donald E. Walker,
Bell Communications Research, Morristown, NJ 07960

David L. Waltz,
Thinking Machines Corporation, Brandeis University, MA 02142
Robert Wilensky,
University of California, Berkeley, CA 94720
Yorick Wilks,
New Mexico State University, Las Cruces, NM 88003

INTRODUCTION

Yorick Wilks

Natural Language Processing is now an industrial process and product as well as a form of theoretical enquiry. Indeed, with the industrial growth of Artificial Intelligence and Expert Systems there is now a danger of difficult and resistant theoretical problems being ignored or pushed aside while products are generated and sold. It is therefore very timely for those in theoretical research in the area of natural language processing and understanding to stand back and survey the partial solutions available to problems in this field, the blind alleys that have been closed off, including some that had been closed for many years but have now been declared reopened, as well as the new theories and representations that have been developed and published since the last such inventory was taken.

This book had its origin in the third of the Tinlap Workshops, held in Las Cruces, New Mexico, in January 1987. The role of these workshops is not to set out and discuss particular applications and implementations of natural language processing systems, but to concentrate on the underlying issues, and to compare solutions and constraints across disciplinary borderlines by drawing into a workshop theoreticians in artificial intelligence, logic, psychology, philosophy and linguistics. The previous Tinlap Workshops were able to crystallize, in the published statements of position from panelists, particular discussions and disputes within the field; and a measure of this is the degree to which those published volumes have continued to sell and to be referenced in the general literature of the field.

The aim of the third Tinlap was again to capture the state of things at the present moment, after a period which had seen a revival of interest in syntactic approaches to analysis; a new and pressing concern with aspects of parallel processing and their role in language understanding; a shift in the aspects of semantics and pragmatics that are of most concern to researchers, as well as an underlying worry that the field has not progressed in the linear fashion that was hoped for at the time of the first workshop in 1975.

The Origins of Tinlap

The first Tinlap was held at MIT in 1975 and was designed with the above goals in mind, but it was also to provide a forum free of the conventional tedium of too many presented papers. The third followed that pattern (as did Tinlap2 at the University of Illinois): the workshop consisted entirely of panel sessions consisting of invited speakers only, and of figures who have made significant contributions to the field. The Chair of each session, in consultation with the members invited, set out a range of questions that express current concerns in the panel's sub-area. The panel members (including the Chair) then provided statements of position not exceeding two thousand words. Those papers were taken as read at the panel sessions at the workshop, and the formal sessions themselves concentrated on interactions, discussion and disagreements among panel members, with the Chair seeking whatever consensus there was and allowing participation of the audience. This book contains revised versions of some of those papers, usually longer than their originals, along with some of the better dialogue that followed.

The Association for Computational Linguistics was involved in planning for the workshop at an early stage, and it, along with the National Science Foundation, the American Association of Artificial Intelligence, and the Association of Computing Machinery, helped provide generous funding for the workshop, as did the Computing Research Laboratory at New Mexico State University, which hosted the original event. All that help is acknowledged here, as are substantial word processing contributions in the preparation of this book by Pat Puckett and the indispensable editorial assistance of Sylvia Candelaria de Ram.

Some Helpful Acronyms

AI:	Artificial Intelligence
ATN:	Augmented Transition Network
CFG:	Context-Free Grammar
CG:	Categorial Grammar
CUG:	Categorial Unification Grammar
CL:	Computational Linguistics
DCG:	Definite Clause Grammar
FOPC:	First Order Predicate Calculus
FUG:	Functional Unification Grammar
GB:	Government and Binding Theory
GPSG:	Generalized Phrase Structure Grammar
HG:	Head Grammar
HPSG:	Head Driven Phrase Structure Grammar
KR:	Knowledge Representation
KRL:	Knowledge Representation Language
LDOCE:	*Longman's Dictionary of Contemporary English*
LFG:	Lexical Functional Grammar
MT:	Machine Translation
NLP:	Natural Language Processing
OALD:	*Oxford Advanced Learner's Dictionary*
OED:	*Oxford Universal English Dictionary on Historical Principles*
PATR:	Parsing and Translation
PDP:	Parallel Distributed Processing
TAG:	Tree Adjoining Grammar

THE QUESTIONS TO THE PANELS

I. Words and World Representations

How have these suddenly become more interesting? Do they offer a way through from the old "primitive" dispute, and do they offer a way out from having to separate world and linguistic knowledge? How does what we know about words fit into the language understanding and generation process, and is that different for understanding and generation?

II. Unification and the New Grammatism

How far does this really differ from the Context-Free Grammar position of the Sixties? Does it yet have any empirical successes in terms of working systems? To what extent are these grammatical formalisms motivated by processing considerations?

To what extent are these processing claims substantiated? Are we converging to some class of formalisms that are relevant for processing and, if so, how can this class be characterized in a theoretical manner?

What are the prospects of these types of formalism becoming the basis for future natural language processing research? Has the processing paradigm now really fundamentally influenced linguistics? Do processing considerations and results show that such systems, when implemented, can be neutral between analysis and production?

Has everyone really been doing unification for decades and just found out? Is it a real advance or just a Hollywood term?

III. Connectionist and other Parallel Approaches to Natural Language Processing

Is Natural Language Processing inevitably committed to a symbolic form of representation? Can syntactic, semantic, or world knowledge be represented in that paradigm if taken seriously? What parts of current Computational Linguistics will fare worst if there turn out to be significant empirical advances with connectionist parsing? Are there any yet (i.e., how far do we trust simulations programmed only on serial machines)?

What new approaches to syntax, semantics, or pragmatics will be needed if this approach turns out to be empirically justified? Will it just bring back all the old views associated with associationism, and will they be changed in the journey? Is parallel parsing just a new implementation or a real paradigm shift?

IV. Discourse Theory and Speech Acts

Is there yet any serious discourse theory with testable computational and empirical consequences? To what phenomena ought a processing theory of discourse understanding/generation address itself that are not already being attended to currently? What aspects of discourse are language problems and which are general AI or Knowledge Representation problems? What makes a theory of discourse a processing theory? Does spoken language affect one's theory of discourse?

Is there any real hope that we will be able to recognize the plans/goals, etc. of a speaker? How much of conversation is carried on through the linguistic window anyway? Do current theories of text and dialogue discourse mesh, and should they?

V. Why has Theoretical NLP Made so Little Progress?

Has Computational Linguistics advanced in this respect since Tinlap2 in 1978? What can Natural Language Processing systems do today in the light of what we would have predicted at Tinlap2? Why are we no nearer to a common notation for systems since Knowledge Representation Language—would be helped by Computational Linguistics textbooks geared to particular programming languages (one such is now in preparation)? Is it a case of just cycling through ranges of obscure syntactic and semantic formalisms (and then rediscovering them every 10 years or so)? Are there serious problems about the overall cognitive paradigm being applied to Natural Language Processing? Are there any serious alternatives to the current paradigms, and what would they imply to Natural Language Processing research directions and goals?

VI. Formal Versus Commonsense Semantics.

What does Montague grammar or situation semantics have to say to Computational Linguistics? Can we distinguish the good parts from what is bad and useless? For what Natural Language Processing applications might these formalisms be particularly appropriate? What have such theories chosen to ignore, in terms of data or intuitions? How are they to be computed: compositionally, randomly? How well can such formalisms mesh with the rest of language representation processes, e.g., discourse and pragmatic analysis?

VII. Reference: The Interaction of Language and the World.

When is a noun phrase a referring expression? How does the meaning of a noun phrase contribute to the success of a referring act? How can a "wrong" description be useful for referring? Is there any role for Russell's analysis of descriptions in a pragmatic theory of referring?

What does it mean for a hearer to identify a referent? What is the relationship between knowing who or what something is and referent identification?

Is referring to events and situations inherently different from referring to material objects? What identification criteria are applicable to events and situations?

VIII. *Metaphor*

How relevant are the philosophical, linguistic, and psychological literatures on metaphor? Can any of the recent work in dialogue, planning, and speech acts be applied to understanding metaphor? Are existing knowledge formalisms, (e.g., conceptual dependency, scripts, semantic networks, KLONE) adequate for metaphor? If not, why not? Given that the recognition of metaphor involves matching together large-scale knowledge structures, are there any existing procedures that do this adequately? How can this matching be done? How might we record the degree of match? Are there additional types of processing necessary for recognizing metaphor?

How should metaphor be represented in semantic representations of text? Are there situations when a metaphor should be "resolved," and others when its tension should remain? How can we recognize those situations?

IX. *Natural Language Generation*

Will the demands of language production bring AI, theoretical linguistics (and of course Computational Linguistics) closer together than the demands of comprehension did in the past? Is there anything special about generation?

Does generation constrain problems differently from understanding, in that it would not matter if some high-powered machine could understand things no human could say, but it would matter if the same machine generated them? Are knowledge structures, of the world as much as language, the same or different for understanding and generation? What is the relation between the message the system wants to convey and its lexical, syntactic, etc. abilities to do it?

- What is the relationship between NL comprehension and generation?

    Is there inherently an asymmetry between comprehension and generation?

    Is comprehension more heuristic than generation?

- Will the demands of language generation bring AI and linguistics closer together than the demands of comprehension did in the past?

    Is there something special about generation?

- Does generation constrain the problem differently from comprehension in that it would not matter if some high-powered machine could comprehend things no human could say, but would matter if the same machine generated them?

- How should the generation and comprehension capabilities of a system be matched? By looking at the sentences or texts a system generates, the user may ascribe comprehension capabilities to the system, which the system may or may not have. In other words how will generation affect user's behavior with respect to the input he/she provides to the system?
- Are knowledge structures of the world as much as language, the same or different for comprehension and generation?
- How does one control for syntactic choice and lexical choice?
- What is the status of different grammatical formalisms with respect to generation? Should the formalism be the same for generation as for comprehension?

Chapter 1

Words & World Representations

Chapter 1

THE WORLD OF WORDS

Donald E. Walker

In the Beginning Was the Word! It is only appropriate that a section on "Words and World Representations" should start with this reminder. It is clear that *word* and *world* are closely coupled concepts. While their similarity in form inspired me to try to trace them back to some common root, none of the dictionaries available to me sustains that conceit, although the **Oxford English Dictionary** does show *word* as one of the forms of *world* in some part of the English-speaking regions during the period 1300-1600.

Selecting words allows us to distinguish different aspects of the world, but the relationship is not a simple one. It would be gratifying to believe that words reflect the form of language and that the world represents their content. However, the history of philosophy reveals that people differ in what these terms mean and which should be taken to be primary, so no simple solution is available to us. It is clear, though, that the shared concern among the participants in this section is to explore the nature of the relationships between the lexicon and knowledge representation.

There have been recent intensifications of interest in the lexicon and in knowledge representation, motivated by both theoretical considerations and application demands. From a theoretical perspective, the lexicon is beginning to assume a new and increasingly important role within linguistics. Correspondingly, knowledge representation has become the dominant concern for artificial intelligence. From the standpoint of applications, the movement toward production systems–for computational linguistics, the development of natural language interfaces; for artificial intelligence, the emergence of expert systems–is requiring practical ways of realizing the underlying concepts. As a result, there now is an interplay between science and engineering in our fields that I view as gratifying. The history of science clearly demonstrates that the physical and biological sciences took off exponentially when the interaction between theory and applications began. I am hoping for similar progress for the language and knowledge sciences.

The authors in this section are addressing a number of critical issues: What are the appropriate units for words and worlds, both theoretically and practically? Will current systems scale up as we add more words and facts?

How can we acquire lexical and knowledge elements in a form that our systems can use? Can material assembled for one application be easily adapted to another? Can we take advantage of existing resources in building the capabilities required?

The section contains a computational linguist, Bran Boguraev from Cambridge University; a computational lexicologist, Bob Amsler from Bellcore; an artificial intelligence specialist, Jerry Hobbs; and a linguist, Judy Kegl. My own remarks are made from a position at the intersection of computational linguistics, artificial intelligence, and information science.

Boguraev talks about "The Definitional Power of Words," reflecting his work on building frames for knowledge representation from dictionary definitions. He and his colleagues have demonstrated that it is possible to establish lexical primitives through a taxonomic analysis of the core vocabulary in a controlled vocabulary, 'learner's' dictionary. One particularly exciting achievement is their use of the grammatical information in the form provided by the **Longman Dictionary of Contemporary English** as the lexical base for the *PATR-II* parser, developed at SRI International.

Amsler in "Words and Worlds" describes his work on the analysis of large text files to determine the lexicons needed to understand them. Existing machine-readable dictionaries do not have sufficient coverage for the task. Two special problems are being addressed. The variety of forms in which proper nouns can be expressed suggests that grammars need to be written for them and parsers developed that can apply those rules. Another important area is phrase collocations: the identification of sequences of words that function as lexical units and should be dictionary entries that are part of the lexicon of a system.

Hobbs considers "World Knowledge and Word Meaning." He believes that it is necessary to explicate the commonsense knowledge people have about the world in order to understand the words they use. His group has been axiomatizing a set of core theories that underlie the way people communicate about objects and events. They have been analyzing texts about mechanical devices and their failures and are developing ways of codifying notions like time, space, causality, shape, and force.

Kegl addresses "The Boundary between Word Knowledge and World Knowledge." Her work entails applying linguistic knowledge to world knowledge to yield word knowledge. She and her colleagues are deriving semantic primitives by determining how the languages of the world encode expressions of objects and events. Their goal is to develop ways of representing lexical items that are neutral with respect to a particular theory, so that lexicons can be shared by different projects.

My own remarks about "The World of Words" reflect a concern for organizing the groups working on the problems that the other authors have considered. I discuss some of the critical issues, point out the broad range of activities that are currently underway, and propose a mechanism for coordinating them.

There are a large number of protagonists involved in the topic area "Words and World representations": lexicographers, lexicologists, computational linguists, artificial intelligence specialists, linguists, cognitive scientists, philosophers, computer scientists, information scientists, publishers, lexical software marketers, translators, industry representatives, funding agency representatives, and professional society representatives. These groups have different backgrounds, motivations, and criteria for evaluation. Yet all have to be convinced that they must work together on shared problems toward a common set of goals.

One of the shared problems is the establishment of multifunctional, polytheoretical databases. There are increasing numbers of dictionaries in machine-readable form, and, as a byproduct of the electronic photocomposition of newspapers, books, magazines, and office documentation, it is possible to get online access to millions of words of text. However, we need to structure these materials so they can be used for many different purposes by people who have different theoretical orientations.

Equally important to accomplish is the development of computational tools for manipulating these data for the range of purposes described by the panelists, as well as to satisfy the requirements of the other protagonists identified above.

To support people who want to use these tools to process the varieties of data available, we have to develop workstation environments that do not require computer sophistication. More important, those environments must be tailored to the special objectives of the users. Although there are similarities between the requirements of lexicographers and translators, for example, the differences are important to identify so that we can model workstations for lexicographers and translators that satisfy their distinctive needs.

There are a number of exciting activities that have been taking place recently that are bringing people together to examine issues involving the lexicon. In May 1986, Antonio Zampolli, Nicoletta Calzolari, Juan Sager, Loll Rolling, and I organized a workshop on "Automating the Lexicon: Research and Practice in a Multilingual Environment." Held in Marina di Grosseto, Italy, its purpose was to explore research efforts, current practice, and potential developments in work on the lexicon, machine-readable dictionaries, and lexical knowledge bases with special consideration to the problems created by working with different languages. We wanted both to identify the current state of affairs and to recommend directions for future activities. We solicited papers that would examine in depth a set of research areas, core problems, application areas, and developing lexical knowledge bases. The papers prepared for the meeting surveyed the role of the lexicon in linguistics, semantics, parsing, generation, lexicography, translation, teaching, psycholinguistics, information retrieval, office automation, and dictionaries for the mass market. They also examined the problems of developing data and knowledge bases that would support the expansion and more effective use of lexical information. As a result we were able to establish a baseline for future work in the field. Of particular value was our bringing together a distinguished group of participants representing the range of protagonists mentioned above.

This workshop was followed immediately by another one on "The Lexical Entry," which was held in conjunction with the Summer Linguistic Institute at the City University of New York in July 1986. The focus there was to determine how different theoretical frameworks and system implementations influence the format for a lexical entry. We were interested in characterizing a general representation or "metaformat" that would subsume the specific ones. The expectation was not that everyone would agree to share a single model. Rather, we hoped to identify the range of parameters that are used and from which different approaches would make a selection.

That workshop, which included primarily research specialists, led to the establishment of a much smaller and more sharply focused "Pisa Working Group" that attempted to create lexical entries that would actually satisfy the requirements of different theoretical approaches. Several meetings were held, and the results served to motivate another large workshop on "The Lexicon in Theoretical and Computational Perspective," at the Stanford Linguistic Institute in July 1987. It had two objectives: (1) the establishment of a structure for lexical entries that will be neutral with respect to theoretical differences so that the information they contain can be shared; (2) the development of community-wide resources that will be widely accessible. The workshop was organized around working groups on syntax, semantics, morphology, and data and knowledge base design.

Collateral developments during this period have been the establishment of an ad hoc working group on "Computational Lexicology and Lexicography" by the European Science Foundation and the establishment of a specialist working group on "Dictionaries and the Computer" by EURALEX, the European Association for Lexicography. A panel on "The Lexicon in a Multilingual Environment," was held at COLING '86 in Bonn in August, 1986. A conference on "Standardization in Lexicography" took place in Saarbruecken in October 1986, and one on "Advances in Lexicology" was organized by the Centre for the New Oxford English Dictionary in Waterloo, Ontario, in November 1986.

Two other related activities were a special double issue on the Lexicon in "Computational Linguistics" during 1987 and a summer school on "Computational Lexicography and Lexicology" in Summer 1988, organized by the European Science Foundation.

This broad range of activities, coupled with the convening of this panel, testifies to the vitality of work on the lexicon. However, the complexities of the issues entailed in accomplishing the goals under consideration demand a more coordinated effort. Bob Amsler likened the organization required to similar efforts in government or industrial circles, which can be characterized as involving a series of directorates, offices, and projects.

Procurement is one major issue. Organized efforts are needed to acquire data, to catalog relevant literature, and to identify people with the necessary skills. A variety of massive databases are essential; they need to include texts, spoken language, graphics, and images. Legal and copyright issues constitute a major set of problems to be considered systematically.

Capturing lexical knowledge is another concern. Establishing a common, shareable lexicon is critical, as is embedding it in the context of a 'universal' grammar. We need to model lexicographers and lexicologists to better understand how they work. Multilingual studies are essential to ensure generality.

Communication and collaboration are central to this effort. Consequently, we need to be concerned with standards and terminology, with effective electronic communication networks, with procedures for data dissemination. Coordination is essential to avoid duplicating research projects and to insure that they complement each other. Conferences and workshops need to be organized to bring people together. Curriculum development and training aids will further the spread of this technology.

Hardware and software support are required. We need to be concerned with workstation design, the development of more effective programming languages that can handle the string and structural features of language, the establishment of database management procedures for massive text files, and the creation of distributed storage systems with fast access times.

These brief statements summarize a complex organizational problem. The Grosseto Workshop, referred to above, actually identified more than 30 major projects that would benefit research and practice in work on the lexicon. The "Introduction" to the Proceedings of that Workshop will provide a more detailed analysis with recommendations for further activities (Walker, forthcoming).

Chapter 1.2

THE DEFINITIONAL POWER OF WORDS

Branimir K. Boguraev

I am deliberate in introducing ambiguity in the title. Part of my thesis in this brief note is going to be that there is a wealth of information relevant to a range of natural language processing functions available and extractable from the definitions of words found in obvious places like dictionaries[1]. This is hardly surprising, given that what is to be found in a dictionary is essentially the result of a substantial amount of work on analyzing and collating data about real language and eliciting collocational and distributional properties of words and applying certain common principles of defining their meaning. Furthermore, I am going to argue that carefully exploited interplay between notions of "words" and "primitives" **can** add substantial leverage to the functionality and coverage of a natural language processing system.

Several factors and related phenomena underlie the current interest in words, and consequently in word resources. Over the last decade there has been the emergence of theories of grammar and grammatical frameworks (e.g., LFG, GPSG, PATR-II, FUG, Lexicon Grammar, Word Grammar) placing heavy emphasis on the lexicon, where elaborate information about the grammatical and logical idiosyncracies of words is stored and used to drive various parsing systems. More relevant to this panel, however, is the progress in both the practical aspects of natural language processing (various techniques for, e.g., performing text analysis or building and customizing natural language interfaces) and the theoretical issues of knowledge representation and access.

It would not be too provocative to state that the current understanding of how to go about building practical systems is sufficient to make such a task tractable. However, realistic natural language processing programs fall in the general class of knowledge based systems in AI, and they all require significant amounts of structured knowledge about the real world, as well as about a particular domain of discourse. There are typically two problems here, one related to the scaling of a prototype up by expanding its knowledge base, and the other related to the activity of transporting or customizing an existing system. In both cases the real culprit is the knowledge acquisition bottleneck. Given the availability online of suitable machine readable resources, namely dictionaries and encyclopaedias, there is strong hope that some model of the common world may be localized and extracted from such sources. Even if individual applications may require additional elaboration of their knowledge bases and the introduction of specialized terms and concepts, these will still have to be related to the common world knowledge. A growing mass of work at present is focussed on making some use of the definitional component of a dictionary entry, where the dictionary itself is regarded as a **knowledge base**, albeit presented in a loose and not very structured fashion. Starting with the assumption that dictionary definitions both employ and imply a taxonomy of genus terms, the ultimate goal is to relate natural language words to this underlying structure which relates together the defining concepts in the dictionary. There are many problems here, ranging from the arbitrariness of dictionary definitions, to the distribution of a particular piece of data over a number of separate entries, to the fundamental differences between dictionaries and encyclopaedias.

Underneath even the most detailed dictionary definition there is still a substantial amount of general knowledge about the world. Without it being formalized and clearly stated, no complete analysis of the descriptive texts typically found in a dictionary can be fully achieved. Still, current views on automatic natural language processing tend to agree that it is hard to pinpoint a boundary between the semantic knowledge that the use of a particular word (sense) implies and the expert background which prompts its use in a specific domain. While it would be unreasonable to expect to find any of the latter in a dictionary source[2], there is sufficient evidence to indicate that most of the former—whether presented in terms of selectional restrictions markers, formulae constructed from semantic primitives, frame-based structures, propositional systems with sortal information encoded in the form of meaning postulates and associated with predicate symbols, or by some other means—can be derived from a suitable dictionary. The idea of using "what is behind words"—structured assignment to thesauri classes or looser descriptions via natural language expressions—to perform functions such as word-sense assignment or lexical disambiguation is certainly not new. Recent proposals for using dictionary definitions to determine relevant context consolidate and extend the pioneering efforts of the Cambridge Language Research Unit of 30 years ago where the structure of the Roget's Thesaurus was applied as an MT interlingua and supported word sense disambiguation.

However, now we are in position to evaluate critically "what is behind words." One of the reasons for the renewed interest in words is the availability, on-line (in the form of machine readable dictionaries and encyclopaedias), of vast resources of information about words. We also have both the technology to process these resources and extract from them what is relevant to computer programs concerned with various natural language activities. Still, given the shallow world knowledge typically contained in dictionaries, perhaps a complete semantic component for a natural language processing system cannot be derived fully automatically by suitable analysis of word definitions. The meaning content of a dictionary holds a promise of a different nature.

While there is no consensus on the kind of representation scheme best suited for capturing the knowledge required for language interpretation and understanding, it is nonetheless possible to identify the distinct classes of propositional systems and type hierarchy systems. The latter utilize, broadly speaking, general notions of frame-like concepts with slot-like role descriptions, organized in an inheritance hierarchy along generalization/specialization axes. Most of the recent work on knowledge representation, whether representative of the strict type hierarchy approach (exemplified by, e.g., FRL, KRL, NETL, UNITS, KL-ONE) or of the hybrid style of KRYPTON and KL-TWO, for example, can be cast into this general mould. For natural language processing, where general world knowledge is just as important as specialized domain- and task-dependent knowledge, the utility of hierarchically structured networks of concepts need not be emphasized. And while it is not entirely clear whether all of the structured information required by the system functions can be derived in a systematic and consistent way from dictionary sources, such sources offer a particularly good and convenient starting point for initial compilation of taxonomically structured knowledge about the world.

Taxonomies for existing dictionaries have been constructed, albeit in a semi-automatic way; more recently, fully automated procedures have been developed to accomplish the same task, and further elicitation of taxonomic structures is underway. Typically, natural language processing techniques and constraints from linguistic theory are applied to the word definitions in the dictionary; in some cases, the analysis process can be made sufficiently elaborate to accomplish not only the identification (and disambiguation) of the superordinate (genus) term, but also further elaboration of the defining concept by extracting additional modifiers and predications.

The resulting frame-like structures with filled-in slots, assigned defaults and specified constraints (insofar as these have been given in the original word definition) allow a fairly accurate characterization of a concept both in a particular domain of discourse and within the relevant fragment of the hierarchy. The networks thus defined can be of enormous utility to a wide range of text and language processing applications. Still, a much more important consequence of the assumption for an underlying taxonomy and the techniques developed for extracting such a taxonomy is the interesting prospect of looking at taxonomic organizations across a variety of existing dictionaries. Perhaps there is a common structure underneath definitions from different sources? Perhaps this common structure reflects a common world representation? It is too much to expect to find the "right" dictionary, which employs a sufficiently detailed and analytically designed taxonomy, directly utilizable by a natural language processing system. On the other hand, it would be unwise to ignore commonalities in the definitional spaces of a cross-section of dictionaries.

From a slightly different perspective, the whole body of work which looks at word definitions in dictionaries bears directly on the issue of deriving lexicons for language processing. Clearly, the techniques referred to above can be applied directly to the task of compiling some lexical semantics from dictionary sources. It turns out that these embody fairly detailed and complex linguistic and general world distinctions. Attempting to use individual word definitions to derive semi-automatically semantic formulae which incorporate selectional restrictions and shallow world knowledge is not an isolated activity. Still, as already noted, dictionaries are not **complete** repositories of linguistic and world knowledge, and it is yet not clear whether a direct mapping from a word definition to a lexical entry derived by means indicated here is going to be an entirely profitable exercise.

In order to exploit fully the wealth of linguistic and general world knowledge embodied in a dictionary, we need to look at the old issue of semantic primitives from a different perspective. It has already been suggested that fixed sets of primitive concepts cannot cope as the granularity of different domains and contexts varies. A lot of questions have also been raised by the issue of exactly how to arrive at a particular set of primitives. It would seem that the work currently being done on analyzing the taxonomic organizations underlying a number of existing dictionaries offers a solution here. At least one dictionary source has been produced by adhering to a principle of using a limited core vocabulary of basic words, **only** in their central meanings, for all the definitions; this controlled vocabulary clearly has not been selected randomly. Apart from allowing a fairly close tuning of a definitions analysis program (it turns out that there exists, in effect, a grammar for writing word definitions), the application of such a program to the core vocabulary itself will yield the taxonomy of defining concepts used in the process of the dictionary writing. Taking this as a guideline for determining a set of semantic primitives, individual word definitions can then be analyzed and corresponding semantic formulae compiled within this primitive vocabulary.

Perhaps the most pertinent point here is that neither this, nor any other dictionary has been developed with the particular intention of being used by a natural language processing program. Given that we now seem to have a slightly better idea of what we would like our systems to do, that a growing collection of texts, from which significant lexical information can be derived, exists in machine readable form, and that we know enough about parsing, a question which would be appropriate to ask is this: what can "reverse engineering" of a dictionary do for a knowledge-intensive language processing system?

Notes

1. By dictionaries I mean monolingual dictionaries of the style exemplified by, e.g., *The Longman Dictionary of Contemporary English, The Collins English Dictionary,* or *Webster's Seventh New Collegiate Dictionary.*

2. Note, however, the CYC project at MCC, whose aim is precisely to derive a formal model of general world knowledge down to some level of detail from an encyclopaedia source.

Chapter 1.3

WORDS AND WORLDS

Robert A. Amsler

For several years now I have been concerned with how artificial intelligence is going to build the substitute for human world knowledge needed in performing the task of text understanding. I continue to believe that the bulk of this knowledge will have to be derived from existing machine-readable texts produced as byproducts of computer typesetting and word processing technologies which have overtaken the publishing industries. However, there are many obstacles to the acquisition of world knowledge from text.

There are some, I am sure, who would argue that world knowledge of the form needed in text understanding will have to be hand-coded and cannot be derived from existing reference books or other texts. My basic argument against those who hold this view is that they are ignoring the magnitude of the task ahead. Whether measured in terms of bytes or man-years, the sum of recorded knowledge is so massive that it is unlikely to be capable of being recoded manually in anything less than man-centuries.

Put another way, there currently exist sizeable publishing empires in this country which every day employ hundreds of people involved directly in the coding of information for new reference texts and revised editions of older reference works. To attempt a recoding of world knowledge solely for use in AI would eventually become an attempt to parallel this effort. It would become a major industry in itself. Thus, it is more likely that, instead of a new knowledge-base industry, we will see an evolutionary change in the methods used by the existing publishing empires to record knowledge in a manner that is of use in producing text both for human consumption and as knowledge bases for computers. Researchers in AI and computational linguistics therefore have some responsibility to determine how the existing printed knowledge can evolve into usable computational world knowledge

Now, of course, I do admit there are subclasses of world knowledge that evidence to date has not shown to exist in print at all. Jerry Hobbs is attempting to codify one such subclass in his work on TACITUS (Hobbs et al., 1986). There are others as well, such as some forms of linguistic knowledge. However, I am concerned about the very large body of knowledge that we try to communicate to people through books, newspapers, and other texts. This knowledge of the outside world, of experiences in which the individual has not and in fact may never personally be involved, is nevertheless shared knowedge known to all of us through reading and listening to the words of others.

Another assumption, and one that has been guiding my work for many years now, is that natural language systems cannot *understand* text for which they do not possess the lexicon. This seems so elemental an assumption that I find it hard to see how to ignore the fact that we do not have a lexicon of any real world text as common as a newspaper.

What is in this missing lexicon? The problem has several parts. First, it now seems clear that even unabridged dictionaries miss sizeable amounts of the lexicon needed to do lexical recognition in a newspaper such as *The New York Times*. Earlier results (Walker & Amsler, 1986) have shown that some of this lexicon was excluded from the dictionaries by choice, such as the proper nouns, but more recent research has revealed that even here the problem is more complex.

Proper nouns are not quite lexical in nature. They possess a grammatical structure which some researchers have noted (Carroll, 1985). This is to say that a typical proper noun has a variety of forms which tend to make the use of a single lexical entry for the proper noun less computationally useful than for a common noun.

Thus we recognize,

International Business Machine Corporation's Thomas J. Watson Research Center at Yorktown Heights, New York,

as the same thing as

IBM Yorktown

or

IBM's Watson Research Center.

What is going on here is that we have a mini-grammar for these types of utterances which allows us to contract their separate parts independently (and even to transform the order of the constituents). Thus, *International Business Machines Corporation* is contractable according to the rules for corporations, namely to forms such as *IBM Corp.* or just its initials, *IBM* (but it cannot be *International B. Machines,* for instance). *Thomas J. Watson* is a person's name, and already has a contracted middle initial. People occasionally can have their names contracted the same way as corporations (e.g., *JFK* or *J.R.* of Dallas TV show fame) but more typically they contract to forms such as *T. J. Watson* and *Watson*. Geographic locations, such as *Yorktown Heights, New York* can contract to forms such as *Yorktown Heights, NY* and *Yorktown*. *Research Center* is a common noun, and as such is lexical, not undergoing this type of contraction and grammatical restructuring.

Finally, one should note that the order of the proper noun constituents in the original full expression was,

<Corporation-owner> <Person-Name> <common-noun>
<geographic-location>.

However, *IBM Yorktown Heights Research Center* has rearranged this ordering. This capability for rearrangement is clearly grammatical in nature.

These and related examples show that (a) most proper nouns have several forms derivable from their most complete representation, and (b) these forms obey a simple grammar of permissible contractions and transformations dependent upon the types of proper nouns involved as constituents of the entire proper noun expression.

Another important aspect of this observation is that it was made as a direct consequence of massive data collection. If one encountered a single form of a proper noun in text, one might be tempted to believe it could be treated by including it in a dictionary just as a common noun. But, examining a very large corpus of text in just the right ways (such as with a proper-noun extraction program and a concordance of its output) shows the proper nouns to stand out as quite distinct from common nouns. There are almost always a dozen different forms for each proper noun, scattered alphabetically according to the initial word of each form. Yet these multiple forms show a pattern of recurrence based upon standard contraction, abbreviation, and transformation operations.

Consideration of a proper noun extraction program points out how important it is to use textual sources in the right way. We now know that counting the instances of isolated words in text is a horrendous misuse of the raw data. To encounter *New York City* and decide that *New* has made an appearance in the text is unacceptable. Lexical events often consist of phrases which bear little more than a historic relationship to the individual blank-delimited words of which they are composed. In what sense is *New York City* **new**? What does *soap* have to do with *soap operas*? These are historic artifacts, and much the way chemical compounds may bear little relationship to the properties of their elemental constituents, observing the spectrum of elements in phrases in isolation doesn't reliably reveal the whole story about the phrases themselves. The problem of detecting such phrases in text and deciding whether they legitimately need their own lexical entries makes clear a distinction between three different degrees of specificity of information and their intended uses.

The first degree of minimal specificity is that contained in published dictionaries which present information for human readers who can be assumed to have a rather complete grasp of world knowledge. Dictionaries offer definitions that are the minimal specification of the meaning of a word capable of evoking its conceptual meaning in the mind of a reader. Dictionaries are so myopic in this regard that they are often inappropriately used to try to teach children the meanings of words, ignoring whether the children possess the accompanying world knowledge needed to understand the dictionary definitions. George Miller (1985) at Princeton has revealed just how little of what a conventional dictionary says can be understood by a child. Dictionaries also tend to split compounds into their constituent isolated words without concern for how the reader will manage to put the right senses of the words back together again. However, this should not be taken as a complete repudiation of dictionaries. They are excellect indexes into the world knowledge needed; they just make no commitment themselves to supply that world knowledge.

The second degree of intermediate specificity is that needed by computational linguistics to build lexicons to be used by programs for parsing, generation, and translation. Computational linguists are required to provide in their lexicons everything necessary to substantiate their program's linguistic competence. If compounds are described by separate entries for each of their components, then rules for the combination of these components must also be included. More likely, the compounds themselves will be given their own entries, since being completely sure a rule is correct requires a great deal more knowledge of the lexicon than is available today. However, parsing, generation, and translation do not necessarily require their programs to construct conceptual structures for the lexical objects they process. One can build parsers, such as the Fiddich Parser, which blithely guess at syntactic categories for words they do not have in their lexicons—and do so so successfully that they complete most parses with acceptable grammatical structures. However, it is clear such a level of understanding is not adequate for more advanced artificial intelligence applications.

The third degree of highest specificity is needed to support artificial intelligence where one must be able not only to parse text, but to understand the meaning of the concepts to which the text refers. Understanding text may require other aspects of knowledge such as visual imagery or knowledge of physical laws, but above all it requires the ability to match incoming lexical entities with stored knowledge about the concepts of which the lexical entities are descriptions. This means that one needs to go significantly beyond linguistic competence.

These three levels of representation directly affect what needs to be stored in a lexicon, and nowhere more than in the nature of what needs to be stored about phrases. For example, whereas the lexicographer can dismiss *elephant house* as the ordinary sense of *elephant* and a sense of *house* which means *a habitation for animals,* the computational linguist needs to distinguish how we know that *cat house* and *dog house* are not instances of this rule, and the knowledge-base researcher needs to distinguish *elephant house* as representing a real world building which appears in zoos, whereas *eagle house* has no such referent or significance. Thus, lexicographers might defend not having an entry for *elephant house* in their lexicons, covering its meaning with a special sense of *house* suitable for this purpose. However, computational linguists would be very critical of the failure to accompany that special meaning with a caveat excluding forms such as *cat house* and *dog house* and perhaps uneasy about the fact that *eagle house* would pass through the parser. The knowledge-base researcher would find the computational linguist's possible problem an absolute obstacle and require an explicit entry for *elephant house* that noted its location in a zoo and other details such as that elephants do not happen to own mortgages on their houses the way people do, just to start off.

What I am implying here is that whereas printed dictionaries have served us well for a few hundred years, it is very likely that we will have to greatly expand their explicitness for computational linguistic needs and even further expand the recorded information for knowledge-base needs. To do this we will have to return to the source materials from which the dictionaries were written, to the text that carries much of our world knowledge. We will have to extract the compound lexical items from these texts and make new decisions about the need to include them in new dictionaries which will serve the needs of AI programs. It is time both to increase the rigor of the lexicographic decisions about including multi-word entries in printed dictionaries, so they will be more usable by computational linguists, and to describe new tests of the adequacy of entries for more advanced knowledge representation disciplines.

Chapter 1.4

WORLD KNOWLEDGE AND WORD MEANING

Jerry R. Hobbs

We use words to talk about the world. Therefore, to understand what words mean, we must have a prior explication of how we view the world. In a sense, efforts in the past to decompose words into semantic primitives were attempts to link word meaning to a theory of the world, where the set of semantic primitives constituted the theory of the world. With the advent of naive physics and research programs to formalize commonsense knowledge in a number of areas in predicate calculus or some other formal language, we now have at our disposal means for building much richer theories of various aspects of the world, and, consequently, we are in a much better position to address the problems of lexical semantics.

In the TACITUS project for using commonsense knowledge in the understanding of texts about mechanical devices and their failures, we have been developing various commonsense theories that are needed to mediate between the way we talk about the behavior of such devices and causal models of their operation (Hobbs et al., 1986). The theories cover a number of areas that figure in virtually every domain of discourse, such as scalar notions, granularity, structured systems, time, space, material, physical objects, causality, functionality, force, and shape. Our approach has been to construct *core theories* of each of these areas. These core theories may use English words as their predicates, but the principal criterion for adequacy of the core theory is elegance, whatever that is, and this can usually be achieved better using predicates that are not lexically realized. It is easier to achieve elegance if one does not have to be held responsible to linguistic evidence. Predicates that *are* lexically realized are then pushed to the periphery of the theory. A large number of lexical items can be defined, or at least characterized, in terms provided by the core theories. The hypothesis is that once these core theories have been formulated in the right way, it will be straightforward to explicate the meanings of a great many words.

The phrase "in the right way" is key in this strategy. The world is complex and can be viewed from many different perspectives. Some of these will lend themselves well to the investigation of problems of word meaning, whereas others will only lead us into difficulties. We could, for example, axiomatize space as Euclidean 3-space, with x, y, and z-coordinates for every point. We could then attempt to define what the various prepositions and verbs of motion mean in this framework. I am quite sure such an attempt would fail. Such a theory of space would be too foreign to the way we talk about space in everyday life. Even if we were to succeed in this limited task, we would not have advanced at all toward an understanding of metaphorical uses of these words.

In contrast, we view our core theories not so much as theories about *particular aspects* of the world, but rather as abstract frameworks that have proven useful in interpreting, generally, a number of different kinds of phenomena. Thus, at the very center of our knowledge base is an axiomatization of "systems," where a system is a set of elements and a set of relations among them. An abstract, "primitive" relation *at* places entities at locations within a system, encoding the basic figure-ground relation. A large number of things in the world can be understood as systems, and a large number of relations can be understood as *at* relations. When we apply the theory to a particular phenomenon, we buy into a way of thinking about the phenomenon, and, more to the present purposes, of talking about it. It is in this way that the metaphorical usages that pervade natural language discourse are accommodated. Once we characterize some piece of the world as a system, and some relation as an *at* relation, we have acquired the whole locational way of talking about it. Once this is enriched with a theory of time and change, we can import the whole vocabulary of motion. For example, in computer science, a data structure can be viewed as a system, and we can stipulate that if a pointer points to a node in a data structure, then the pointer is *at* that node. We have then acquired a spatial metaphor, and we can subsequently talk about, for example, the pointer *moving around* the data structure. Space, of course, is itself a system and can be talked about using a locational vocabulary.

Also central in the knowledge base is an axiomatization of "scales," which is a particular kind of system whose relations are a partial ordering and an indistinguishability relation (encoding granularity). Once we develop a core theory of scales, we can use the predicates it provides to characterize a large number of lexical items, such as "range", "limit", and the comparative and superlative morphemes. For x to range from y to z, for example, is for y and z to be endpoints of a subscale s of a scale, and for x to be a set of entities which are located *at* elements of s. By choosing different scales, we can get such uses as

The buffalo ranged from northern Texas to southern Saskatchewan.

The students' SAT scores range from 1100 to 1550.

The hepatitis cases range from moderate to severe.

His behavior ranges from sullen to vicious.

Our desire to optimize the possibilities of using core theories in metaphorical and analogical contexts leads us to adopt the following methodological principle: For any given concept we wish to characterize, we should determine the minimal structure necessary for that concept to make sense. In efforts to axiomatize some domain, there are two positions one may take, one exemplified by set theory and the other by group theory. In axiomatizing set theory, one attempts to capture exactly some concept one has strong intuitions about. If the axiomatization turns out to have unexpected models, this exposes an inadequacy. In group theory, by contrast, one characterizes an abstract class of structures. If there turn out to be unexpected models, this is a serendipitous discovery of a new phenomenon that we can reason about using an old theory. The pervasiveness of metaphor in natural language discourse shows that our commonsense theories of the world ought to be much more like group theory than set theory.

Our approach to space and dimensionality illustrates this. Rather than defining dimension in the classical manner of linear algebra, in a way that requires a measure and arithmetic operations, we have sought to be able to build spaces out of less structured components. Thus, we have defined a two-dimensional space as a set of elements that can be located on two different scales that are independent in the sense that the order of two elements on one scale cannot be predicted from their order on the other. A space can then be defined corresponding to any set of scales. Real space is an instantiation of this theory, and so are various idealizations of it. But metaphorical spaces are also instantiations. We can, for example, talk about salary and quality of life as different dimensions relevant to job choice.

We have concentrated more on specifying axioms than on constructing models. Thus, our approach is more syntactic than semantic, in the logical sense. Our view is that the chief role of models in our effort is for proving the consistency and independence of sets of axioms, and for showing their adequacy. Many of the spatial and temporal theories we construct are intended at least to have Euclidean space or the real numbers as one model, but they are also intended to have discrete, finite, and less highly structured models as well.

Not only do people seem to have single theories for multiple phenomena, they also seem to have multiple theories for single phenomena. Where this is so, where for example several competing ontologies suggest themselves, we attempt to construct a theory that accommodates both. Rather than commit ourselves to adopting one set of primitives in the stead of another, we try to show how each set of primitives can be characterized in terms of the other. Then one need not make claims of primacy for either. Generally, each of the ontologies is useful for different purposes, and it is convenient to be able to appeal to both. Our treatment of time illustrates this. One possible approach is to take the time line as basic, and to say that events and conditions have associated time instants or intervals. In this view, there is a change in the world if an entity is in one state at one point in time and in another state at another point in time. This view is reflected in language in the clock and calendar vocabulary. Another approach, one I think corresponds better with the way we really view the world most of the time, is to say that there is a primitive relation *change* between conditions or situations, that these conditions and changes can co-occur, and that the time line is just an idealized sequence of changes that many other events co-occur with. This view seems to be deeply embedded in language, in, for example, verbs describing changes of state. Rather than be forced into one ontology or the other, we have shown how each can be defined in terms of the other.

In addition to being cavalier about the match between the core theories and the way the world really is, we are being cavalier about whether the axiomatizations fit into the classical mold of a few undefined, "primitive" predicates and a large number of predicates defined in terms of these primitives. We take it that one can rarely expect to find necessary and sufficient conditions for some concept p. There will be few axioms of the form

$$(\forall\ x)\ p(x) \equiv Q$$

The most we can hope for is to find a number of necessary conditions and a number of sufficient conditions, that is, a number of axioms of the form

$$(\forall\ x)\ p(x) \supset Q$$

and a number of axioms of the form

$$(\forall\ x)\ R \supset p(x)$$

It is generally hopeless to aim for *definitions*; the most we can expect is *characterizations*. This amounts to saying that virtually every predicate is a primitive, but a primitive that is highly interrelated with the rest of the knowledge base.

One way this can happen is illustrated by the predicate *at*. There are very few facts that one can conclude from the fact that one entity is *at* another in an arbitrary system. The predicate is used first as a way of relating many other concepts, especially concepts involving change, with each other. So there are axioms that say that when something moves from one point to another, it is no longer at the first and is now at the second. Its second use is as an entry point into spatial metaphors. There are a number of axioms of the form

$$(\forall\ x,y,s)\ p(x,y)\ \&\ q(y,s) \supset at(x,y,s).$$

When we see a spatial metaphor and ask what would imply such a usage, axioms like these enable an interpretation.

The predicate *cause* is another illustration of the roles of primitive predicates in the knowledge base. We do not attempt to define causality in terms of other, more basic concepts. There are a few things we know about causality in general, such as the transitivity of *cause* and the relation between *cause* and temporal order. But otherwise almost all we know about causality is particular facts about what kinds of particular events cause what other kinds of particular events. We should not expect to have a highly developed theory of causality *per se.* Rather we should expect to see causal information distributed throughout the knowledge base.

Another example of characterization rather than definition is provided by natural kind terms, like "metal". We all know from Putnam that we can't hope to define such terms in ways that will survive future scientific discovery. Even if we were able to define them in ways consistent with current science, the definitions would be very distant from common sense. Nevertheless, we know a great many properties of metals, and this knowledge plays a role in the interpretation of many texts we encounter. Therefore, the knowledge base contains a number of axioms encoding things like the fact that metals behave in a certain way when subjected to increasing forces.

The TACITUS project is fairly new, and we have not yet characterized a large number of words or axiomatized very many core theories. But already the range of words we have been able to handle indicates the promise of our approach. Here are some examples. The word "range" has already been discussed. Assemblies and environments are both systems of particular kinds, and we can say that an assembly "operates" if it engages in its normative behavior in an environment. The word "immediately", etymologically, predicates of an ordering relation between two events that a third relevant event does not occur between them. This fact can be expressed in terms provided by the core theories of scales and time. The word "brittle" can be characterized within the same theory of materials acted upon by forces that was useful in specifying some properties of metals, mentioned above. The concept "wear", as in "worn bearings" or "a worn-out shirt", was one of the original targets of our research effort. Wear is the cumulative small-scale loss of material from the surface of an object due to the abrasive action of some external material. We have been able to state this formally in terms of predicates from core theories of granularity, change, force, and the topology and cohesion of pieces of material. The diversity and complexity of the set of words we have been able to handle encourages us in the belief that lexical semantics should be integrated with efforts to formalize commonsense knowledge.

An old favorite question for lexical theorists is whether one can make a useful distinction between linguistic knowledge and world knowledge. The position I have articulated leads one to an answer that can be stated briefly. There is no useful distinction. In discourse comprehension and generation, both kinds of knowledge are required and, in our work so far on interpretation, both are handled in the same way. Defining or characterizing words can only be done as an adjunct to an effort to build theories useful for understanding phenomena in the world. In fact, the only reason I can imagine for maintaining such a distinction is for preserving discipline boundaries.

There is, however, a useful, related distinction in kinds of knowledge bases one might build. The knowledge base we are building is geared toward communication. There are other efforts, such as those in qualitative physics (e.g., De Kleer and Brown, 1985), which are geared toward the prediction of physical events in the absence of complete information. In such efforts, one is less concerned about metaphor and more concerned about detailed correspondence with the world. It wouldn't disturb me if with our knowledge base we failed to predict when a valve would close, but I would be disturbed if we could not cope with spatial metaphors for, say, economic information.

So far we have spent more time developing the core theories than in characterizing words in terms of them. What we have done in the latter area has primarily been for exploratory and illustrative purposes. Moreover, the entire effort is so new that frequently when we try to characterize a word we discover another core theory or two that needs to be axiomatized first. So we have barely scratched the surface in constructing the kind of knowledge base required for genuine text processing. What hope is there for scaling up? There are two points to make here. First of all, Maurice Gross is fond of pointing out that other fields, such as astronomy and botany, have faced just as formidable a task of classification and cataloguing as we face, and have thrived on it. When we have a better idea of what we want to do, there will be people enough to do it.

Secondly, there is promise in the recent attention given to automatic processing of already existing on-line dictionaries and other knowledge sources. I can imagine that work eventually converging in a fruitful way with our research. I like to characterize the difference between the TACITUS project and recent projects aimed at encoding all the knowledge in an encyclopedia by saying that rather than encoding the knowledge in the encyclopedia, we are trying to encode the knowledge required by someone before he even opens the encyclopedia, just to be able to read it. The same holds true of a dictionary. As we build up a larger and larger knowledge base and further implement the procedures that will use this knowledge in text comprehension, we will be more and more in the position of being able to use the information in large, on-line dictionaries. Work on extracting semantic hierarchies from on-line dictionaries (Amsler, 1980; Chodorow, Byrd, and Heidorn, 1985) will not merely reveal a set of semantic primitives for some domain. These semantic primitives will be concepts that have already been explicated in core theories in the knowledge base, so that this automatic analysis will have in turn yielded more valuable results. We will have extended the knowledge base itself using these on-line resources.

Acknowledgments

The research described here is a joint effort with William Croft, Todd Davies, Douglas Edwards, and Kenneth Laws. The opinions expressed here are, however, my own. The research is funded by the Defense Advanced Research Projects Agency under Office of Naval Research contract N00014-85-C-0013.

Chapter 1.5

THE BOUNDARY BETWEEN WORD KNOWLEDGE
AND WORLD KNOWLEDGE

Judy Kegl

I will focus my comments on linguistic considerations concerning the interrelation between words and world representation and will argue that word knowledge must be kept distinct from world knowledge. Knowing everything about a referent object or event with which a word is associated is not enough to allow one to use a word appropriately. World knowledge must be supplemented and constrained by linguistic knowledge to yield an appropriate account of word knowledge.

Let's start with a relatively straightforward example, one which is now so commonplace that I am unsure of who to cite for its introduction into the literature. Consider the word *dance/danser* in both English and French. These cognates might at first glance appear to be almost interchangeable glosses for one another. Certainly, when looking at the event we think of as dancing both English and French speakers see and experience the same physical event. Details of the exact instantiation of dancing might vary from culture to culture, but I think we would agree that we all share the same concept of what constitutes a dancing event. Yet speakers of English and French do not use their "words" for this event in parallel ways. In English, for example, we use the verb *dance* to refer to both a translatory and a non-translatory event (where translatory means to move along a path from one place to another). So, for example, the English sentence *John and Mary danced across the room* is ambiguous. It can mean either "John and Mary went from one end of the room to the other while dancing" or "John and Mary were located at the other end of the room dancing." French, on the other hand, allows only the non-translatory reading where John and Mary are at some location engaged in the act of dancing. French speakers have no problem describing the translatory event of dancing from one end of the room to the other, they just don't use the word *danser* in this context. They speak of crossing the room while dancing. Somewhere along the road between French and English world knowledge and word knowledge seem to have diverged. What's interesting about such examples is that this divergence isn't a freak occurrence. The divergence seen with *dance* and *danser* extends to a whole class of related verbs. In other words, the behavior of these verbs is a reflex of some language-specific regularities.

However, even though there exists a considerable amount of freedom with regard to what aspects of our world knowledge of an object or event are encoded in its linguistic alter ego (the word), the range of possibilities is still severely constrained. Not everything we know about an object or an event is a candidate for inclusion in its linguistic representation. For example, color is a salient property we associate with the objects around us, but no language in the world exhibits a linguistic classifier system based on color. Shape, solidity, and flexibility, on the other hand, are at the heart of a large majority of the world's classifier systems. Time and space seem to have equal status in the world of conceptual knowledge, yet languages prefer to speak of time in spatial terms (at 6:00, from Tuesday to Thursday, toward evening, in 1976, Winter is fast approaching) and not *vice versa*.

From the time of the Byzantine Planudes through the writings of Hjelmslev (1935) and even into the more recent work of Gruber (1976) and Jackendoff (1983), the claim has been made that motion and location play a special role in the organization of language. Even abstract verb classes (verbs of cognition, perception, emotion, etc.) involve figurative extensions of basic motion/location relations (to feel down, to think something through). When we stop to think about it, many possibilities for classification come to mind, but the world's languages seem to select their options from a very restricted set. Determining these preferred encoding strategies across languages is one way to get at a linguistically relevant set of semantic primitives. The relevant linguistic phenomena to examine are verb classes (cognition, perception, emotion, motion/location, change of state, bodily care, *etc.*), thematic roles (source, goal, theme), and predicate argument structure, mappings between semantic roles (agent, patient), and grammatical relations (subject, object), and grammatical functions such as causation. All of these phenomena straddle the boundary between linguistic conceptual structure and conceptual structure in general.

Acquisition work by the Clarks (E. Clark, 1973, H. Clark, 1973) presents some ties between perception and language and raises some interesting issues concerning the interface between perceptual and linguistic knowledge, and the mechanism by which a child might use perceptual knowledge as a bootstraping device to link words and world knowledge into an already existent innate linguistic knowledge. Moving to evidence from language typology, we find that even though grammatical relations and semantic roles (agent, patient) are evidently part of universal grammar, the link between them is subject to variation and must be determined on the basis of language-specific evidence. Otherwise, how could Nominative/Accusative languages (languages where the object is the marked case) map agent to subject and patient to object, whereas Ergative languages (those where subject of a transitive is the marked case) do the reverse, mapping agent to object and patient to subject. This is a simplified statement of the facts (see Levin, 1983 for more detail), but it is explicit enough to make my point here which is that certain links between world knowledge and linguistic knowledge are in a very constrained sense arbitrary.

Recent work on lexical conceptual structures coming out of the Lexicon
Project at MIT casts some of the words and world representation issues in a
new light. Hale and his colleagues (Hale and Laughren, 1983, Hale and
Keyser, 1986) have proposed a level of representation called lexical conceptual
structure (LCS) which follows from and extends Jackendoff's work on predicate decomposition. This work involves breaking the definition of a predicator
into a series of subcomponents of meaning, subcomponents which prove to be
relevant to the predicate argument structure of these lexical items. The LCS
offers insight into the mapping between lexical representations and syntactic
configurations. In my opinion, when we speak of lexical semantic representation we must keep in mind that the semantic representation of a word relevant
to its functioning as a linguistic entity is separate from the much wider range
of information which must be considered to be part of its meaning. For example, connotation is relevant to the meaning of a word but it is not part of its
lexical semantic representation.

Consider another cross-linguistic discussion. The meaning of a word
like *thirst* has the potential for yielding multiple LCSs only some of which
might be relevant to its linguistic behavior. Take the sensation of being thirsty
which we share with all other human beings, and let's agree for the sake of
argument that we can all share the same concept of a thirst event. When we
look at how that event is spoken of across languages, we find that it is linguistically encoded in a variety of different ways. In some languages the lexical
semantic representation for "to thirst" might be non-translatory (I have thirst,
Thirst is at me, I am at thirst (in a state of being thirsty)); or it might be translatory (I go to thirst, I am getting to be thirsty, Thirst has come upon me, *etc.*).
Notice that even within the set of translatory versus non-translatory options the
thematic roles assigned to *thirst* can vary. In some instances it serves as the
theme (the entity which moves or is located), and in other instances it serves as
an anchorpoint which the experiencer moves to (goal) or is located at (location). I am sure if we looked hard enough we would also find examples where
a source is involved (I am running from thirst, Thirst comes from me). All of
the above figure/ground relations and translatory/non-translatory options are
compatible with the meaning of *thirst*, and they all pick from the same set of
building blocks comprised of motion/location relations and thematic roles.
Still, which encoding to use as the basis of a LCS for a verb of thirsting is a
language-specific choice. And, certain specific syntactic and semantic consequences will follow from that choice—similar in nature to the syntactic and
semantic differences between *dance* and *danser*.

Actually, the work on LCSs raises two even more basic questions: What
is a word? And, what does it mean to know a word? A word is not the header
associated with a lexical entry. That is simply a label associated with a given
word. A word is a more abstract entity which is probably best thought of as a
LCS plus information concerning what components of that LCS are projected
into the syntax, its predicate argument structure. The label *move* in English,

for example, is associated with at least two words, one non-translatory (I saw it move), and the other translatory (She moved to the other side of the room). In fact, some languages give distinct labels to these two words.

Knowing a word entails not only knowing what it means, but also knowing how to use it. Part of knowing a verb is knowing the various ways it can realize its arguments, and if it permits more than one way, what sets each of the alternatives apart. Examination of this aspect of lexical knowledge gets us into the nitty gritty of what word representation is all about. It also brings to light some of the more perplexing problems which must be faced in the process of developing "reverse engineering" techniques for extracting information from dictionaries. I'll mention not only the problems, but also the potential benefits to be gained from systematic examination of learner's dictionaries and large corpora of texts. Atkins, Kegl and Levin (in press) discuss the explicit and implicit information to be found in learner's dictionaries such as the *Longman Dictionary of Contemporary English* (LDOCE), the *Oxford Advanced Learner's Dictionary of Contemporary English* (OALD), and the *Collins English Learner's Dictionary.* In this paper, we pointed out complex form/meaning interdependencies which can only be extracted from existing dictionaries by detailed examination of converging information provided in the three central components of a dictionary entry: the syntactic code, the sense information, and the example sentences.

Consider the problem. Many verbs exhibit transitivity alternations where they appear as either transitive or intransitive. See the examples below which were discussed in the Atkins, Kegl, and Levin paper:

Indefinite (Unspecified) Object Alternation:
(1) a. Mike ate the Cake.
  b. Mike ate. (=Mike ate food or a meal.)

Characteristic Property Alternation:
(2) a. That dog bites people.
  b. That dog bites. (=That dog is a biter.)

Reciprocal Alternation:
(3) a. Anne met Cathy.
  b. Anne and Cathy met. (=Anne and Cathy met each other.)

Reflexive Alternation:
(4) a. Jill dressed herself hurriedly.
  b. Jill dressed hurriedly. (=Jill dressed herself hurriedly.)

Causative/Inchoative (also Anti-Causative or Ergative) Alternation:
(5) a. Janet broke the cup. (=Janet caused the cup to break.)
  b. The cup broke. (How the cup broke is left unspecified.)

Instrumental Alternation:
(6) a. The scissors won't cut the denim.
  b. The scissors won't cut.

The preceding examples not only participate in transitivity alternations, but the interpretation assigned to their intransitive forms and the thematic role assigned to their subjects varies according to the verb class to which each belongs. When examining pairs such as those above, it quickly becomes clear that a simple transitive/intransitive distinction will not suffice. There is a complex interaction between verb class, sense, and transitivity which must be recognized. Work on extracting significant lexical information from machine-readable dictionaries such as the research described by Boguraev (1986) requires extremely complex computations on a database not originally designed with such a use in mind. Although learner's dictionaries are phenomenally comprehensive, they aren't as consistent in their presentation of the lexical data as one might hope. Therefore, a lot of cleaning up needs to be done before even the best machine-readable dictionary can reveal the form/meaning inter-dependencies mentioned above. The project is, however, well worth the effort. One suggestion I would like to make is that we not confine ourselves to decoding simply the syntactic code and sense portions of the dictionary. The example sentences have a lot to offer. Contrary to their role in etymological dictionaries or more general purpose dictionaries where they serve to document the chronological occurrences of a lexical item or its attested occurrences in literary texts, example sentences in learner's dictionaries are another form of code. The sentences which exemplify certain verb classes or types of transitivity alternations are parallel in form, so much so that one can often determine the possibilities for syntactic patterns and verb class membership from the examples alone. And, frequently, the examples cue the user into usage patterns that the entry itself has failed to include in its metalinguistic components. Finally, a pair of sentences and their associated interpretations is frequently the most effective means of conveying cross-classificatory information to a user. Even if a dictionary were able to exhaustively convey this information in its code, its not clear that such information would be easily understood by the user. Furthermore, the more we develop tools for extracting dictionary information from carefully chosen example sentences, the closer we will get to extracting such information from unrestricted texts.

Determining verb class membership and the syntactic and semantic properties of a given lexical item also depends upon world knowledge that the user brings to the dictionary, knowledge which is pre-assumed by the sense definitions. In analyzing dictionary entries in LDOCE and OALD, we found many inconsistencies in the presentation of lexical entries which only became obvious when we examined what one would get from the explicit and implicit regularities presented alone, without certain commonsense and experiential knowledge we are assumed to bring to the task. Unless the "reverse engineering device" also comes to the task with such assumed knowledge, we won't reap the maximum benefits from this dictionary research.

A final postscipt to this discussion concerns current efforts to develop a theory neutral lexicon which can be used by a variety of parsing and generation programs. Such a goal can be achieved, but I think it is important to keep in mind how that end product will be achieved and what it has to offer theory-based parsers and generation systems. The neutral lexicon must be reductionist in nature. It can only be arrived at by continually breaking into subcomponents those units currently utilized by well-articulated linguistic theories. Then we will still need a series of overlay systems which will combine those commonly shared units into the chunks made reference to in each individual framework. Thus it seems that building a neutral lexicon requires a well-articulated lexicon from each theory purporting to use this neutral lexicon and a well articulated set of rules to translate the neutral lexicon into a form the framework can utilize. On the optimistic side, although we work hard to maintain our individual identity, most linguists do seem to agree on most of the basic units of analysis as is evidenced by the fact that we continually translate the data from one theory into another in order to argue against it or in order to use the basic facts in support of our own analyses. Work toward a neutral lexicon will, if nothing else, lead us to a better understanding of the subsets of data successfully handled in different frameworks and to a more precise characterization of those points on which we agree and disagree.

Chapter 2

Unification & the New Grammatism

Chapter 2.1

COMIT ==> PATR II*

Gerald Gazdar

Here is the history of linguistics in one sentence: once upon a time linguists (i.e., syntacticians) used augmented phrase structure grammars, then they went over to transformational grammars, and then some of them started using augmented phrase structure grammars again, <space for moral>. Whilst we are in this careful scholarly mode, let us do the same service for computational linguistics: once upon a time computational linguists (i.e., builders of parsers) used augmented phrase structure grammars, then they went over to augmented transition networks, and then many of them started using augmented phrase structure grammars again, <space for moral>. There are people who would have you believe in one or other of these stories (e.g., Chomsky, 1983, p. 65, for the first). And, of course, there is an element of truth in each of them. If an unrestricted rewriting system is an "augmented phrase structure grammar," then we can say that Chomsky (1951) propounds an augmented phrase structure grammar [1].

Turning to computational linguistics, let us consider two fairly well-known exemplars, one for the old grammatism (COMIT—Yngve, 1958) and one for the new (PATR II—Shieber, 1984). Both are computer languages, both were designed for computational linguistic purposes, notably the specification of natural language grammars with a view to their use in parsers. The two general criteria that Yngve explicitly notes as having motivated the design of COMIT, namely "that the rules be convenient for the linguist— compact, easy to use, and easy to think in terms of" and "that the rules be flexible and powerful— that they not only reflect the current linguistic views on what grammar rules are, but also that they be easily adaptable to other linguistic views" (1958, p. 26) are indistinguishable from two of the three general criteria that motivate the design of PATR II (Shieber, 1985, pp. 194-197) (the third—computational effectiveness—may have been too obviously pressing in the late 1950s for Yngve to have thought worth mentioning explicitly). Both have been implemented on a variety of hardware, and substantial grammar fragments have been written in both.[2]

Both COMIT and PATR II are, in some sense, and not necessarily the same sense, augmented phrase structure grammar formalisms. In examining the differences between them, it will be convenient to divide the topic into (i) consideration of categories, and (ii) consideration of rules.

Looking at the category formalisms first, both formalisms allow categories to have an internal feature structure, but there the resemblance ends. A COMIT category consists of a monadic name (e.g., "NP"), an optional integer "subscript," and a set containing any number of attribute-value pairs (called "logical subscripts"). Attributes are atomic, but values are sets containing between 0 and 36 atomic members. This is a sophisticated and expressive feature system by contrast to the impoverished phonology-based binary systems that most transformational syntacticians seemed content to assume, though scarcely to use, during the 1960s and 1970s. A PATR II category, however, is an arbitrary directed acyclic graph (DAG) whose nodes are labeled with atomic names drawn from some finite set. Thus it easy to see how to translate a set of COMIT categories into a set of PATR II categories: the only minor complication concerns how you choose to encode the COMIT integer subscripts. But translation in the other direction is in general impossible, for all practical purposes, since COMIT logical subscripts do not permit any recursive structure to be built.[3]

Switching our attention now to rules, we observe that both COMIT and PATR II allow one to write rules that say that an expression of category A can consist of an expression of category B followed by an expression of category C. But a COMIT rule is a rewriting rule whose primary concern is that of mapping strings into strings, whereas a PATR II rule is a statement about a permissible structural configuration, a statement that concerns itself with strings almost incidentally. A rule with more than one symbol on the left-hand side makes no sense in the PATR II conception of grammar, but it makes perfectly good sense when the function of a rule is to change one string of categories into another string, as in the COMIT conception. COMIT rules give you unrestricted string rewriting; PATR II rules permit concatenation only. Thus COMIT rules cannot, in general, be translated into PATR II rules, and PATR II rules, thanks to the category system employed, cannot, in general, be translated into COMIT rules. COMIT rules are inextricably embedded in a procedural language: the rules are ordered in their application, every rule has an address, every rule ends with a GOTO-on-success, and rules can set and consult global variables in the environment (the "dispatcher"). PATR II rules, by contrast, are order independent, side effect free, and pristinely declarative. Both languages allow the user to manipulate features in rules, but whilst COMIT offers the user a small arsenal of devices—deletion, complementation, merger—of which the last-named appears to be the one most used, PATR II offers only unification. But are "merger" and "unification" two names for the same concept? The answer here is no: merge (A,B), where A and B are attribute values (hence sets), is the intersection of A and B if the latter is nonempty, and B otherwise.

There is nothing too surprising in any of the foregoing: as one might expect from the chronology, PATR II stands in much the same relation to

COMIT as Scheme does to Fortran. If anyone wanted to do COMIT-style computational linguistics in 1987, then they would probably be better off using Icon than they would be using PATR II. What is distinctive about the new grammatism, as canonically illustrated by PATR II (but also exemplified in CUG, DCG, FUG, GPSG, HPSG, JPSG, LFG, UCG, ...) is (i) the use of a basically type 2 rule format (single mother, unordered, no explicit context sensitivity) under (ii) a node admissibility rather than a string rewriting interpretation, with (iii) a recursively defined tree or DAG based category set, and (iv) unification as the primary operation for combining syntactic information. It would be interesting to learn of any computational linguistic work done in the 1950s or 1960s that exhibits more than one of these characteristics.

Acknowledgements

I am grateful to Geoff Pullum for some relevant conversation and to Victor Yngve for making copies of unpublished COMIT work available to me. This research was supported by grants from the ESRC (UK) and SERC (UK).

Notes

1. The notation Chomsky used mostly suggests a context sensitive rewriting system which allows null productions (hence type 0 rather than type 1). However, one nonstandard augmentation that is employed throughout the work is the "sometimes" notation, as in the following example from page 30.

    Y2 → y, sometimes

    This remarkable innovation does not seem to have found favor in later work except, perhaps, as the precursor of the "variable rules" that became fashionable in sociolinguistics in the 1970s.

2. For some example COMIT grammars, see Dinneen (1962), Fabry (1963), Satterthwait (1962), Weintraub (1970), and Yngve (1967).

3. The concern in this paper is only with what each formalism can naturally express, not with what you can do if you start playing tricks. Since both COMIT and PATR II are Turing equivalent, anything that can be expressed in the one, can be coded up somehow or other in the other one. Thus, for example, given some Godel-numbering scheme for DAGS, every PATR II feature structure could be mapped into a COMIT integer subscript (ignoring the 2^{15} upper bound on the latter). But nobody in their right mind would do this.

Chapter 2.2

UNIFICATION AND THE NEW GRAMMATISM

Steve Pulman

What Are We Talking About?

The prototypical unification grammar consists of a context-free skeleton, enriched with a set of *feature + value* specifications on the grammatical symbols in the rules and associated lexicon. These feature specifications may involve variables, and may be recursive (i.e., the values may be interpreted as referring to a whole category). Whereas parsing and generating sentences using grammars with atomic grammatical labels involves a test for equality between symbols in a rule and those in a tree, in unification grammars the test is whether two non-atomic descriptions "unify," i.e., can be made identical by appropriate mutual substitutions of terms. This mechanism can be used to enforce identity and co-ocurrence restrictions between feature values, and to "percolate" such values between nodes. Thus, to take a simple example, a rule like:

$$A \text{ --> } B\ C$$
$$foo(A) = foo(B)$$
$$baz(B) = baz(C)$$

where the equations specify constraints on the possible values of the features "foo" and "baz", can be understood as "percolating" the value of *foo* from *B* to *A*, or vice versa, and as enforcing agreement between *baz* values on the daughter categories. But these are not separate operations or procedures: in fact, they are not operations or procedures at all. They are order independent, fully declarative statements about what must be true for a tree to be well formed whose implementation by unification has these desirable effects. Thus unification provides a neat and manageable solution to the problem of feature agreement, and feature percolation between nodes in a phrase structure tree: a problem which has produced more *ad-hoc* and underspecified "solutions" than almost any other in linguistics. (Nor has the computational paradigm done any better: the usual solution in NLP has been to decorate CF rules with arbitrary bits of Lisp code).

This high-level syntax in terms of equations may translate down into a form suitable for unification of terms, resulting perhaps in a rule like:

A[foo(X)] --> B[foo(X), baz(Y)]   *C[baz(Y)]*

or for unification of graphs, perhaps represented more like:

    [[mother   [category A [foo X]]]
     [daughter1 [category B [foo X]
     [baz Y]]]
     [daughter2 [category C [baz Y]]]]

The actual "unification" used may range from strict (first order) logical unification to more or less arbitrarily powerful pattern matching (Kay, 1979), with many other variants aimed at capturing specific types of linguistic regularity (Gazdar, Klein, Pullum, and Sag, 1985; Bresnan, Ed., 1982). There is no ultimate formal difference between term and graph unification, although they differ in the styles of grammar writing they encourage. In term unification, the terms must be fully specified, perhaps via some system of default values for features. In graph unification, without further stipulation, non-distinct graphs will unify, encouraging a style in which rules and lexical entries may be radically under-specified.

What Can You Do with Unification Grammars?

Assume that we are talking about ordinary unification (i.e., allowing for category valued features, but not for negation, disjunction or other types of testing or pattern matching). A CFG enriched with such unification is still an extremely powerful system. Given the ability to manipulate category valued features we can generate some context-sensitive languages directly (at least). We can use the feature system to mimic a Turing machine (Ritchie, 1986) (though this may not be reflected in weak generative capacity of the resulting grammar), and can simulate or implement many other apparently widely diverse grammatical formalisms: Fillmore type case grammars, categorial and dependency grammars, indexed grammars, some aspects of systemic networks, and so on. We can express such grammars in a wholly declarative way in the confidence that there is a theoretically clean and fairly efficient computational interpretation of them.

Furthermore, viewed simply as a computational technique, unification can be used for several other types of linguistic structural manipulation beyond those involved in morphological or syntactic analysis:

(i) building up explicit, possibly decorated, parse trees themselves during the course of recognizing a sentence, as is done in, e.g., *Definite Clause Grammars* (Pereira and Warren, 1980).

(ii) building up logical forms compositionally by using extra features to represent the function-argument structure of a constituent as is done in, e.g., the PATR formalism (Shieber, 1987). With ingenuity, the effects of function application, composition, and so on can be simulated using logical variables within a feature system. More simple predicate-argument structure can of course be built directly.

(iii) assigning prosodic contours on the basis of syntactic and lexical structure, by associating values for relative prominence and direction of pitch movement to the components of a constituent (Bell, 1986). Unification ties in all these values in such a way that the absolute pitch value of some constituent may ultimately depend on that of some higher level constituent, or of some other phrase some distance away. To the extent that prosody is syntax driven at all, this is a theoretically clean way of deriving default intonation contours from the parse tree of a sentence.

(iv) expressing sortal (selectional) retrictions on combinations of functions with arguments, for example, for lexical disambiguation purposes (Alshawi et al. 1987). Sort lattices of various types can be encoded within a unification based formalism.

Unification as a Contribution to Linguistic Theory

It should be clear from the foregoing that there are at least two different ways in which we could assess the notion of unification, and unification grammars. Given a particular notion of unification as incorporated in a linguistic theory (say, that defined in Gazdar et al., 1985), we can ask whether it enables us to express linguistic generalizations clearly, and whether it meshes in satisfactorily with other mechanisms used within that theory (for example, default feature specifications, or co-occurrence restrictions). In short, we are assessing unification as a claim about human linguistic ability. Depending on the formal properties of the type of unification at issue, this may or may not be a meaningful thing to do: if we have a system that can do anything, it is not news to be told that it is adequate for syntactic description.

In fact, it strikes me as most unlikely that everything one would want to say about the syntactic structure of language would turn out to be expressible cleanly within one particular flavor of unification grammar (*pace* LFG, FUG, GPSG). Even if this did turn out to be the case, it would actually be mildly disturbing, given current dogma about modularity, to find that a mechanism conceived of originally for syntax turned out to be so easily adaptable for other, possibly unrelated, kinds of symbolic manipulation. It is almost certain that any theory with unification as a component will be capable of simulating most of the features of any other such theory, when regarded merely as a notation. Unification is a very powerful symbol manipulation tool: a programming language, in fact. Thus arguments about whether X-UG is better than Y-UG, for many values of X and Y, are liable to be as ultimately unproductive (except perhaps of entertaining rhetoric) as most other competitive linguistic arguments.

Unification Grammars as a Linguistic Lingua Franca

In my view, a more useful way of thinking about unification, from the point of view of computational linguistics at least, is to see it as merely a useful computational procedure with a well-defined semantics and efficient implementations. It seems to me that the real role of unification in grammatical formalisms will be to provide a kind of normal form of guaranteed computational tractability, or perhaps better, an assembly language into which different linguistic theories can be compiled. Take the example of feature percolation given above: as far as the linguist is concerned, the first statement involving explicit equalities says everything there is to say about when a tree is or is not well formed. The linguistic theory need not be committed to any of the concepts presupposed in the translation to the second format where the equations are implemented via unification: for example, the notion of a logical variable need not figure in the linguistic theory at all, although it must figure in the implementation.

Thus the relation between a prototypical unification grammar of the type outlined above, and a particular linguistic theory, would be akin to that between the compiled code which executes a program, and the original raw form of the program (or even some higher level description). We have already seen that many different linguistic theories can be translated into a unification grammar format: the original insights and theoretical content of the theories is presumably independent of this translation. The grammarian says what he wants to say about the structure of the language, in some high-level declarative formalism, and for the purposes of parsing or generation, this high-level description is compiled out into a lower level, simple unification formalism, for which there exist well-understood computational interpretations.

This compilation process serves several purposes: the practical one of ensuring that you can actually do something with the grammar: parse, or generate sentences. A second purpose, somewhat akin to the requirement of Turing machine reducibility on psychological theories, is achieved by the fact that the existence of such a compilation serves as a guarantee that the original theory is consistent and has a coherent computational interpretation. (The version of GPSG in Gazdar et al. (1985) turns out to have some problematic features in this respect.) Finally, in supplying such a normal form, a unification formalism provides a rational basis for the comparison of different grammatical theories: you have to compare like with like, and this can more easily be done via translation into a common format. This is an aspect of unification formalisms which has been explored for formalisms like LFG and GPSG using the PATR formalism by the CSLI foundations of grammar group (Shieber, 1987).

Chapter 2.3

UNIFICATION AND SOME NEW
GRAMMATICAL FORMALISMS

Aravind K. Joshi

The key idea in the unification-based approaches to grammar is that we deal with informational structures (called feature structures) which encode a variety of linguistic information (lexical, syntactic, semantic, discourse, perhaps even cross-linguistic) in a uniform way and then manipulate (combine) these structures by means of a few (one, if possible) well-defined operations (unification being the primary one). The feature structures consist of features and associated values, which can be atomic or complex, i.e., feature structures themselves. In other words, the values can be from a structured set. The unification operation builds new structures and, together with some string combining operation (concatenation being the primary one), pairs the feature structures with strings (Shieber, 1986).

How Does the Unification Formalism Differ from the Standard Context-free Grammar Formalism?

In a pure CFG one has only a finite number of nonterminals, which are the category symbols. In a CFG based grammar one associates with each category symbol a complex of features that are exploited by the grammar in a variety of ways. In the unification formalism there is really no such separation between the category symbols and the features. Feature structures are the only elements to deal with. Of course, the traditional category symbols show up as values of a feature (*cat*) in the feature structures. The notion of nonterminal symbol is flexible now. If we multiply out all features and their values down to the atomic values, we will have a very large number (even infinite under certain circumstances) of nonterminal symbols. Of course, this means trouble for parsing. Clearly, the standard parsing algorithms for parsing CFG's cannot be extended to unification formalism because of the exponential blowup of computational complexity, including the possibility of nontermination. One could focus only on parts of feature structures, not necessarily the same parts for different feature structures, and thereby, have a flexible notion of nonterminal on the one hand and, perhaps, control the computational complexity on the other hand. This aspect of unification formalism has not received much attention yet, except in the very interesting work of Shieber (1985).

To What Extent has the Unification Formalism been Motivated by Processing Considerations?

First of all, we should distinguish at least two meanings of processing considerations. One has to do with the efficiency of computation and the other has to do with computational formalisms, which are well defined and whose semantics (i.e., the semantics of the formalism) also can be well defined. Although the unification formalism has been developed largely by researchers who are, no doubt, interested in the efficiency of computation, the primary motivation for the formalism has to do with the second meaning of processing considerations. The standard CFG based formalisms (augmented in a variety of ways) can do all the computations that a unification-based formalism can do and vice versa; however, the semantics of the formalism (not of the language described by the grammar) is not always well understood. The same is, of course, true of the ATN formalism. The unification formalism does give an opportunity to provide a well-defined semantics because of its algebraic characterization (Pereira and Shieber, 1984). How this understanding can be cashed into efficient algorithms for processing is still very much an open question. Good engineering is based on good theory—therein lies the hope.

Are We Converging to Some Class of Formalisms that are Relevant to Processing and, if so, How can this Class be Characterized in a Theoretical Manner?

Most of the grammatical formalisms, especially those of the so-called nontransformational flavor, have been motivated, at least in part, by processing considerations, for example, parsing complexity. We could say that these formalisms are converging if convergence is defined along several dimensions. GPSG, LFG, HG, HPSG (CFG: context-free grammar, GPSG: generalized phrase structure grammar, LFG: lexical functional grammar, HG: head grammar, TAG: tree adjoining grammar, HPSG: head-driven phrase structure grammar, FUG: functional unification grammar, CG: categorial grammar, PATR: parsing and translation) all have a context-free grammar explicitly or implicitly, use feature structures of some sort or another, and a lexicon. Unification formalism by itself is not a grammatical theory but a formalism in which different grammatical theories can be instantiated. Some of these grammatical theories explicitly incorporate unification formalism as one component of the grammar (e.g., GPSG, LFG, HPSG, FUG, PATR based grammars, etc.), while some others (e.g., TAG, HG, CG, etc.) do not explicitly incorporate unification formalism, as the feature checking component is not explicitly specified in these grammars as they are formulated at present. The unification formalism is a nice way of incorporating this feature checking component in these grammars, in fact, the string-combining operations (in HG and CG) and the tree combining operation (in TAG) can themselves be formulated within the unification formalism generating feature structures in an appropriate manner. In fact, these different grammatical theories differ with respect to the

domain of locality over which the unifications (*a la* Shieber), i.e., a set of constraints across a set of feature structures, are defined. For example, for a CFG
based unification formalism, the domains of locality are the context-free rules,
e.g.,

$$X_0 \ R \ X_1 \ X_2.$$

The unifications are defined over feature structures associated with X_0, X_1, and
X_2. For a tree adjoining grammar, the domains of locality are the elementary
trees (structures, in the general case), both initial and auxiliary. These domains
of locality define the unifications across the feature structures associated with
the components of the domain and thereby determine how information flows
among these feature structures. These domains also determine the kinds of
word-order patterns describable by these different grammatical formalisms. In
this sense, all these grammatical formalisms could be said to converge. This is
not surprising as the unification formalism is a very powerful formalism, in
fact equivalent to a Turing machine. As far as I can see, any reasonable grammatical formalism can be instantiated in the unification formalism, as it is
unconstrained in the sense described above. The particular constraints come
from the particular grammatical formalism that is being instantiated.

There is another sense of convergence we can talk about. Here we are
concerned with the weak generative capacity, strong generative capacity, parsing complexity, and other formal language and automata theoretic properties.
It appears that a proper subclass of indexed grammars with at least the following properties may characterize adequately a class of grammars suitable for
describing natural language structures, a class called "mildly context-
sensitive" in Joshi (1985), (MCG: mildly context-sensitive grammars, MCL:
languages of MCGs). The properties are: (1) context-free languages are
properly contained in MCL, (2) languages in MCL can be parsed in polynomial time, (3) MCG's capture only certain kinds of dependencies, e.g., nested
dependencies and certain limited kinds of crossing dependencies (e.g., in the
subordinate clause constructions in Dutch, but not in the so-called MIX (or
Bach) language, which consists of equal numbers of a's, b's, and c's in any
order), and (4) languages in MCL have the constant growth property, i.e., if
the strings of the language are arranged in increasing order of length, then any
two consecutive lengths do not differ by arbitrarily large amounts; in fact, any
given length can be described as a linear combination of a finite set of fixed
lengths. These properties do not precisely define MCG but rather give only a
rough characterization, as the properties are only necessary conditions and
further some of the properties are properties of structural descriptions rather
than the languages, hence, difficult to characterize precisely. TAG, HG, some
restricted IG (IG: indexed grammar), and certain types of CG all appear to
belong to this class. Moreover, certain equivalences have been established
between these grammars, for example, between TAG and HG (Vijay-Shanker,
Weir, and Joshi, 1986). Some natural extensions of TAG also seem to belong
to this class. The processing implications of this convergence are not at all

clear, because the polynomial time complexity, first of all, is only a worst case measure, and secondly, it has to be considered along with the constant of proportionality, which depends on the grammar.

Do Processing Considerations and Results Show that such Systems when Implemented can be Neutral between Analysis and Production?

The pure unification formalism (i.e., with unification as the only operation and no non-monotonic aspects in the feature structures) is bidirectional, in the sense that the order in which unifications are performed does not matter. In this sense, they can be considered neutral between analysis and production. However, as soon as one adds operators that are not commutative or associative or adds values to feature structure which exhibit non-monotonic behavior, we no longer have this bidirectionality (and also, perhaps, disallow the possibility of giving well-defined semantics). The proponents of unification formalism hope to keep these amendments under control. How successfully this can be done is very much an open problem.

To the extent a formalism is declarative (and this applies equally well to the particular grammatical theories instantiated in a unification formalism) it can be neutral between analysis and production. The processes which manipulate these formalisms may or may not differ for analysis and production. Neutrality between analysis and production is a property shared by a variety of grammatical formalisms. This kind of neutrality is not the key selling point for unification formalism, in my judgment.

Is it a Real Advance or just a Hollywood Term?

We have already stated the difference between a CFG based formalism using feature complexes in a variety of ways and the unification based formalism. A well-defined formalism whose mathematical properties (syntactic, semantic, and computational) are well understood is always an advance, even though some earlier theories may have used the same pieces of information in some informal manner. Clearly, before the advent of the CFG formalism, people had worked with related ideas (e.g., immediate constituent analysis, even part of Panini's grammar are in a CFG style!); however, no one would say that CFG is just a Hollywood term (or a Broadway term, given the location where CFG's were born). The mathematical and computational insights that CFG has provided have immensely helped linguistics as well as computational linguistics. The unification formalism shows similar possibilities although the mathematical or computational results are not yet at the level corresponding to the CFG formalism. So in this sense, it is not a Hollywood term, it is an advance. How big an advance? We will have to wait for an answer to this question until we know more about its mathematical and computational properties. Personally, I would like to see some results on some constrained unification formalisms, in the sense that the flow of information between feature structures is constrained in some systematic manner. Such results, if obtainable, could give us more insights into the computational properties of these formalisms and their suitability (not just their adequacy) for describing natural language structures.

Acknowledgments

This work is partially supported by DARPA grants NOOO14-85-K-0018 and NOOO14-85-K-0807, NSF grants MCS8219196-CER, MCS-82-07294, 1 RO1-HL-29985-01, U.S. Army grants DAA6-29-84-K-0061, DAAB07-84-K-F077,U.S. Air Force grant 82-NM-299, AI Center grants NSF-MCS-83-05221.

Chapter 2.4

DISCUSSION: UNIFICATION & THE NEW GRAMMATISM

Fernando PEREIRA: It is very important to distinguish views of unification grammar and unification grammar formalisms, and they very often get confused and people start to talk at cross-purposes. And I distinguish four different fields which overlap in certain ways. One is what I might call the mathematical view, which approaches these formalisms as devices of formal language theory: the same way as one might study context free grammars or index grammars, one might study unification grammars. We can look at the formalism from a more computer science oriented point of view, in particular as regards the design of computer languages for processing linguistic information. We can take a linguistic point of view when we try to reuse the formalisms for expressing linguistic theories. And finally, we can look at the more psycholinguistic point of view, where we are trying to use formalisms to express or help in expressing language processing mechanisms. And I think it's important to distinguish this kind of processing from the processing that is involved in designing a computer language. The desiderata are rather different in general. Now, my view about unification, or my interest in unification grammar formalisms are basically of the first and second kind, basically mathematical and computer science views. And I see these formalisms as providing a very radical idealization of information combination in language processing, where you deal with the abstract partial descriptions of sentences or other utterances in general.

Now, as I see it the main contribution of unification grammar formalisms in general is that one has abstracted away from specific machine details, from specific data structures, to a fairly general notion of information combination in language processing. One can see then that the unification grammar is a sort of partial specification of a language analysis or generation process, although of course only partial: It has to be filled in by specific processing algorithms, by specific models of sentence processing by people. The questions that come up when we think of unification grammar and its idealization are of various kinds, but the ones that I'm interested in are questions like How realistic is the idealization? Are we actually idealizing too much? And in particular, how do we cope with highly disjunctive descriptions which lead to overcommitment and combinatorially explosive problems of analysis? Another problem is how do we deal with locality? Very often in unification grammars you have very long-distance dependencies between information contents, which leads to combinatorial problems. There are problems of implementation for worst-case. Even in the case where the formalisms are decidable, they have very poor worst- case complexity characterizations, and there may be other subformalisms that have better (for instance, polynomial) parsing times. On the implementation side, but looking not at implementation on the computer but rather how this could be used as part of theories of language processing in people, How good are these abstract information combination operators? How are they at capturing what information combination goes on when people actually process sentences?

One last comment I want to make along those lines, is that I like to see a unification grammar from this perspective as giving a partial specification, which but might be partially realized by the implementation mechanism. For instance, you might have a nondeterminacy in the grammar as to which particular processor is going to take what particular path in the search space, and it might fail if that path leads to an inconsistency. By having these more specialized kinds of algorithms, partial algorithms, you might be able to capture performance concepts and certain preferences in processing. So in the same way in computer science one often has partial specifications. I take the view that unification grammar formalisms follow the same distinct kind of usefulness and content as, say, logical specifications in the specification of algorithms.

Steve PULMAN: If you're coming to unification grammar formalisms from a mostly linguistics background as I did, the first thing that strikes you is, it's a really neat way of handling problems that were always glossed over in the books, how to get features to trickle up and down trees in an appropriate way. Those of you who have taught undergraduate syntax classes, relying on well-known textbooks, will have had the embarrassing experience of getting halfway through a derivation on a blackboard and realizing that there isn't anything there that will get [+ wh] from the bottom to the top. And unification provides a very neat mechanism of doing that. Once you then start to read around and see what people do with unification as a mechanism, you begin to realize that there are a lots of different flavors, as Pereira said, and also that, in terms of linguistic theories, very often the particular flavor comes along with a view of what constitutes a category. For example, if you think that categories like NP and VP are atoms with associated clumps of properties, then the type of unification that you're likely to invoke in your grammar is going to be something pretty much like ordinary, what I'll call Prolog style unification, whereas if you think that there's no essential difference between categories and features, as in the generalized phrase structure grammar framework, that categories are simply sets of features, where features are pairs of name and value, then you're likely to have a type of unification which is a little bit richer, in the sense that you can combine things which are not completely specified, things that if you treated them literally as prolog terms wouldn't unify.

The next thing that strikes you is—purely as a mechanism—how flexible all this is. And we've used unification grammars for simulating or for implementing different types of linguistic theory. It's very easy to assign case roles to noun phrases in the style of Fillmore or Jackendoff by associating the right information with the verb and passing the case role features up through a tree so that, in the course of actually parsing the sentence and assigning the constituent structure, you get this extra information assigned. You can do the same thing for other aspects of semantics like ?? quantificational structure of sentences by having particular features whose values are actually semantic items.

You can use unification to build up what might be done in a different framework by function application. Function composition type—that gets a little bit tricky, but it's possible to do it. Another application used recently is using unification to assign prosodic contours to sentences by cheating, pretending that prosodic contours are things that can be assigned in a kind of atomic way and you can capture the interrelationship between the prosodic values and particular constituents in the global structure of the sentence by imposing various constraints that unification allows you to implement very efficiently. Once you've realized all these things, you start to get a little bit suspicious about linguistic theories that want to make strong claims about unification as a contribution to cognitive science or whatever your term for that brand of psychological theorizing is, because with a little bit of experience you realize that inside these frameworks you can simulate almost anything else that you want to simulate, and you tend to want to back off a little bit and say, "Hang on, what we've got here is not something that should be viewed in the way that linguists have usually viewed a formalism," namely, where the formalism is what captures the generalizations. Rather you might want to think of it as something that is a low-level language in which the particular grammars you'll want to write will compile into, so that the actual generalizations are not there written in grammars in the usual way.

A unification grammar is actually the result of having written some higher level grammar and having that compiled out. That's the kind of thing which I think you can see has been expressed clearly in the work that Shieber and his colleagues did in comparisons of LFG and GPSG, by translating both into a PATR-style format. And as I said in the paper, my end view is that the usefulness of unification grammar formalisms is in providing a kind of a ling assembly language expressing grammatical theories.

Aravind JOSHI: One of the questions that was asked was about processing considerations. By processing, I think one means at least two things. One is the effiency of computation, and the second aspect is whether one can have a well-defined semantics for the particular formalism. I think that the unification framework is not really motivated by efficiency of computation. In my judgment, it's much more motivated by the second aspect, namely it provides well-defined semantics because you can have various kinds of augmentations of the standard phrase structure grammar and construct efficient computational procedures. But the problem is for particular formalisms, it's very hard to state what the formalism is. And I think it's an advance, in that sense. Now whether this understanding, this semantic understanding of the formalism, can be cached into algorithms is an open problem But one assumes that if you have a good theory, it's likely to lead to good engineering.

Another aspect of unification that I'd like to bring out, maybe something that can be discussed, is locality. I'm not sure I'm talking about the same thing by this as Pereira did though there ought to be some kind of connection. In the standard unification formalism, there is a context free skeleton behind the scenes. So there are rules of the kind X0 goes to X1 X2. And unifications (this is a technical term used by Shieber) are defined over the feature structures associated with X0, X1, X2. F0, F1, and F2 are the feature structures associated with X0, X1, X2. And then you specify certain equations that hold among these feature structures, and these are called the unifications. So the Domain of specification of these unifications is this rule. The Domain of locality, of course, specifies how the unifications are defined. It also determines the flow of information among the features in D. In other words, the information has to rise up to this Domain of locality in order for certain constraints amongst F0, F1, F2 to be checked. And that can cause some unnecessary flow of information, depending on the choice of the domain of locality. The domain of locality also determines the kind of word-order pattern that will be described within the framework. So one of the things that would be of interest would be to study unification formalisms by looking at different domains of locality for different types of grammars, for example, the categorial grammar, the tree adjoining grammars that I have been interested in, and in particular, in a grammar like the tree adjoining grammar where the elementary trees serve as the domain of locality. Although we don't have concrete results yet, the idea is that by looking at different domains of locality, you might get certain constrained unification formalisms because of the flow of information that's constrained. For example, the agreement can be defined between NP and V rather than NP and VP.

What's the future of unification? Well, there are two directions in which one can look for the future. One is that there will be computational environments around unification-based grammars and useful tools will be developed for writing grammars, so that's sort of the engineering aspect. On the theoretical side, I think that the important question as I see it is whether one can look at constrained formalisms within the unification framework; that could contribute to computational efficiency. That's not clear, but it might also explain why different grammatical formalisms are in principle between the same sort of things.

Martin KAY: The reasons why I like unification grammar are in fact not the reasons that have come up so far. If unification grammars had all the properties ascribed to them, I wouldn't like them quite so much. Unification grammars, it seems to me, constitute the only formalism for grammar that there has been since context-free grammars that have many of the extremely desirable properties that context-free grammars had. Context-sensitive grammars don't have them, transformational grammars certainly didn't have them, and most of the other things we've encountered in between don't either. Namely, that on all of these dimensions that Pereira mentioned—mathematical, computational, linguistic, psychological, and so forth—they have a very clean profile, they can be studied within each of those four domains without there being any unnecessary intrusion from properties that they acquire from the other domains. So, for example, you can do linguistics within a unification-based framework, secure in the knowledge that a large number of choices about how the associated computations will be done will still be open to you. You make no commitment about the kinds of strategies that will be used in the computation, but you are nevertheless assured that a rich set of strategies will be available to you. To put this another way, adopting a framework like unification makes practical sense of the distinction between competence/performance, in a way which I think is very important for linguists in general, computational linguists in particular.

Now, one of the things that it seems to me is the most interesting about unification grammar and that does not come with context-free grammar, for example, is that it provides for a great many different kinds of modularity. And modularity in linguistic descriptions seems to me to be a kind of thing that is justifiably sought after. It enables us, for example, to write formal grammars, which divide their subject matter into sensible chapters in much the same way that a traditional grammar does, and remain reasonably secure in the knowledge that when these things are put together, they will constitute a coherent whole. Now that is something that does not necessarily flow from the view of transformational grammars that says they have an essentially context-free backbone, and then a set of features decorate the trees that are constructed thanks to that context-free backbone. In my own view of the way the details ought to be settled in unification grammar, which I have called Functional Unification Grammar, there are no type-2 rules. There is not a set of context-free rules which provide the basic decorated set of trees, because it's important, to me, that the information that is provided in a context-free rule should be capable of being contributed by a different set of chapters from this grammar that you want to write. Some of it will come from the transitivity systems of the grammar, some of it will come from considerations of functional sentence perspective, whatever it might be. But there is not one place where, for example, word order or category dominance information has to be placed. So, one of the things I would like to see coming out of a unification grammar and which seems to come out of it when you do it in terms of Functional Unification Grammar is this: A lot of the stuff, which linguists for the most part don't put in the grammar itself because they claim that it's part of the theory and therefore include in the textbook about the grammar, and not the grammar itself, can in fact go into the grammar without you, in fact, having to repeat it for each individual case to which it applies. So, for example, if you believe in lexical precedence rules of some sort, you have, according to most views, two approaches that you can take. You can either specify a set of stipulations about the way all grammars will be written, i.e., either you are writing in the formalism or you are not, or you must state a linear precedence fact for each rule in the way they have always been done in a context-free grammar. Within something like Functional Unification Grammar, you can specify for those languages where they seem to be appropriate, and specify the same information in other ways in places where it seems not to be appropriate. The same thing goes for such things as head feature constraints, and so forth and so on.

Now what I have just said is, of course, an antitheoretical set of remarks. The whole point about stating these things in the metatheory and not in the theory is that they constitute what you believe about natural language and therefore what you as a scientist claim to have discovered. I think I'm just about running out of my time, so all I will say about that is that I in fact don't think that any of those remarks are remarks about the data we are studying, none of them in fact make claims about natural language, and I therefore wish to be honest on that score.

Mitch MARCUS: It seems to me that it's a little funny to have a session at a theoretical issues conference on a programming language. It's a little like having a session on Algol at an algorithms conference, and I think it's worth asking why that's the case. People tend to use two words when they talk about unification grammar, noting as other people do, as Pereira does and as Shieber does, that unification grammar is a funny thing to say, that people talk about two ways of using it. One, as Pulman said before, it's a kind of assembly language in which one might implement or compile into a theory but, when one changes language and then starts to talk about expressing theories, it's as if one would talk about again using Algol to "express" an algorithm. There's an implication in the word "express" that there's something much closer between this thing which is putatively a tool and the theory than there might be otherwise. And I'd like to look at what it is about unification grammar that leads people to view things in this way and argue that that's very dangerous, and I believe not a good thing.

Here are some things that I think are quite good and important first: First of all, unification grammar formalisms lead people to think of theories that are monotonic, where one works with partial descriptions and one works with a quality between the entities described. My own work at the moment is in such a framework, and to that extent a unification formalism would be appropriate for me to use. Something which is much more suspect, if viewed incorrectly, is this notion that there's a well-defined semantics for unification. That's true, but again people make the mistake of thinking that that maps over into a semantics for their theory. One might have a well-defined semantics, say, for Algol, God knows not Lisp, but the point is that if you implement something in that language the semantics don't transfer. So say we had a good semantics for atoms in Lisp, for example. One might use those atoms to implement parsing nodes, to implement frames, to implement individuals in the world, but the semantics clearly don't transfer.

So what I want to do is quickly describe a series of ways in which I believe unification grammar is not an ideal programming language in which to build theories, in that it doesn't lead one to think about theories of what I believe to be the right kind. One wants a programming language that allows the right kinds of things to fall out naturally. One can write structured programs in Basic, but you'd never discover the notion of structured programming looking at Basic, except by counterexample.

The first is that unification formalisms are not restrictive. This actually is in contrast to the extended context-free formalisms. As Allen once noted, a wonderful insight of ATNs was that they had this context-free part, in which most of the facts of language could be expressed, and then kitchen sink in which to put everything you couldn't fit in. This is the sense in which the research program of GPSG, to try to force everything into a context-free formalism, is just the right thing. I believe that one makes progress by trying something restrictive and working it out. To the extent that unification grammar is extraordinarily not restrictive, the tool tends to seduce one into not looking for restrictive theories.

The second thing is that unification formalisms are not modular in a rather different sense than Martin had in mind. Some work by Uszkoreit on a categorial unification grammar takes a categorial grammar on one side and Kampian discourse representation structures on the other, and some work on representing the lexicon on the third, and puts them together all implemented in unification grammar, as they say. I'd like to suggest that UG in this context might not stand only for Unification Grammar but also for Universal Glue. And to the extent that that's true, it doesn't lead one to ask the kinds of questions that I believe need to be asked. I believe that one ought to ask questions like is there a separate sentence structure for phrase structure, for subcategorization, for anaphoric phenomena, for semantics for the lexicon. What's very wonderful about unification formalisms is that they allow one to think about the pipelining of information through the system. One problem with many systems that have been implemented using these formalisms is that they use that freedom to ignore the fact that one might indeed want separate modules.

The third thing to say is that unification grammars are by and large purely declarative. There are people who are very good in programming in them. But to the extent that we're trying to do computational linguistics (by which I don't mean writing competence grammars for a useful purpose and throwing them into something), that makes them wrong. But again, the activity that I'm interested in is trying to figure out what kind of processing the human mind does, and to the extent that unification grammar doesn't really allow one to consider directly these questions, unless it's used as an assembly language, in a very abstract sense, I think that's a problem.

The fourth thing to say is that it's not powerful enough. The intrinsic formalisms that are used don't seem to work in the current sense. The next thing to say is that they're too powerful. So people have theories of things like priority, union, and overwriting, that in many cases destroy the basic monotonicity that I find so compelling to begin with. Another sense in which they're not powerful enough is you can't express your theories in unification frameworks. As Pulman noted before, the formalism does not capture the generalizations. You have to say the generalizations on the side, and in many cases to implement them in the grammar.

So, the sense in which it's too powerful is that in fact constraint propagation is really a kind of informational action at a distance, as other people have said, and it's just crucial that people ask themselves the kind of questions that both Joshi and Pereira raised, as to how do we keep information local. And these frameworks, if I look at the kinds of things people have implemented using them, have not led people to ask these kinds of questions. So in summary, I think that unification grammar isn't a bad tool. In many ways there's a trend that it really nicely summarizes. But it's a long, long way from the right thing yet.

Larry BIRNBAUM: This is addressed to linguists on the panel. I'd like to know what new, empirical results have been discovered by linguists using this kind of formalism.

Gerald GAZDAR: I think I'd like to answer that by actually addressing a point Marcus made at the very end, about formalism not expressing the generalizations. And I think there was a confusion there in that what we're talking about here are really two types of formalisms, in terms of their goals. You get all these names, FUG, GPSG, LFG, and so on, and they all look very much the same, but actually they conceal two different families. Now these families are not different technically or mathematically, really, but they are different in terms of the goals they were addressed to. If you take FUG and PATR II, these formalisms are not intended to express linguistic generalizations as such: particular empirical claims about the way languages work. And if they did, their progenitors would be distinctively twitchy about the fact that they did, because they'd be worried about these things being wrong. These really are intended as general purpose computational linguistics programming languages.

Now by contrast, there are these formalisms, like GPSG and LFG, which are not intended as general purpose computational linguistics formalisms, but are meant to embody particular linguistic claims, and the proponents of those formalisms make a whole raft of claims of what the details of those formalisms buy you in terms of linguistic generalizations. I wouldn't want to start giving you a list of what LFG thinks the LFG formalism buys you or what the GPSG formalism buys you, but there are such lists, in a sense. So I think one needs to distinguish these two subcategories of unification grammar formalisms. Mathematically, they are all in the same ballpark and it's reasonable to have a common panel to talk about them, but there are two sets of people out there with two sets of intentions.

Steve PULMAN: I would endorse what Gazdar said about there being two families of unification out there, and presumably LFGers and GPSGers think that their notion of unification is saying something new linguistically. The people using unification grammars as a tool, have I think made as many new discoveries about language using unification as there have been made using Lisp, for the same reason: that it's a device for encoding what you have already discovered. It may be the case that working within that framework forces you to think of things in a different way, but I guess that in my experience that's more to do with the fact that you're using a context-free skeleton than the fact that you're using unification.

Larry BIRNBAUM: What has been the progress towards reducing search on the computational side of this framework?

Fernando PEREIRA: If you take the view of some of these formalisms as programming languages, we have the same problems as with any other programming language. There are problems for which in those programming languages you can write efficient algorithms, and there are problems for which you cannot. Given the generality of languages the like of PATR II, you can write lots of grammars for which the parsing will be exponential, say. Now, that doesn't mean that, for things you are interested in characterizing, you cannot write things that parse in polynomial time or even linear time, in some cases. When looking at these formalisms as programming languages, you have to judge them by programming language criteria, not by the kind of criteria that one might use in judging a formalism that tries to capture a certain linguistic theory or certain linguistic generalization. And then someone might say, oh, but wait a minute, this thing is exponential, or np complete or intractable in some way, and clearly a language cannot be intractable (well, some people say that) so the formalism cannot be capturing the right thing. That's a different kind of argument. It's an argument you might direct at the linguistic theories based on this kind of formalism, but not at programming languages.

QUESTION: In comparing unification grammar to a context-free grammar, and saying that the importance for linguistics is similar in the two cases, that leads me as a linguist to ask the following question. One of the things that was important and is important about context-free grammar is that it was possible to go searching through the languages and constructions of the world and come up with cases that looked like they might not be handleable in a context-free way. And if those problems could be solved, then Gazdar's program, to show that context-free grammar was sufficient to handle the kinds of structures that we find in linguistics, would work out. And if you couldn't handle them, then maybe some augmentation was required. That all makes perfect sense to me. Is it the case that one could in principle search for empirical counterexamples to the use of unification as the basis for writing a grammar? I think the answer is no, from what little I know about the mathematics of it. So if the answer to that is no, then I think there's a problem.

The comment that I wanted to make is that when computer scientists talk about what they do, they talk in a way that I think is admirably clear. But now, when they talk about linguistics, they use all words that I as a linguist am very uncomfortable with, like express, generalizations, and capture. I think it might have been Pereira who used the word "capture." We, in linguistics use these terms, I think, because we often don't know quite what we're doing. They're dangerous words. If you would, think a little bit about why we don't just say describe, or explain, which are two words we might have inherited from the philosophy and history of science, whose meanings are relatively clear (you know how to describe something, how to explain things). When you don't know what you're doing, you say "capture" or "express." The issue of what it is that a formalism does in a linguistic is a very, very hairy one. There's a simple case, for example: the use of binary features in phonology. If in fact you never need ternary features, and you say that the set of feature values is the zero, one set, you have expressed the generalization that there are no ternary features in a very direct way, and your system will never give you any ternary features. But those cases are simple, and not very common, and not as interesting. The other case, which I think is the more general case, and the interesting and difficult case, is where your formalism might allow you do to all sorts of things, many of which you don't want to do, but, this formalism, in doing things that you don't want to do, would force you to alter the way you did something else. And the something else is something you know something about, and you know how to do the other thing correctly, or in a reasonable way, and the formalism says to you, "If you want to do this way-out thing, you're going to have to alter the way you do something you have confidence in." Therefore, the system as a whole won't do some bad things for you, because the combination of your formalism for part A of your enterprise, and knowledge that you have about how part B should be done, suffices to rule out the bad consequences. It seems to me that's the notion of how formalisms capture generalizations that we want to rely on, and I would appreciate comments on the extent to which this unification business helps in that enterprise.

Steve PULMAN: I think there's another dimension in which you can think about regarding falsifiability, because one of the original points back on context-free grammar was that, okay, there may be some things that can be done, but they can't be done very elegantly. And I think, it's clear that you can certainly say that about simple unification formalisms. There are some things like unbounded dependencies which can be done, but the actual gory code is not very elegant, and that's what makes you want to back off and say, That's not my theory, that's simply the implementation of it.

Mary WOOD: I'm glad this issue's coming up, of the role of a formalism within a linguistic theory. There's been some nice work done within the unification camp, mainly by Shieber, on comparing the power of, say, LFG, FUG, and PATR II, and doing interreductions and trying to show what are real substantive variations and what are so-called mere notational variants. Well, of course they aren't mere notational variants; they follow through in lots of other ways. Pollard has some nice comments, also, on the way in which two initially equivalent linguistic, or even computational formalisms can cash out in very different ways and directions, with different degrees of elegance. But what I would like to see, is a good comparison of a unification and a non-unification version of the same grammar. The only one I know where that easily could be done is categorial grammar, where I think a close comparison of a Steedman type classical categorial grammar and Uszkoreit type unification categorial grammar, might bring up some very interesting points about exactly what it is that using unification is giving you, or how it's pulling your analysis. And to go back to the tool kit metaphor, if you've got a tool kit with a lot of really nice screwdrivers, you're probably not going to use very many nails.

QUESTION: Your discussion of the unification grammars is focussed primarily around the family of unification grammars, and you've started to mention things that aren't easily represented within unification grammars. I'd like to just a little bit hear what looking at unification grammars has revealed to you about the non-unificational class. What are the pressing problems, what do you see then as just not representable, or as real problems? Could you explicitly talk about a grammar like Government and Binding and what the problems are? Does the unificational framework just not apply to that or does it reveal something about that kind of model?

Martin KAY: It seems to me that unification grammar would actually be an extremely good candidate for a formalism within which to try to formalize GB, if anybody was actually interested in doing it. There are indeed questions relating to the theoretical status of unification grammar, which seemed to me to be interesting, and of two kinds. One, somebody asked about before: Is this indeed the case that you can do things that you want to do with unification? And I don't think anybody quite believes that it is, but one is able to do so many of them that there's been a general agreement that we ought to understand at least those better before we go on to the others. But, for example, there are phenomena involved in coordination, which have caused people to propose that another operation in the same family with unification, namely generalization, ought to be part of the same toolkit. And the other sort of question is, of course, the sort of question that formal linguists have been asking for a long time, namely, given that we have a general, very clear and fairly well-understood framework from all the various points of view that I mentioned, what then are the kinds of restrictions that might be appropriate to introduce?

Using the tool metaphor again, the difference between a computationalist and a linguist is that the computational linguist wants the wrench that you can use on any nut, whereas the linguist wants one that you can use on as few nuts as possible. The less it will do, the better it is, as long as it will help everything that actually comes along. One perfectly reasonable strategy, and one which has a perfectly good patrimony within linguistics, is that one should first of all devise a fairly clean and simple tool, and then start writing the footnotes. It's unkind, I think, to say that it's inappropriate to bring up a discussion of this sort in what purports to be a theoretical issues conference. This sort of discussion has gone on in the annals of the LSA ever since the word "formalism" was first introduced. Some of the discussion is of whether we should have traffic rules, and whether we shouldn't have traffic rules, and whether there's a cycle and whether there isn't a cycle, and all of those programming language questions. If they didn't look like programming language questions, I think it's because they were poorly formalized.

Fernando PEREIRA: One point that I wanted to mention is this issue of locality that came up. One problem that one has, both from the theoretical point of view in terms of theoretical complexity, and from the practical point of view in implementation of unification grammars, is that information can be transferred around the grammar. Arbitrarily large amounts of information can be transferred. For me, one of the most interesting questions, and I have to say I don't have good answers to this question is: How does one bring some form of locality — that is, some form of the mechanism by which you are forbidden from carrying arbitrary amounts of information arbitrarily far — in an analysis into these formalisms? If you can do that, then you might alleviate the worst-case computational complexity situation of these grammars, which I must emphasize is not something that comes in practice often, if at all, but you also might have developed formalisms that are more restricted, for which might be more easily falsifiable, in a way that Kirk was suggesting one should try to do, and I couldn't agree more.

Aravind JOSHI: I think that's one of the attractive areas that I find, namely, how to constrain the flow of information within the unification system. And the brief discussion I gave about domains of locality is really, I think, possibly a key to this point. One of the things that we have looked at is to say that the only place where the information will flow is with the feature structures associated with the nodes of elementary trees, which are described, and the only communication that takes place between two elementary trees is via certain nodes at which they get composed. So this constrains the flow of information. Whether this constrains it enough to really make it less powerful than the general one is an open question, or at least one is able to formulate one case of constrained flow of information. And I would expect that a similar thing could be done in the categorial framework because its domain of locality is not the same as the context-free skeleton, although it looks so superficially but, since each category symbol is encoding much more information, its domain of locality is larger. So I think that's an interesting avenue, and I think it should contribute to possibly more efficient algorithms.

The one thing that concerns me in this kind of approach, although I advocated it, is the following: looking at the history of this field, one takes a very general framework and then asks how you can constrain it. The history of that enterprise has not been very successful: as an example, in the days that transformational grammars were active, one of the activities was how to constrain transformational frameworks. Well, I don't think anything really interesting came out. What actually happened was people started working for a more restrictive formalism, just as Gazdar started with context-free, and then asked the question, is that enough or do we need to augment it. Given that history, I sometimes feel a doubt whether starting with the most general formalism like that and then asking what the constraints are is going to work. On the other hand, it doesn't mean that it will not work.

Gerald GAZDAR: I share Joshi's doubts, about working from the outside in. I don't think it's quite fair to say too that nothing of interest came out of the attempts to constrain transformational grammar. I think it's true to say that nothing of mathematical interest came out of it, but I think quite a lot of empirical interest came out of it. On another point, it doesn't seem to me that there's much alternative to the use of unification in grammar formalisms. If one runs through the things people have done, they're all things that have been, as it were, subsumed by unification grammar formalisms, If you look at context-free grammars, people who like context-free grammars, myself included, don't want to use pure, simple context-free grammars of grammatic symbols, they want to have a feature system, they want to have a structured feature system. And more or less everybody who's taken some formalism that they like, be it phrase structure or dependency or categorial, and beefed it up with a feature system, ends up with a problem of how you put information together. And there aren't an awful lot of ways of doing that, and the most straightforward and intuitively natural way, once you get your head round it, is unification. A lot of this discussion has been about, you know, falsifying unification grammars, alternatives to the unification grammar, and so on, and that seems to me kind of odd, because the alternatives we know about, nobody seems to have any great interest in using.

Aravind JOSHI: I actually think something extraordinarily useful came out of the attempts to constrain transformational grammars following Ross's thesis. In fact, most of sort of modern sort of GB-ish grammar came out of just that. There was recognition that if you had these constraints, in fact you didn't need to constrain the rest of it at all, so it went through range where essentially the rule was roughly you can move anything anywhere. And then all of the work was on the constraints, and of course the latest forms out of MIT have nothing but constraints. So in a most interesting way, the attempt to constrain transformational grammar led to in fact a total abandonment of classical transformational grammar, and led to enormous amounts of work on coming up with what systems of constraints look like, thereby moving the interest entirely out of the first area into the second. Now it's possible that could happen with unification grammar, and that there would be natural families of constraints that might follow through from that, and that would be just delightful, and unification would be the equivalent of the rule move alpha, move anything anywhere, and that would be just fine. So I think some interesting things did follow from that.

Chapter 3

Connectionist & Other Parallel Approaches

to Natural Language Processing

Chapter 3.1

CONNECTIONIST MODELS: NOT JUST A NOTATIONAL VARIANT, NOT A PANACEA

David L. Waltz

Prologue

My current research centers on memory-based reasoning, a connectionism-informed descendant of associative memory ideas. Memory-based reasoning holds considerable promise, both for cognitive modeling and for applications. In this model, rote memories of episodes play the central role, and schemata are viewed as epiphenomenal. This model is described in considerable detail in (Stanfill and Waltz, 1986) and will not be explained here; however, as I have prepared this paper, it has served as the background against which I have critically examined both connectionist and more traditional AI paradigms.

Connectionist and Heuristic Search Models

For most of its history, the heuristic search, logic, and "physical symbol system" (Newell, 1980) paradigms have dominated AI. AI was conceived at about the same time that protocol analysis was in vogue in psychology (Miller, Gelanter, and Pribram, 1954); such protocols could be implemented on the then-new von Neumann machines fairly well. Protocol analysis suggested that people operate by trial and error, using word-like objects as primitive units. AI has stuck almost exclusively with heuristic search and symbol systems, using them in a wide variety of natural language processing models and programming languages, ranging from ATN's, most other natural language parsing systems, and planning-based models (e.g., for pragmatics) to Prolog and Planner (Hewitt, 1972).

Meanwhile, it seems highly implausible that anything resembling heuristic search is used much below the level of consciousness; certainly no one would believe that a neuron executes heuristic search. The small amount of evidence marshalled to support the hypothesis of subconscious search (Marslen-Wilson and Tyler, 1980) could be explained in many other ways. Such models as Marcus' deterministic parser (Seidenberg, Tanenhaus, and Leiman, 1980) have attempted to move away from heuristic search, yet were cast largely in heuristic search terms. One problem that Marcus' parser was attempting to solve was the mismatch between psychological data and heuristic search models; garden path sentences were an exception, where backtracking seems an appropriate model. Even there, it seems that to understand garden path sentences people generally back up and completely reprocess sentences, using a "trace" stored in a sort of audio buffer (Rumelhart, Hinton, and Williams, 1986).

Connectionist systems have stirred a great deal of excitement for a number of reasons: (1) They're novel. Connectionism seems to be a good candidate for a major new paradigm in a field where there have only been a handful of paradigms (heuristic search; constraint propagation; blackboard systems; marker passing). (2) They have cognitive science potential. While connectionist neural nets are not necessarily analogous to neurons, they do seem brain-like and capable of modeling a substantial range of cognitive phenomena. (3) Connectionist systems exhibit non-trivial learning; they are able to self-organize, given only examples as inputs. (4) Connectionist systems can be made fault-tolerant and error-correcting, degrading gracefully for cases not encountered previously (Waltz and Pollack, 1985). (5) Appropriate and scalable connectionist hardware is rapidly becoming available. This is important, both for actually testing models, and because the kinds of brain and cognitive models that we build are very heavily dependent on available and imaginable hardware (Pylyshyn, 1980; Backus, 1987); and (6) Connectionist architectures also scale well, in that modules can be interconnected rather easily. This is because messages passed between modules are activation levels, not symbolic messages.

Nonetheless, there are considerable difficulties still ahead for connectionist models. It is probably premature to generalize based on our experience with them to date. So far all systems built have either learned relatively small numbers of items, or they have been toy systems, hand built for some particular task. The kinds of learning shown to date are hardly general. It seems very unlikely to me that it will be possible for a single, large, randomly wired module to learn everything. If we want to build a system out of many modules, we must devise an architecture for the system with input and output specifications for modules and/or a plan for interconnecting the internal nodes of different modules. Finally, connectionist models cannot yet argue that they offer a superset of traditional AI operations: certain operations such as variable binding cannot yet be performed efficiently in connectionist networks.

Best Match vs. Exact Match

It is not possible to specify completely the conditions for any sort of decision—including decisions on natural language understanding and parsing—in a manageable set of logical rules and heuristics. By inserting a sentence in an appropriate context, even extremely rare or unusual structures and interpretations can be made to seem the most natural.

Rule systems can be constructed to handle such cases, but at the expense of requiring arbitrarily large numbers of rules with arbitrarily long sets of conditions. Connectionist models inherently integrate all available evidence, most pieces of which will be irrelevant or only weakly relevant for most decisions. Moreover, one does not have to find logically necessary and sufficient conditions; connections between actions and the facts of the world can be represented as statistical correlations. In Feldman's terms (Shastri and Feldman, 1985), connectionist reasoning is evidential rather than logical.

Reasoning that is apparently logical can arise from connectionist models in at least two ways.

(1) A programmer can encode individual alternatives for lexical selection, phrase structure, etc., as nodes which compete with or support each other; the processing of a sentence then involves clamping the values of some input word nodes, and allowing the whole network to settle. For "regular" inputs, strong pathways, which "collaborate" in reinforcing each other, can give the appearance of rule-like behavior. Given similar inputs, one can expect similar outputs. Most natural language connectionist work has been rule-like in this sense (Waltz and Pollack, 1985; Cottrell and Small, 1983; Small, 1980; Selman and Hirst, 1985).

(2) The appearance of rule-based behavior can also result from learned connectionist networks or associative memory models. If a system can find the activation pattern or memory which is closest to a given current event or situation, it can exhibit highly regular behavior. Such systems degrade gracefully. Unlike connectionist models, associative memory models can also tell when a new event does not correspond well to any previous event; they can "know that they don't know" (Stanfill and Waltz, 1986; see also Grossberg, 1987).

In contrast, systems based on logic, unification and exact matching are inevitably brittle (i.e., situations even slightly outside the realm of those encoded in the rules fail completely, and the system exhibits discontinuous behavior). We see no way to repair this property of such systems. (See also Nilsson, 1983, and Pentland and Fischler, 1983.)

Match with Psychological Results

Psychological research on categorization (Smith and Medin, 1981; Rosch and Mervis, 1975; Lakoff, 1979; Berlin and Kay, 1969) has shown that category formation cannot be explained in a classical logical model; that is, the conditions of category membership are not merely logical conditions (result of expressions with connectives 'and' 'or' and 'not'). Rather, categories are organized around "focus concepts" or prototypes, and exhibit graceful degradation for examples that differ from the category focus along any of a number of possible dimensions (Lakoff, 1979). Connectionist systems seem well suited for modeling such category structure (though such modeling has not been explored very extensively; Hinton and Anderson, 1981).

Massive Parallelism

Restricted natural language is not natural language. One cannot make progress in natural language understanding unless one can run large problems and see the results of experiments in finite time. Small scale experiments (involving on the order of hundreds of nodes or less) are inadequate to really explore the issues in computational linguistics. One needs a model with a realistically large vocabulary and range of possible word senses and interpretations, in order to convincingly argue that the model is appropriate and adequate.

Fortunately, dramatic strides are being made in computer architecture at just the time that connectionist theoretical models are being explored. These fields are not unrelated. Connectionist models (Quillian, 1968; Fahlman, 1979) served as initial inspiration to designers of new generation hardware (e.g., Hillis, 1985), though many parallel architectural ideas were already being explored in the pursuit of greater speed. This followed the realization that we were approaching asymptotes for speeds possible with serial uniprocessors. I believe that developing appropriate hardware will prove to be the easiest part of building full-scale natural language systems.

Integration of Modules

Connectionist models allow for much easier integration of modules than is possible with symbolic/heuristic search-based systems. Generally, symbolic systems require either a very simple architecture (e.g., the traditional phonetic-syntactic-semantic-pragmatic bottom-up model of classical linguistics) or a sophisticated communications facility (for example, a blackboard) in order to build a system composed of many modules. In the blackboard model, each module must in general have a generator for complex messages as well as an interpreter for such messages.

In contrast, connectionist models allow an integration of modules by links that can go directly to the nodes (concepts or microfeatures) that co-vary with the activation patterns of other modules, and messages themselves can be extremely simple (e.g., numerical activation levels, or markers; Hendler, doctoral dissertation, 1986). In some cases, link weights can be generated based on an analysis of the statistical correlations between various concepts or structures; in other cases weights can be generated by learning schemes (Rumelhart and McClelland, 1986). Nonetheless, still there is a potentially large set of cases where weights will have to be generated by hand, or by yet-to-be-discovered learning methods. Clearly, every concept cannot be connected to every other directly. (This would require n^2 connections for n concepts, where n is at least 10^6.) Some solutions have been suggested (e.g., the microfeature ideas in Waltz and Pollack, 1985) but none seems easy to program.

Fault Tolerance

Since a large number of nodes (or modules) have a bearing on a single connectionist decision (e.g., lexical selection or prepositional phrase attachment) then not all of them need to be active in order to make a correct decision; some variation of values can be tolerated. In a modular connectionist model, input information can be fed to syntactic, semantic, and pragmatic modules directly. Thus, an unparsed string of terms can suggest a particular topic area to a pragmatic context module, even without any syntactic processing; such topical context can in turn be used to influence lexical selection. At the same time, the range of possible syntactic structures allows certain lexical assignments and precludes others; semantic information such as case role restrictions likewise can have a bearing on lexical selection (see Waltz and Pollack, 1985, for further discussion).

Learning

Learning is one of the most exciting aspects of connectionist models for both the AI and psychology communities. For example, the back propagation error learning (Rumelhart, Hinton, and Williams, 1986) and Boltzmann machine (Sejnowski and Rosenberg, 1986) methods have proved quite effective for teaching input/output patterns. However, such learning is not a panacea. Some researchers believe that one can start with a very large randomly interconnected and weighted network and potentially generate a fully intelligent system, simply by presenting it with enough raw sensory inputs and corresponding desired outputs. I doubt it: the learning space corresponding to raw sensory inputs (e.g., visual and audio) is astronomically large, and learning to perceive via feedback ("punishment/reward" ?) seems both cognitively and technically unrealistic.

Key Problems for Connectionist Language Models

Learning from "Experience"

As suggested above, learning is both a key achievement of connectionism and a key open issue for a full cognitive system.

The difficulty for cognitive learning theories of any sort is the observation that perception has to be prior to language. In turn, perception itself seems to require *a priori*, innate organization. Just how large must an innate component be? I believe it will have to account at least for such phenomena as figure/ground organization of scenes, the ability to appropriately segment events (both to separate them from the experiences that precede and follow them and also to articulate their internal structure); the notion of causality; and general structuring principles for creating memory instances. This suggests to me that a large portion of a learning system must be wired initially, probably into fairly large internally regular modules, which are subject only to rudimentary learning via parameter adjustment. This conclusion follows from the observation that if brains could completely self-organize, this method, being simpler than present reality, would have been discovered first by evaluation. My guess is that such total self-organization would require far too long, since it requires exploring a vast space of weight assignments. Even given extensive *a priori* structure, humans require some twenty years to mature. I think that we cannot avoid programming cognitive architecture.

Variable Binding

Some operations that programmers have traditionally taken for granted have proven difficult to map onto connectionist networks. One such key operation is variable binding. Assume that we have devised a good schema representation or learning system and stored a number of schemata: what happens when a new natural language input triggers a schema and we would like to store this instance in long-term memory? It seems that we need to create an instance of the schema with the particular agents, objects, patients, and so on, bound to case roles. It is not obvious how this ought to be done in a connectionist model. Some experiments in designing general connectionist schemes for variable binding have been performed (Touretzky, 1986), but these methods seem very awkward and expensive in terms of the numbers of nodes and links required to store even a single relation.

Another possibility is to make a copy of the entire schema structure for each new instance, but this seems to lack neurophysiological plausibility. A more appealing direction is suggested both by Minsky (Minsky, 1980; Minsky, 1986) and Feldman and Shastri (Feldman and Ballard, 1982; Shastri and Feldman, 1985): a very large number of nodes are randomly connected to each other such that nodes that have never been used before form a kind of pool of potential binding units for novel combinations of schemata and role fillers. When a new instance is encountered, all the participants which are active can be bound together using one or more of these previously unutilized binding nodes, and those nodes can then be removed from the "free binders pool."

There are important open questions in any case: for example, are different modules responsible for sentence processing, perceptual processing, short-term memory and long-term memory (Fodor, 1982)? If so, how are these interconnected and "controlled"? If not, how can we account for these different processing modes?

Timing and Judging When Sentence Processing is Complete

Connectionist systems for language processing have assumed that sentences will be preceded and followed by quiescent periods. The resulting pattern of activations on nodes in the system can then be read whenever appropriate, and the time sequence of node actuations interpreted as desired (Pollack and I are guilty of this sloppiness). There is a real difficulty in knowing how and when one should interpret the internal operation of a system. Should we wait until activation levels on nodes have settled, i.e., changed less than a certain amount on each cycle? Should we wait for activity to either be completely on or completely off in various nodes? Should we wait a fixed amount of time and then evaluate the network activation pattern? If so, how do we set the clock rate of the relaxation network relative to the rate at which input words arrive? What should be done to the activation pattern of a set of nodes after a sentence has been "understood"? Should the levels be zeroed out? Should they remain active? Under what circumstances and by what methods should items be transferred to (or transformed into) long-term memory? Are the nodes used in understanding the same ones responsible for long-term memory storage or is there some sort of copying or transfer mechanism?

All these questions need crisper answers and principles. It does seem clear that processing must be approximately complete soon after the completion of a sentence so that processing of the next sentence can start, since sentences or clauses can occur with very little separation. This suggests that expectations play an important role in sentence processing and further that really important material ought to appear or be expected well before the end of a sentence if the processing of the next sentence is not to be interfered with.

Debugging and Understanding Systems

In general, it is difficult to tell exactly what systems with distributed knowledge representations know or don't know. Such systems cannot explain what they know, nor can a person look at their structures and tell whether they are in fact complete and robust or not, except in very simple cases (Hinton, McClelland, and Rumelhart, 1986). The only way to test such systems is by giving them examples and judging on the basis of their performance whether they are suitable or not. This problem is a quite serious one for systems that are designed to be fault tolerant. A fault-tolerant system, for instance, might usually work quite well, even though one module is seriously defective; however in marginal cases, a counterproductive module could cause performance to be much worse than it ought to be. The problems of debugging a system in which some modules may compensate for and cover up the errors of others seem quite intractable.

Generating Applications

Natural language processing work has suffered and still suffers from a shortage of good ideas for applications. We don't know quite what we'd do with such systems even if we could successfully build them. In part this is because the actions that a computer can easily carry out are radically different from those that a person can do. In part the difficulty is that typing is a slow and error-prone input method; if speech were available, natural language processing might rapidly increase in importance. On the other hand, bulk processing of text databases (Sabot, 1986) seems a promising applications area.

It may be impossible to use human-like learning methods for connectionist systems (or for any computer-based language processing system). It may also be undesirable. Unlike people, computers are capable of remembering literally the contents of large text files and complete dictionaries while at the same time they lack perceptual and reasoning facilities. The combination suggests that infant-like learning may not be appropriate for computer-based language systems, even if a brain-like machine can be built.

Chapter 3.2

TOWARD CONNECTIONIST SEMANTICS

Garrison W. Cottrell

Introduction

Much of the study of language has centered around the study of syntax, to the detriment of semantics and pragmatics. Part of the reason for this may be akin to the motivation of the besotted gentleman on his hands and knees beneath a streetlamp, who, when queried as to why he is looking on the sidewalk for the keys he lost in the alley, replies: "Because the light is better here!" I believe it is time to start mucking about in the alley; the keys are there. I also think we have a new flashlight: Parallel Distributed Processing.[1] PDP mechanisms allow us to build machines whose fundamental operations include best fit search, constraint relaxation and automatic generalization. These are useful properties for processing language. I think the application of these models to NLP will change our view of what constitutes "semantics". I will argue that in order to deal with meaning seriously, we have to move beyond the folk-psychological level of symbols, and represent the microstructure of symbols. This is more than a granularity issue. It also has to do with the grounding of meaning in perception. It is on the level of microfeatures that I believe this grounding occurs, and PDP gives us a way to express this interface between language and perception.

My discussion of these issues will take the following course.[2] First I describe my previous work on word sense disambiguation in a PDP framework as a springboard for the rest of the discussion, and to give a sense of how lexical semantics might fit into an overall parsing model. Next I motivate a new model of word meanings through an example. I try to show that PDP has a natural way of expressing these meanings, and I give a sketch of how connectionist semantics could be learned. Finally, I briefly discuss metaphor.

Word Sense Disambiguation

One of the fundamental problems of natural language processing is word sense disambiguation. Determining the correct sense of a word for a particular use involves the interaction of many sources of knowledge: syntactic, semantic, and pragmatic (i.e., "everything else"). In previous work (Cottrell, 1985) I have shown how word sense disambiguation can be modeled as a constraint relaxation process between competing hypotheses instantiated as nodes in a network representing linguistic knowledge. The representation is one that I have fancifully called **proclarative**: disambiguation happens as the result of activation spreading through a knowledge base where constraints between hypotheses are represented by positive and negative links between them. Figure 1 shows the basic structure of the model.

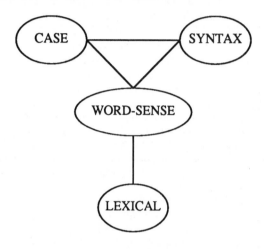

Figure 1: Sources of knowledge and constraint paths for disambiguation.

The model operates as follows: First, words activate all of their lexical entries. These, in turn, activate syntactic and semantic (case) structures, which represent relations between word senses. It is feedback from these developing representations that provides support for the correct meanings and syntactic classes of the words. At the same time, bindings of constituents to roles in both syntax and semantics are mutually constraining one another to decide such things as prepositional phrase attachment. Thus parsing into a case structure is modeled as a three-way constraint relaxation between the lexical entries of the words, the possible syntactic representations, and the possible semantic relations. Syntactic and semantic information are accessed in parallel and operate simultaneously to determine the correct parse. This was shown to be a useful model of the human disambiguation process, as evidenced by explanations of various psycholinguistic and neurolinguistic results.

One of the major weaknesses of that model was the representation of "meaning." Each meaning of a word is represented by a unit with an "awkward lexeme" (Wilks, 1976) as a label. Certainly, the label on a node is not important; it is the way the node connects up to other nodes that determine its relationship to other "meanings." But I think this is a general failing of almost all NLP programs currently in existence: the meaning of a word is best represented not as a symbol, but as an aggregate of connected microfeatures. I will next try to show why.

What is Meaning? (A Thought Experiment)

It has been said that all words are polysemous to a degree. Let's take a fairly safe example: **truck**. This seems hardly polysemous, but it turns out we can bend the meaning, at least the image formed, in fairly continuous ways. Consider *Billy picked up the* **truck**. If you are like me, you get a picture of a small, probably plastic truck. In a symbolic system we might have a rule that if a usually large object is the object of a picking up action, then we should "toy-ify" it, either looking up the entry for "toy truck" or by applying a "toyification" transformation to the representation we had already retrieved: it weighs less, it is much smaller, it is composed of plastic. Of course, in *Superman picked up the* **truck**, we have an exception to the rule. And in *Bobby picked up the toy* **gun**, the application of the toy-ifying rule would need to be modified so that the size is not reduced. One can imagine that the list of rules and their application criteria might get a bit unwieldy.

One answer to this is, "Yes, the world is complicated". The problem is that this is not an isolated phenomenon. Rather, it pervades our conceptual landscape. The concepts that people use are not fixed entities, nor are they entities that vary discretely along a small number of dimensions. They **covary** in a continuous way. In *Tommy lugged the* **truck** up the hill, we imagine a heavier toy truck than the one Billy picked up, but a lighter one than Superman did. It might even be the same truck—*Billy picked up the* **truck** and handed it to Tommy. Tommy lugged it up the hill. In this case it is **Tommy** that we imagine is smaller than Billy! Thus the interpretation we derive of the words in a sentence is the result of constraints between the meanings of the individual words, as well as the usual list: the structure of the sentence, the context in which it is spoken, the relationship between the speaker and the hearer, the shared knowledge, etc. People are very good at tasks like this that involve the application of multiple, simultaneous constraints. I claim that the "rules" that I attempted to describe above can emerge from the regularities of interaction among the internal structures of the concepts themselves, rather than an application of explicit rules to atomic concepts.[3] There is no reason that this could not be implemented in a "symbolic" system that has a constraint propagation mechanism, and continuous-valued levels of properties. The problem is that the modification would alter it so radically that we might as well have started with a connectionist model.[4]

A Modest Proposal

In this section I will draw on previous work of others to lay out how a connectionist model can represent the kind of meanings that I think our experiment with **truck** point to. The basic idea is that meanings are connectionist schemata. These are assumed to be embedded in a system like the one I described above for word sense disambiguation—that is, they are getting input from other schemata concerned with syntax and larger semantic (case) structures.

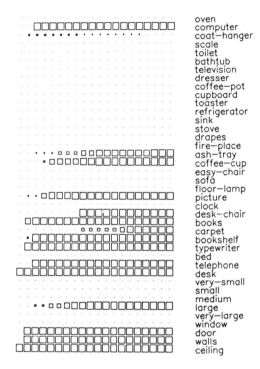

oven
computer
coat—hanger
scale
toilet
bathtub
television
dresser
coffee—pot
cupboard
toaster
refrigerator
sink
stove
drapes
fire—place
ash—tray
coffee—cup
easy—chair
sofa
floor—lamp
picture
clock
desk—chair
books
carpet
bookshelf
typewriter
bed
telephone
desk
very—small
small
medium
large
very—large
window
door
walls
ceiling

Figure 2. Probing the model with "desk" and "ceiling". The size of the square indicates activation value of the unit, and time moves from left to right. (From McClelland and Rumelhart, 1986, reprinted by permission).

Connectionist Schemata

Rumelhart et al. (1986) have demonstrated how a connectionist model of a schema can do something no implementation has done before: represent smoothly varying constraints between the slot fillers. The demonstration model represents the information we have about rooms. Each unit of the model represents one of forty possible descriptors and contents of a room: size, walls, ceiling, bathtub, stove, etc. The connection strengths between the units of the schema model were derived from people's reports of what they expected to find in each kind of room. (The weights were set according to the conditional probability that one item was reported given another item was reported.) Things that occurred together often were given a strong positive weight, things that never occurred together were given a negative weight. For example, every room has walls and a ceiling. These have a strong positive connection between them because they always co-occur. Probing the model consists of "clamping on" some units, which then activate positively connected units, and inhibit ones negatively associated with them. The office schema, for example, can be accessed by probing the model with "desk" and "ceiling" (to simulate that the context is "room"). The result is that units representing the prototype office become activated—accessing the schema is a matter of pattern completion. This corresponds to filling in the default slots in the schema (see Figure 2).

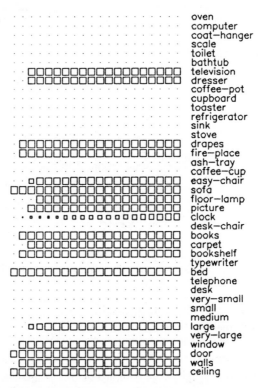

Figure 3. Probing the model with "bed" and "sofa". (From McClelland and Rumelhart, 1986, reprinted by permission).

The "prototype" rooms are shown to be peaks in a "goodness surface" in the space of unit activations that reflects the number of constraints satisfied between units of the model and the clamped inputs. The activation of the units travels up the goodness surface to the corner where the elements of the office schema become activated, maximizing goodness in the context of the clamped "desk" unit. This type of pattern completion is a typical way to access information in connectionist models.

An interesting variation on this is when two items are probed together that do not normally co-occur. For example, if the model is probed with "bed" and "sofa" what results is a large, fancy bedroom with a fireplace. The goodness space has been warped by these two inputs to form a new stable peak, where the filler of one of the slots, "size-of-room", has constrained what will be in the contents of the room in a way that is intuitively pleasing.

It is possible to train a connectionist model to exhibit this blending of meanings, and to do so at the more micro-level I am advocating for word senses. McClelland and Kawamoto (1986) trained a network to assign case roles to nouns presented in a matrix as VERB-SUBJ-OBJ-MODIFIER. The representation of the input was a set of features for each syntactic slot that were linked to output feature schemata for each case role. The model was trained on a set of sentences in this format, and then tested on novel sentences. When given the novel sentence *the doll moved*, the model interpreted the doll as *animate*, because of the shared features between doll and humans and a tendency to assign animacy to agents. Thus, the model adjusted the meaning to fit the situation. The point is that distributed connectionist representations that represent symbols such as "doll" as a set of features and constraints can *relax* those constraints depending on external constraints—inputs from combinations of features in the schemata of the other words in the sentence.

These models assumed the elements of the schemata—the micro-features—were chosen by the modeler. The next section deals with how the features themselves might be learned, and how they might be grounded in perceptual processes.

Learning

A problem with any representation of meaning in terms of features is the infinite regression of features defined in terms of features. What is the basis clause of the inductive process of building a semantic represpresentation? I believe that semantics must fundamentally be based in perception of and interaction with the environment. Powerful new algorithms have been discovered that allow connectionist networks to develop their own internal representations of their environment. Surprisingly, a rather useful network is one that does an identity mapping (Figure 4).

The network has an input and output layer connected through a smaller layer of *hidden units*. By forcing the network to reproduce the input on the output through this narrow channel, it has to learn an efficient encoding of the input at the hidden unit layer. Such networks are self-organizing systems that learn to represent the important features of their environment.

These systems have been used to encode natural images and speech signals (Cottrell, Munro and Zipser, 1987; Elman and Zipser, 1986). The internal representations devised by these two systems (auditory and visual) can then be the "environment" to a third system which would take into account

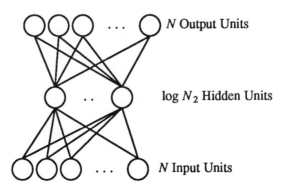

Figure 4: A network that develops an efficient encoding of its environment.

covariances between the two of them in a unified abstract encoding of sound and light (see Figure 5).[5]

By learning recurrent connections at the coding layers, these become pattern completion devices (auditory and visual schemata). Now it will take only one of the input modalities to evoke the other. The input of an image would activate the image encoding, which in turn would partially activate the unified encoding of associated sounds and images. This can be filled out by pattern completion, enabling the unified encoding to feed back and activate the encoding of the word associated with the image; that is, an image will evoke a word and a word an image. While this is an oversimplified sketch, the important point is that connectionist systems use a uniform representation medium for both modalities and thus afford the modeler an ease of communication between visual, proprioceptive and auditory inputs. Thus, this approach promises a computationally viable way to ground the infinite regress of meaning in associations between speech sounds with other perceptual representations generated from interactions with the environment. While this is just the base case of the induction, it has not been addressed by other approaches.

Metaphor

A second problem for a model of meaning is the question of metaphor. How could a connectionist system learn the metaphorical mappings that are such a big part of language? Connectionist schemata that have many stable states reflecting related meanings may account for much of what we call "metaphor." But how might new meanings be learned that are more radical transformations of old ones? For example, how might we learn that *I feel* **up** *today* means one's mood is elevated? Our identity mapping networks can be put to good use here in the following way.[6] Suppose we divide up the input pattern in Figure 4 into portions corresponding to a function, an input and an output. So

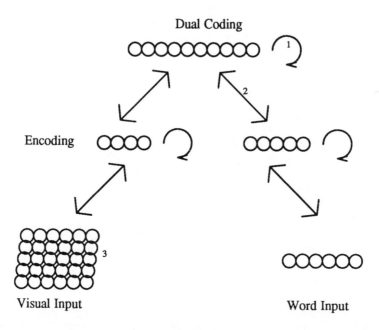

Figure 5. Automatically learned inter-modal encoding. The inputs and outputs of the network in Figure 2 have been overlain in this diagram, and correspond to the lower left and lower right parts. The final layer is a joint encoding of the hidden unit layers of the modality-specific codes. Conventions: [1] *return arc indicates cross-connection within layer of response units;* [2] *broad arrow shows total connection between layers;* [3] *array of response units indicates system of units as for a patch of visual input.*

the triple (F a b) represents F(a) = b, and given (F a b) the network produces (F a b). If we add a pattern completion network on the output layer, we can now give the network (F a *) (where * represents no input) and it will produce F(a,b), computing that F(a) equals b. In fact, within resource limitations, we can give it F(*,b) or even *(a,b) and have it invert the mapping or induce the relationship between the arguments. In ambiguous cases it will produce blends of the possible answers.

Now, assume that we have enough units in the argument positions that we can represent anything we want, and that we have trained it with functions and arguments from several disparate domains. Suppose we now give the network a function F with an argument c that is not in the domain of F. One characteristic of these networks is that they map similar inputs to similar outputs. The degree of overlap between the features of c and the features of elements of the domain of F will determine the coherency of the mapping. If c is sufficiently similar to a previously learned input, it will map c to an output similar to the previous one. It is able to do this because the mapping reflects constraints it has learned between the features of the inputs and outputs of F. If c is sufficiently different from other inputs it has learned in the domain of F, the result will be uninterpretable. Somewhere between these two is metaphor[7].

Conclusion

I have attempted to show in this paper that word meanings are more of a moving target than we would like to think, and that they **covary** depending on constraints between them. The connectionist approach to semantics has a natural way to capture these smoothly varying constraints and meanings. I also have sketched how these meanings can be grounded in perceptual encodings and how some aspects of metaphor might be captured in this framework.

Acknowledgements

I would like to thank Mike Mozer, Harold Pashler, and Dave Rumelhart for helpful comments on this paper. Remaining errors in judgment are mine.

Notes

1. I will assume familiarity with the connectionist, or PDP paradigm. The best introduction is Rumelhart and McClelland (1986).

2. I will restrict myself here to lexical semantics. The generalization to logical form is left as an exercise for the reader.

3. I am not claiming that these are simply first order interactions; relations between feature clusters also need to be captured.

4. Another reason for starting with a connectionist model is the existence of powerful learning algorithms that can derive constraints between features, as we will see below.

5. A similar idea has been independently proposed by Chauvin (1986).

6. The following network is implemented, as McClelland would say, in "hopeware."

7. This represents a slight generalization of an idea of Dave Rumelhart's: his model did not include the function in the input.

Chapter 3.3

CONNECTIONISM AND EXPLANATION

Eugene Charniak

I gather that the panel on connectionism was picked to have a variety of viewpoints represented, some very pro, some very against, and me—I take an extreme waffle position. I really like connectionism, and I wish it would work for me. But so far it can't and theoretical breakthroughs would be needed to change things. I will try to explain here why I see things this way.

Before I start, however, it would be a good idea to clear up one possible source of confusion. My recent work has been on the problem of explanation in stories: how, given a story one can assign a motivation to a character based upon his or her actions. I also believe that the processes which are needed to do this will shed a lot of light on traditional parsing issues. The source of confusion comes from the fact that my recent models of explanation have involved a process of "marker passing," or "spreading activation." Basically I am using a breadth-first search in an associative network to find connections between concepts, in the hope that such connections will suggest explanations. My typical example is

Jack wanted to kill himself. He got a rope.

Here the connection between **kill** and **rope** would be the clue.

Many people upon seeing this work hook me up with the connectionist school. This is not correct. I do not consider myself a connectionist, and real connectionists do not consider me one either. At best my marker passer might be seen as indicating "localist" (as opposed to distributed) connectionist leanings, since some of what Jerry Feldman and his students do has some of the same flavor. But marker passing is only a small part of my system, and after it is finished I feel free to use deduction, unification, search, and, heaven forbid, *cons.*

Nevertheless I am sympathetic to connectionism, and to give some idea why, let me discuss a minor knowledge representation problem which I recently encountered. I have already noted that I am interested in the problem of explanation in language comprehension. One obvious idea is to use the objects in a story as a source of possible explanations. So, upon seeing a sentence like

"Jack got some milk"

we might suggest explanations like

"He will eat cereal"

"He will drink the milk"

etc. Presumably we know that milk is put over cereal, and that milk is a beverage, and beverages are typically used for drinking. Thus it seems reasonable
to index activities by the objects that get used in them (there could be other
ways to index as well) and then, given an action like Jack's getting milk, look
at milk, and the things above milk in the "isa hierarchy" for the actions which
are indexed there. Naturally one must then decide between the possibilities, or
put off the decision in hopes of further information, but how this is might be
done need not concern us here.

Now consider the following facts which one might wish to express.

1) Shopping takes place at stores

2) Supermarket-shopping is one kind of shopping

3) Supermarket-shopping takes place at supermarkets. (It has other distinc-
    tive characteristics as well, but we will ignore these)

4) Supermarkets are one kind of store.

Facts in this form lead to what I have taken to calling a square formation,
because when written down as an associative network they form a square, as
shown in the figure.

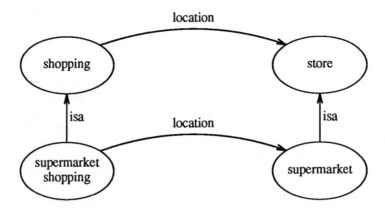

Figure 1: Associative Network.

I suspect that this is quite common in these kinds of representations,
because often one wants to store the information at many levels of generality.
For one thing, if we were only told that Jack went to the store, one might still

want to infer that he will shop, and secondly, many facts about specific kinds of shopping can be expressed at the higher level, and thus save space by not including them at all the lower nodes in the hierarchy: for example, the fact that shoppings typically start by going to the store.

So far so good, but now consider what happens when one uses the object hierarchy for finding explanations for

"Jack went to the supermarket."

It will suggest supermarket shopping, which is fine, but it will also suggest plain old shopping, since supermarkets are stores, and we use the suggestions from all (or at least many) levels of the isa hierarchy (remember that for milk we wanted suggestions from both **milk** and **beverage**). The problem is that we have redundancy. It appears superficially that we have two independent suggestions as to Jack's motivation for going to the store, one being supermarket shopping, and one being shopping, but really they are the same. Somehow this has to be weeded out.

I do not mention this as an example of a really tough problem. It is pretty easy to think of ways to get rid of the unwanted motivations, or, as my current system does, consider both and rank the more specific as better. Rather this is the kind of minor annoyance which we have to put up with all the time. I can solve it, but it sure would be nice to have a representation in which such things never came up in the first place.

It may be wishful thinking, but it seems that this problem would not come up if I were to use a connectionist model of knowledge representation. For those of you not familiar with connectionist networks, let me just give an example of some work by Rumelhart which has some relevance to my problem. Rumelhart was trying to show how one could model schemata (which are pretty much the same as frames and scripts) using connectionism. What he did was to create nodes corresponding to the various objects one finds in a house: bathtubs, couches, clocks, etc. He asked people to create typical rooms, and set the strength of connection between nodes so they were proportional to how often the objects were found in the same room. For example, sink and bathtub would be highly connected, as would sink and refrigerator, but refrigerator and bathtub would be negatively correlated. He would then turn on some nodes, like clock and sink, and look to see what else got turned on. As you might expect, things common to kitchens would light up in this case. If one put in just chair the system would not be able to decide on the location but some things, like wall and ceiling would light up anyway, since all of the places which use chairs would have them. Perhaps bathtub would be turned off as well, since chairs typically are not found in bathrooms.

The point is that connectionist networks are very good at filling out patterns from incomplete information, and doing this on the basis of lots of special cases. It should not take too much to imagine how this might work for my problem. One would give the system nodes for supermarkets, baskets, shopping, food, pushing baskets, bakery-shops, taking a number to be waited on, etc. One would also provide many examples of common patterns to assign the weights between nodes (or possibly put in weights by hand). Then if you put in supermarket you would get supermarket-shopping, along with baskets, etc., whereas if you put in store, you would not get the details, but only those things which all shoppings could agree upon, like a buying event, going to the store, etc. Thus we get the effect of an isa hierarchy without the precise mechanism, and the square problem goes away.

To keep my mind flexible I occasionally think about how my work would look in a connectionist model—the above observation was the result of one of such times. I find it interesting that the problems I run into never seem to have counterparts in the connectionist view of the world. It really is a different way of thinking about things.

So why don't I adopt the view? The answer is clear if we take the earlier thought experiment about a connectionist model of shopping events and really ask what it would look like in detail. One can, as I mentioned, create nodes for the various objects used in various stores, and for the various actions done in them. But suppose I get in a sentence like "Jack went to the supermarket" and I want to infer that he will be shopping. I can have a *supermarket-shopping* node, but to infer that **Jack** will be shopping by this method I would need a *Jack-supermarket-shopping* node. Given that I never heard of Jack prior to this story, this is obviously problematic. How would such a node be created? What would it be connected to? Furthermore, this problem is compounded by a second, which we might call the "infer everything" problem. The square problem cannot come up in a connectionist model because there is only one body of nodes, and it is their joint action which makes up the explanation, by, in effect, creating a "picture," albeit a very abstract one, of the situation which is envisioned as the explanation. If this *picture* is all one has, then it has to have everything filled out since it is not clear how, without learning more, it could be modified. Thus, if this picture is to have any explanatory power, it would have to include nodes for things like

> "Jack get basket"
>
> "Jack pick up food"
>
> "Jack put food in basket"
>
> "Jack take food to checkout counter"

etc. So it is not just that we would need a new node for

> "Jack supermarket shopping."

We would need nodes for everything else as well. In normal AI knowledge representations this is not necessary. It is perfectly possible to **construct** new data structures (based upon deductions from the general plan for shopping) which represent the details of Jack's activity. I cannot see how this could be done in a connectionist scheme.

More generally, the problem of representing new propositions in connectionist networks is a real mess. The connectionists know about this however, and there has been some work on the topic. The basic idea is that one uses the state of the entire network to represent a proposition rather than concentrating it at a node. So, one might have one set of nodes which represent the first argument of a proposition, one for the second, and one for the predicate, and each set of nodes could indicate different individuals, depending on the pattern. The networks could be trained so that, say, if "father-of" was the proposition, it would tend to like "jack" as argument one, and "ann" as argument two, assuming one wanted to store the fact that Jack is the father of Ann. Using the connectionist ability to complete patterns, one can also see how such a network might fill in **jack** if both **father-of** and **ann** were put into the appropriate places. David McClelland does something like this in his work on case assignment using connectionist networks.

There are other ways to represent propositions as well (perhaps best being the work of David Touretzky), but they all lose what is so nice about the unsophisticated version of the networks. Before, the network as a whole represented the situation as a whole, and filling in gave us things like motivation, etc. Now the network just represents a single proposition. Filling in gets us the rest of the proposition, which is nice if one wants to find propositions on the basis of partial content, but I already know how to do that. AI has a whole bag of tricks for solving this problem, and by and large they do it much better than connectionist versions. What I want is something to fill in the context, but this the proposition representations schemes have not been able to do.

This is not to say that the problem is unsolvable. In my imagination, just beyond an obscuring haze, is an idea that one might combine the "entire scene" type networks and the propositional ones. One would have a network in which lots of connected propositions are all represented at once, with special sets of nodes for the objects which bind their variables. Geoff Hinton believes in something like this, and while I am around his infectious enthusiasm I can almost believe it too.

But I have not been able to penetrate the haze, and thus I think it is still fair to say that connectionist networks cannot represent propositions at all. To the degree they can it is like a horse walking on two legs— it does not do it very well, and you lose all that is distinctive about the creature. I use a horse because I want to gallop. If I have to walk I would rather do it in Lisp.

Chapter 3.4

PARALLEL DISTRIBUTED PROCESSING AND ROLE ASSIGNMENT CONSTRAINTS

James L. McClelland

My work in natural language processing is based on the premise that it is not in general possible to recover the underlying representations of sentences without considering semantic constraints on their possible case structures. It seems clear that people use these constraints to do several things:

To assign constituents to the proper case roles and attach them to the proper other constituents.

To assign the appropriate reading to a word or larger constituent when it occurs in context.

To assign default values to missing constituents.

To instantiate the concepts referenced by the words in a sentence so that they fit the context.

I believe that parallel-distributed processing models (i.e., connectionist models which make use of distributed representations) provide the mechanisms that are needed for these tasks. Argument attachments and role assignments seem to require a consideration of the relative merits of competing possibilities (Marcus, 1980; Bates and MacWhinney, 1987; MacWhinney, 1987), as does lexical disambiguation. Connectionist models provide a very natural substrate for these kinds of competition processes (Cottrell, 1985; Waltz and Pollack, 1985).

The use of distributed representations also seems well suited to capturing many aspects of the way people exploit semantic constraints. For choosing between two distinct alternative interpretations of a constituent, local and distributed representations may be approximately equivalent, but distributed representations are much more natural for capturing contextual shading of the interpretation of a constituent. In a distributed representation the pattern of activation that is most typically activated by a particular word or phrase can be subtly shaded by constraints imposed by context; there is no need to limit the choice of alternative shadings to a pre-specified set of alternatives each represented by a differnt single unit. Similarly, filling in missing arguments is not a matter of choosing a particular concept, but of filling in a pattern that specifies what is known about the filler, without necessarily specifying a particular specific concept.

In previous work, Alan Kawamoto and I (McClelland and Kawamoto, 1986) implemented a parallel-distributed processing (PDP) model that can use semantic constraints to do the four things listed at the beginning of the article, though it was limited to processing only one clause at a time. While it would be possible to use such a mechanism clause-by-clause, semantic constraints are often required to decide which of several clauses a phrase belongs to. For example, in the sentence:

1) John ate the cake that his mother baked at the picnic.

we attach "at the picnic" to the main clause (as the place where the cake was eaten), whereas in

2) John ate the cake that his mother baked in the oven.

we attach "in the oven" to the subordinate clause (as the place where the cake was baked). Clearly these attachments depend on knowing that baking can take place in ovens, not at picnics, and eating can take place at picnics, not in ovens; I would also claim that the relative merits of both attachments must be taken into account to get the attachments right. It seems, then, that a mechanism is needed that can consider the possibility of attaching a phrase to more than one possible clause.

This article sketches out a model that aims to achieve multi-clause capability. The model has not yet been fully implemented, so the paper is quite speculative. However, I think the model promises to take us some distance toward a better understanding of the interaction of syntactic and case-role analysis. In particular, it suggests that with the right connectionist architecture, the four uses of semantic constraints enumerated above become intrinsic characteristics of the language processing machinery.

Representing Structure and Content

To begin, let us consider how to represent the structure of a sentence in a PDP mechanism. To do this, we make use of the notion that a structural description can be represented as a set of triples. For example the correct role structure of Sentence 2 can be represented with a set of triples such as the following:

- (P1 AGENT BOY) (P1 ACTION ATE) (P1 PATIENT CAKE)

- (P2 AGENT MOTHER) (P2 ACTION BAKED) (P2 PATIENT CAKE)

- (P2 LOCATION OVEN)

An individual triple can be represented in distributed form by dedicating a set of units to each of its parts; thus we can have one set of units for the head of the triple, one for the relation, and one for the tail or slot-filler. Each of the three parts of a triple can then be represented in distributed form as a pattern of activation over the units. The idea of using this kind of three-part distributed representation was introduced by Hinton (1981) to represent the contents of semantic nets; the extension to arbitrary tree structures is due to Touretzky and Hinton (1985) and Touretzky (1986).

For the fillers, or the tail of a triple, the units stand for useful characterizers that serve to distinguish one filler from another. Hinton (1981) used the term **microfeatures** for these units; these features need not correspond in any simple way to verbalizable primitives. Different slot fillers produce different patterns on these units; and the different possible instantiations of a filler are likewise captured by differences in the pattern of activation on the units.

For the relations, the units stand for characteristics of the relation itself. Note that this differs from most other approaches in treating each role or relation as a distributed pattern. This has several virtues. For one thing, it immediately eliminates the problem of specifying a small set of case roles, in the face of the fact that there seem to be a very large number of very subtle differences between roles that are in many ways very similar. Further, the use of distributed representations allows us to capture both the similarities and differences among case roles. The idea has been proposed on independent linguistic grounds, as well.

For the head of each triple, the units stand for characteristics of the whole in which the filler plays a part. Thus the pattern that represents P1 is not some arbitrary pointer as it might be in a Lisp-based representation, but is rather a **Reduced Description** of the constituent that it stands for (Hinton, McClelland, and Rumelhart, 1986; Lakoff, personal communication). In particular, the pattern representing P1 would capture characteristics of the act of eating and of the participants in the act. There would be less detail, of course, than in the separate representations of these constituents where they occur as separate fillers of the tail slot.

Syntactic and Case-role Representations

Sentences have both an augmented surface structure representation and a case-role representation. In the present model, then, there are two sets of units, one that represents the syntactic structure triples, and one that represents the case-structure triples. I have already described the general form of the case-role triples; the syntactic triples would have a similar form, though they would capture primarily syntactic relations among the constituents. So, for example, the set of syntactic triples of Sentence 2 would be something like:

(S1 SUBJ BOY) (S1 VERB SAW) (S1 DOBJ CAKE) (CAKE MODIFIER S2)

(S2 SUBJ MOTHER) (S2 VERB BAKED) (S2 DOBJ T=CAKE) (S1 LOC-PP OVEN)

There are, correspondingly, two main parts to the model, a syntactic processor and a case-frame processor (See Figure 1). In this respect, the model is similar to many conventional parsing schemes (e.g., Marcus, 1980; Kaplan and

Bresnan, 1982). The microstructure is quite different, however. One of the key things that a PDP microstructure buys us is the ability to improve the interaction between these two main components.

Syntactic Processing

The role of the syntactic processor is to take in words as they are encountered in reading or listening and to produce as its outputs a sequence of patterns, with each pattern capturing one syntactic structure triple.[1]

In Figure 1 the syntactic processor is shown in the midst of processing Sentence 2. It has reached the point where it is processing the words "the cake". The output at this point should tend to activate the pattern corresponding to (S1 DOBJ CAKE) over a set of units (the *syntactic triple units*) whose role is to display the pattern of activation corresponding to the current syntactic triple. Note that these units also receive feedback from the case-frame processor; the role of this feedback is to fill in unspecified parts of the syntactic triple, as shall be discussed below. The syntactic triple units have connections to units (the *case-frame triple units*) which serve to represent the current case-frame triple.

The connections between these two sets of units are assumed to be learned through prior pairings of syntactic triples and case-frame triples, so that they capture the mutual constraints on case and syntactic role assignments. The inner workings of the syntactic processor have yet to be fully worked out, so for now I leave it as a black box.

The Case-frame Processor

The role of the case-frame processor is to produce an active representation of the current case-frame constituent, based on the pattern representing the current syntactic constituent on the syntactic triple units and on feedback from a set of units called the *working memory*. The working memory is the structure in which the developing case-frame representation of the sentence is held. As constituents are parsed, they are loaded into the working memory, by way of a network called an I/O net.[2]

Within the working memory, individual units correspond to combinations of units in the current case-role representation. Thus, the representation at this level is *conjunctive* and is therefore capable of maintaining information about which combinations of case-role units were activated together in the same case-role triple when the patterns activated by several triples are superimposed in the working memory (see Hinton et al., 1986, for discussion). Of course, early in a parse, the loaded constituents will necessarily be incomplete.

Pattern Completion

The working memory provides a persisting representation of the constituents already parsed. This representation persists as a pattern of activation, so

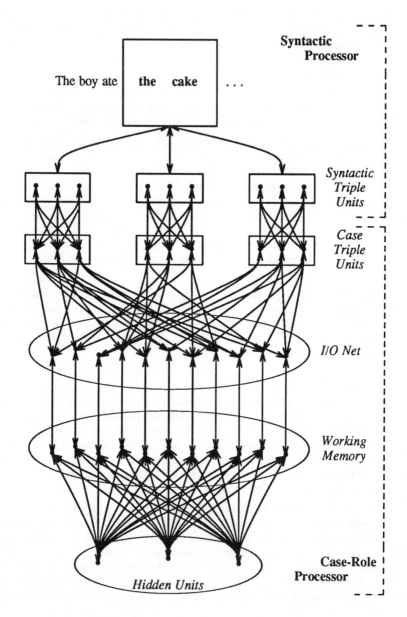

Figure 1. A diagram of the model.   See text for explanation.

that it can both constrain and be constrained by new constituents as they are encountered, through interactions with a final set of units, called the *hidden case-role units*. These units are called "hidden" because their state is not visible to any other part of the system; instead they serve to mediate constraining relations among the units in the working memory. The process works as follows. Connections from working memory units to hidden units allow the pattern of activation over the working memory to produce a pattern over the hidden units. Connections from the hidden units to the working memory units allow these patterns, in turn, to feed activation back to the working memory. This feedback allows the network to complete and clean up distorted and incomplete patterns (that is, representations of sentences). The connections in the network are acquired through training on a sample of sentences (see St. John, 1986, for details). The connection strengths derived from this training experience allow it to sustain and complete the representations of familiar sentences; this capability generalizes to novel sentences with similar structure.

What This Model Can Do

The model I have described should be able to do all of the kinds of things listed at the beginning of the paper. Consider, for example, the problem of interpreting the sentence "The boy hit the ball with the bat." This requires both assigning the appropriate reading (baseball-bat) and the appropriate role (instrument) to the bat. The syntactic triple for this constituent (S1 with-PP BAT) would tend to activate a pattern over the coresponding to a blend of baseball bat and flying bat as the tail of the triple, and a blend of the possible case-roles consistent with "with" as the the pattern representing the relation portion of the triple. These in turn would tend to activate units representing the various possible filler-role combinations consistent with this syntactic constituent. But since the other constituents of the sentence would already have been stored in the working memory, the completion process would tend to support units standing for the baseball-bat as instrument interpretation more than others. Thus, simultaneous role assignment and context-sensitive selection of the appropriate reading of an ambiguous word would be expected to fall out naturally from the operation of the completion process.

Filling in default values for missing arguments and shading or shaping the representations of vaguely described constituents is also a simple by-product of the pattern completion process. Thus, for example, on encountering "The man stirred the coffee", the completion process will tend to fill in the pattern for the completion that includes a spoon as instrument. Note that the pattern so filled in need not specify a particular specific concept; thus for a sentence like "The boy wrote his name", we would expect a pattern representing a writing instrument, but not specifying if it is a pen or a pencil, to be filled in; unless, of course, the network had had specific experience indicating that boys always write their names with one particular instrument or another. A similar process occurs on encountering the container in a sentence like "The container held the cola". In such cases the constraints imposed by other constituents (the cola) would be expected to shape the representation of "container", toward a smallish, hand-holdable, non-porous container. Again, this process would not necessarily specify a specific container, just the properties such a container could be predicted to have.

I have not yet said anything about what the model would do with the attachment problem posed by the sentence "The boy ate the cake that his mother baked in the oven." In this case, we would expect that the syntactic processor would pass along a constituent like (S? in-PP OVEN), and that it would be the job of the case-role processor to determine its correct attachment. Supposing that the experience the network has been exposed to includes mothers (and others) baking cakes (and other things) in ovens, we would expect that the case-role triple (P2 LOC OVEN), where P2 stands for the reduced description of "mother-baked-cake", would already be partially active as the syntactic constituent became available. Thus the incoming constituent would simply reinforce a pattern of activation that already reflected the correct attachment of oven.

Current Status of the Model

As I previously stated, the model has not yet been implemented, and so one can treat the previous section as describing the performance of a machine made out of hopeware. Nevertheless, I have reason to believe it will work. CMU connectionists now have considerable experience with representations of the kind used in the case-frame processor (Touretzky and Hinton, 1985; Touretzky, 1986; Derthick, 1986). A mechanism quite like the case-frame processor has been implemented by St. John (1986), and it demonstrates several of the uses of semantic constraints that I have been discussing.

Obviously, though, even if the case-frame processor is successful there are many more tasks that lie ahead. One crucial one is the development of a connectionist implementation of the syntactic processor. I believe that we are now on the verge of understanding sequential processes in connectionist networks (see Jordan, 1986), and that this will soon make it possible to describe a complete connectionist mechanism for language processing that captures both the strengths and limitations of human language processing capabilities.

Acknowledgements

I would like to thank Geoff Hinton, George Lakoff, Brian MacWhinney, and Mark St. John for discussions of the topic of this paper and/or for specific comments on the first draft. Supported by ONR contract N00014-82-C-0374, NR 667-483.

Notes

1. Note that this means that several words can be packed into the same constituent, and that as the words of a constituent (e.g., "the old grey donkey") are encountered, the microfeatures of the constituent will be gradually specified. Thus the representation of the constituent can gradually build up at the output of the syntactic processor.

2. The I/O net is equivalent to Touretzky and Hinton's (1985) "pull-out net." Its job is to ensure that the characteristics of only one of the constituents stored in the working memory are interacting with the case-frame triple units. See Touretzky and Hinton (1985) for details.

Chapter 3.5

POSSIBLE IMPLICATIONS OF CONNECTIONISM

Wendy G. Lehnert

As far as I can tell the most exciting thing happening in AI these days is the invasion of the brain people (a.k.a. the connectionists). The connectionists haven't really invaded the AI community in the sense of making a planned assault—it just seems that connectionism is the sexiest thing around. The AI community has very suddenly become very interested in connectionist techniques, and it is only a slight exaggeration for me to say that all the first year graduate students I meet express an interest in connectionism. So perhaps it would be useful to talk about the status of connectionism with respect to the old formal/commonsense semantic arguments. Let's try to pigeon-hole this new paradigm in terms of our old formal/procedural/episodic/semantic distinctions and see what happens.

What About Symbols?

The first thing we have to grapple with is the fact that the connectionists are operating within a sphere of assumptions that is problematic to mainstream AI research. The cornerstone of mainstream AI is the idea of symbol manipulation. Interestingly, many of the most exciting efforts in connectionism (the "Parallel Distributed Processing" [PDP] models described by Rumelhart and McClelland, 1986) do not utilize explicit symbols at all. But this does not prevent PDP systems from manipulating information: it just means that a concept in a PDP system is not present in that system as an explicit data structure. Concepts (and attributes and categories) manifest themselves as patterns of activation distributed throughout a strongly connected network of nodes, where the nodes by themselves signify nothing in particular. Distributed representations of this sort can be manipulated to exhibit useful I/O behavior, but our traditional ideas of data and control fail to provide the descriptive framework needed to understand these systems.

The implications of this are important. In mainstream AI, a successful system can be said to embody a theory of human information processing. But this claim is evaluated on the basis of what we understand about that program. An explanation at the level of machine code is not very useful, but a high-level flow chart might be. The PDP systems do not lend themselves to this explanatory aspect of AI very readily.

"The strength of this more complicated kind of representation
does not lie in its notational convenience or its ease of implementation in a conventional computer, but rather in the efficiency with
which it makes use of the processing abilities of networks of simple, neuron-like computing elements."
(Hinton, McClelland, and Rumelhart, 1986).

In some sense, the task of understanding how a given PDP system works is
very much like trying to understand machine code. This should not be surprising, given the intimacy of PDP models with low-level computing mechanisms,
but it does tend to alienate those elements of the AI community who are
interested in "understanding" their programs in traditional information processing terms. It is no small accomplishment to stop thinking in terms of
primitive symbols, data structures, and procedures, in order to start thinking in
terms of input vectors, linear thresholds, and necessary conditions for stabiliza-
tion.

While the presence or absence of explicit symbols may at first seem to
be an insurmountable hurdle to any intelligent comparisons between AI and
connectionism, it is sobering to consider what the connectionists have accom-
plished using distributed representations. Connectionists have traditionally
looked at "low-level" information processing problems: motor feedback,
stereoscopic vision processing, visual letter recognition, and lexical access for
natural language are typical examples. If the AI community has been slow to
embrace the lessons of connectionism, it is because mainstream AI is more
concerned with "high-level" information processing: text comprehension,
problem solving, scene recognition, and inductive learning are closer to the
heart of mainstream AI. But now we are beginning to see connectionism
"trickle-up" into higher task orientations.

Connectionist systems are now being designed to:

1. *Translate sentences into case-frame representations*
    (McClelland and Kawamoto, 1986)

2. *Index causal chains for narrative recall*
    (Golden, 1986)

3. *Handle the script activation problem*
    (Sharkey, Sutcliffe, and Wobcke, 1986)

4. *Index memory for a case-based reasoner*
    (Stanfill and Waltz, 1986)

5. *Store and retrieve relational data*
    (Hinton, 1986)

These tasks are firmly situated in the realms of "high-level" information
processing—or at least they used to be. No one is claiming to have solved
these problems, but one cannot resist the feeling that a breath of fresh air is
clearing a musty old closet.

The TWITIT Methodology

Connectionists are generally attentive to the physical properties and limitations of the human brain. At the same time, they experiment with programmable systems and bend an occasional constraint as needed. They are exploiting an interesting mix of science (brain theory) and engineering (TWeak It Til It Thinks). On the one hand, connectionists are more constrained than traditional AI researchers: AI people do not think in terms of hardware constraints. On the other hand, connectionists have no shame when it comes to actually making something work: The business of finding a correct set of weights (or initial values, or network architecture, or whatever) is closer to the Quest for the Holy Grail than any knowledge engineer has cared to go. The AI community became understandably nervous about the TWITIT paradigm for system design shortly after Samuel's checkers-playing system failed to extrapolate up to chess. I suppose we never quite got over that one.

Even so, as far as methodological styles go, the connectionist enterprise seems capable of accommodating both "neats" and "scruffies" (Abelson, 1981). The neat AI camp can optimize learning rules, establish tests for Boltzmann-equivalence, and worry about decidability as a problem in linear algebra. While all this is going on, the scruffies can revel in the pursuit of graceful degradation, operate on the basis of elusive concept definitions, and learn from experience. Wherever the chips may fall, it is nevertheless true that the connectionist turf is up for grabs in the mainstream AI community. What is the relationship between formal logic and connectionism? Theories of reminding and connectionism? Opportunistic planning and connectionism? Teams are just now forming and the sides are still being chosen.

A ROSE is a ROZE is a ROZ is a WOZ

Having said all that, maybe we can now try to say something about our original topic of discussion: how the connectionists weigh in on the formal/procedural/episodic/semantic scales.

To begin, let's consider the problem of representing word meanings. In traditional AI there are basically two competing approaches to the representation of word meanings. (1) The formalist fans assume a componential view in which a word's meaning is represented by a set of semantic features. (2) The episodic enthusiasts assume a structuralist position in which the meaning of a word must be defined in terms of its relationship to other words and available memory structures. Interestingly, there are PDP models inspired by both viewpoints. Hinton, McClelland, and Rumelhart (1986) describe componential systems, while McClelland and Kawamoto (1986) discuss structuralist PDP systems.[1]

If we look a bit closer at the PDP models for lexical access, we discover that they are governed by remarkably predictable task orientations. The componential systems are all concerned with the problem of mapping single isolated words to their word senses, while the structuralist systems are all trying to resolve word senses during sentence comprehension. *Plus ça change....*

On the surface, at least, it seems that connectionist techniques can be applied to any traditional view one wants to promote. But there are some undercurrents afoot that might tip the balance away from a fully neutral position of non-alignment. The undercurrent to watch is the question of learning.

One of the reasons why connectionists (at least the PDP variety) are preoccupied with learning is because they see no other systematic way to approach the design of large (at least 100,000 nodes) networks which cannot be understood as static data structures. Coincidentally, a similar preoccupation with learning has risen in recent years among the proponents of episodic memory. It is easy to build a limited prototype that illustrates the utility of episodic memory structures—but it is much harder to scale up from that to a practical system which utilizes a lot of episodic knowledge effectively. This parallel is at least suggestive of some common ground, although the Lisplovers and the TWITIT set will have to stretch considerably in bringing their respective methodologies together. I think it will happen. The episodic camp is populated primarily by closet psychologists, and the TWITIT group seems to be dominated by closet neurologists. Whatever other differences exist, both groups build systems in order to test their theories and this requires a healthy respect for engineering. The engineering components of both groups are sufficiently *simpatico* to encourage a few curious adventurers into crossing over.

The formalists operate with a very different methodological style, one that is dominated by a much more philosophical orientation. The formalists prefer to study knowledge in a competence framework rather than a performance framework. This is the study of knowledge as it might be if we could factor out the imperfections of the human mind that conceives it. Never mind the fact that "Three dogs ate four bones" is problematic only for graduate students—these are the problems we can study without reference to performance criteria or subject data or anything else that relies on a concern for human memory organization. References to "semantic memory" confuse the issue (as do those who take formal semantics seriously as a model of human memory), but the difference in methodological styles is obvious.[2]

The advocates of semantic features, quantification, and distinctions of intension/intention are almost never people who design psychological experiments or worry about models of human information processing as a precursor to intelligent information processing.

Given all this, it seems to me that the formalists will be even more uncomfortable with the TWITIT mentality than they were with the old-style scruffies. Of course there will always be room for people who want to nail down optimal annealing schedules and mathematical foundations. So the job prospects for formalists look healthy if the connectionists stage a complete takeover of AI in the next decade. As for the scruffy AI types, it seems that the future depends on whether one is primarily a closet psychologist or a latent engineer. The engineers will undoubtedly find work in the brave new world (they always do), but the closet psychologists will be interesting to watch. They will either retreat with queasy feelings of paradigm failure, or stage a revolution that's tough to call. If the connectionists should ever come to dominate AI, we will have to deal with the very real possibility that we might be able to simulate something without really understanding it very well at all. But that's another panel discussion altogether.

Notes

1. A number of research efforts which qualify as connectionist efforts are not PDP systems since they employ "local" representations rather than "distributed" representations. The work of Small; Cottrell and Small; Waltz and Pollack; and Charniak fall into this category.

2. This point was nicely illustrated by Drew McDermott's commentary on Geoff Hinton's invited talk at AAAI-86. McDermott said that whatever else might be nice about connectionism, the connectionists really ought to stop worrying so much about learning. In retrospect, I would have predicted this.

Chapter 3.6

DISCUSSION:
CONNECTIONIST AND OTHER PARALLEL APPROACHES
TO NATURAL LANGUAGE PROCESSING

Gary COTTRELL: A lot of people are worried about this approach, especially if they're in the "symbolic camp," and I'd like to lay out what I think some of the possibilities are for connectionist approaches to natural language. Let me say at the outset that I am mainly interested in NI, or Natural Intelligence, and how it processes languages, versus, say, a competence model. This is the kind of process that I think is necessary for understanding, for determining the senses of words. Word sense disambiguation is something that's often ignored by computational linguists. I may get some argument on that, but it involves the interaction between a lot of different sources of knowledge, and that's something I think connectionism is good at. For example, discourse context. "I am taking the car" means one thing if you're a teenager or if you're sitting in front of a Lisp machine. Grammar, of course is important, meaning frequency—"Bob threw a ball": most of you thought of somebody propelling a small round thing rather than hosting a formal dance. Semantic associations are important— "Deep pit" (I think this is Steve Small's example): "deep" can mean "far down" or "abstract," the "pit" can be "fruit pit" or "hole in the ground," but only two of those senses go together. And they mutually constrain one another to determine the correct meaning. Pragmatic information is important. "The man walked on the deck": it's probably a ship's deck rather than a card deck. And this is Graeme Hirst's example—"Nadja swung the hammer at the nail and the head flew off": pragmatic and syntactic information helps us determine whether that it was the hammer's head and not the nail's head, or Nadja's head.

So my thesis attacks some aspects of this problem in a connectionist framework, the localist one, from Rochester. I added a three-layer, four-component system. The major difference between this and other systems at the time was that I didn't place syntax first or semantics first, but rather, that access to those two systems was in parallel. At the lexical level, I had a unit for every word in the language I wanted to worry about, and then at the word-sentence level, were lexical entries that were activated by the lexical items as they came in. Then, if a word was ambiguous, it would [have] more than one lexical entry, and they would be mutually inhibitory and compete at the word-sentence level. Who won that competition was determined by feedback from the third level, where if a lexical item is part of an active right-hand side of a syntactic production, then it gets more feedback than when it isn't, and if a word sense is part of a developing case frame—my semantics was a case semantics—then it gets more feedback than something that didn't participate in the developing representation of the parse.

Now, I've become a distributed connectionist, and I think that meanings are best represented not as these awkward lexemes, as Yorick Wilks has called them, but units at this level are better represented by what Rumelhart calls "connectionist schemata." I'm going to do a little thought experiment. This is aimed at those people that didn't read my paper, because the ones who did have seen it. Consider the word "truck." This is a fairly solid word, and doesn't seem polysemous. Yet, in the sentence "Danny picked up the truck," suddenly it turns small and light, probably plastic, so we might in a symbolic system have a rule that if a truck is the object of a picking-up action, then it becomes a toy truck. But then, there are always exceptions to the rule, and there might be an exception in the first case, if Danny's picking up a rental truck. So there are a lot of exceptions to the rules, plus the meaning of "truck" varies rather smoothly. In "Tommy lugged the truck up the hill," it's a little bigger truck than the one you imagined in the first case. And in "Danny picked up the truck and handed it to Tommy. Tommy lugged it up the hill," now, not only the truck is a little bigger, but the Tommy is a little smaller than Danny.

The point here is that words are not represented very well by a list of their alternate meanings. Rather, they vary smoothly along a fairly, I would guess, large number of dimensions. One can imagine doing this same experiment with rooms, and having your image of a room varying smoothly; and Rumelhart actually did this and built a connectionist model from it. He had a couple of people imagine five different kinds of rooms, and he had forty descriptors of what might be in a room or descriptors of a room, and had them say what was in the room they were imagining and what wasn't. So he'd have them imagine a living room, a kitchen, etc. and then he used the results of that to wire up a network, where if two items co-occurred, then there was a positive link between them, and if they didn't occur very often, there was a negative link between them, so that sofa and fireplace became positively connected. Bathtubs rarely occur with sofas, and we actually get a winner-take-all net for the size of the room, because it's either small, medium, large, or very large, and it's not any of those at the same time.

My point is that word senses can be represented in the same way, where these units represent more microfeatures, such as "boy" might be represented by HUMAN, ANIMATE, YOUNG, MALE, etc. What happens when you access this model—here are the forty descriptors, and here he's actually clamped on "ceiling" to imagine we're talking about a room and "oven" so we're asking the model, "Think of a room with an oven in it." Time here goes from left to right, and the sizes of these squares are the activation of the units.

What the network does is fill out a pattern which corresponds to your proto-type, to the network's prototype kitchen, so kitchen has a coffee pot, a cup-board, etc., in it. This is his version of the connectionist schemata. So this same network will do different things. If you start it on "bed" or "sofa," you'll get the other five rooms that were stored in it. But the interesting thing is you can get stable states that weren't actually stored explicitly in the net-work. If you turn on two things that don't normally co-occur, such as "bed" and "sofa," it fills out a pattern that can correspond to a large, fancy bedroom. It has a fireplace in it, and that's an intuitively pleasing result. So the fillers of some roles in this schema constrain fillers in other roles, and you actually get a room that's halfway between a living room and a bedroom. In size, it's a large bedroom, and it's a nice, smooth result. So that's what I imagine is happening at my word sense level instead of my awkard lexemes.

So much for how I think lexical semantics should be represented, How might such a thing be learned? Here we have a robot with a mohawk. This is probably everybody's first idea of how you might do semantics, how you might ground semantics, in that we have inputs coming in from different chan-nels, and they get their own codes for those channels, a visual code for vision, an auditory code for what comes in your ear, and what we'd like is some sort of intermodal code that joins those things together, so that when we see those things together, and Mom says "dog," we develop an intermodal code that represents both of those together, and in some sense represents meaning of the word "dog."

Jay McCLELLAND: I'm going to focus my remarks on the topic of distributed representations in connectionist networks. I guess one way of thinking of the thesis of this talk is that the connectionist enterprise might give you something, even if you're a symbol processor, that you can take home with you and use to make your machines better, more sensitive to constraints, more capable of deal-ing with the flexibility of natural language. The notion is that distributed representations might be thought of as being a way of looking at the micros-tructure of what people have typically thought of as symbols, sort of these encapsulated objects that can't be ripped apart. Now actually this view is not completely unlike the kind of view that says, say, instead of having an NP node you have a description there of the constituents in a parse tree, or some-thing like that, and I don't mean to say that nobody else has been using some-thing like distributed representations, but the connectionist distributed represen-tations give us several sorts of further benefits, compared to the kind I've seen in other kinds of work. They're continuously shadable, they're malleable by context, and they're active. And by "active" I mean that they do things, they cause other representations by virtue of the connections that you have in the network already, and they take a lot of the work out of the control structure of your model and sort of put it into the knowledge that's encoded in the network.

Well, I've been thinking about this, along the following lines, and I should say that my thinking here is heavily based on some work that Touretzky and Hinton have done with similar kinds of ideas. The basic notion is to look at a tree as a set of triples, a very familiar notion, in which each triple consists of some whole, some part and some relation that specifies how the part relates to the whole. While I've said whole, relation, part, here, one could think of superordinate, relational constituent, or of a taxonomic hierarchy this way also. On this view, we can imagine that we have a set of units to represent each of the constituents of each triple, or of a triple, so that we represent the filler in a triple, not by a symbol, ball number 37 or something, but by a distributed pattern that represents the characteristics of the ball as instantiated in this context to the best of our current ability. The pattern for the whole provides what George Lakoff has suggested to me you might indeed want in your representational system, namely, some kind of a summary description of the contents of the entire set of triples that go into this particular constituent. So, for example, suppose we're trying to capture the structure of a case frame, say, underlying a proposition, in which we have some sentence and several constituents, say, an agent, a patient, some verb in the sentence, we can imagine that the pattern for the whole would be a summary description of the whole sentence that would capture such features, if the sentence involved breaking that it's a discrete action, that it results in the destruction of the patient, and so on. The role, say, for the instrument slot, would specify that the instrument was in the causal chain of events, but that it wasn't necessarily the instigator of that causal chain, that it was controlled by the agent, and so on.

I just briefly want to say one little thing about the role of learning. The job of learning in these kinds of networks is not only to figure out what the constraints are among the features, but to figure out what the right descriptors are, what the right features should be in these distributed representations. It turns out that the set of features that are needed cannot be determined a priori from considering the individual sentences that need to be comprehended. You need to know what the whole ensemble of things that needs to be comprehended is. The set of primitives that you need is dependent upon what distinctions need to be made to capture some sort of corpus of linguistic material you're trying to cope with. So any attempts to prespecify enough descriptors to cover the whole space is doomed, and we've found this repeatedly in our work. If we were to say, "Let's just make up a set of descriptors," it doesn't work. But the learning algorithms that we've begun to develop are helping us to allow our networks to figure out for themselves what descriptors they need in order to solve the tasks that they are confronted with. And so, I think that the connectionist learning algorithms provide a way not only of tuning up connections among the descriptors once they're established but also of figuring out what kinds of descriptors you need within your distributed representations in order to get the job done. I think that if you're a symbol processor, you could see connectionism as providing you with a set of tools for building more flexible, more context-sensitive, more malleable symbolic structures in which the particular elements of your descriptions that make up the microstructure of your symbols would actually be things that connectionism would provide you with means for discovering, and without requiring you to necessarily prespecify them all in advance.

Wendy LEHNERT: I can date my own entry into this movement on the order of months ago. It seems to me 1986 was a very significant year in some sense, and I'd like to point out a paper that first brought it home to me, which appeared in the AAAI that August. It's called "Mixing binary and continuous connection schemes for knowledge access," by Sharkey. If you look at the paper, what it seems to be about is the problem of script activation: restaurant scripts, and so on and so forth, utilizing a technique called simulated annealing. Now those of us who know about scripts understand what that problem is. That's a very "scruffy" problem, and you have to be fairly scruffy to want to work with scripts in the first place. Simulated annealing, on the other hand, is something you tend to know about only if you're a theoretician or someone who perhaps works with VLSI layout. It's not a scruffy technique, and indeed if you look at the paper, you see equations and annealing schedules. This is what you call a real paradigm shift, and when I first saw the paper, I recognized it to be an editor's nightmare. Who is going to try to review a paper that tries to synthesize, in this case, a problem from one paradigm with a technique from a completely different one? I happen to know enough about simulated annealing to feel I could read the paper, but when I was done I wasn't at all sure, and it motivated me to learn a little bit more about this class of techniques called connectionism.

Robust information processing is a real challenge for mainstream AI, and it seems to me that if anybody, I don't care who they are, claims to have any kind of a handle on these capabilities, we really ought to take the time to stop and look and assess the situation to see if we can benefit from it. So I'm willing to stop and look. I haven't really crossed over into the connectionist camp, because I'm not building connectionist systems, and I don't imagine I ever will. But I have found a few ideas out of the connectionist literature that I've been able to incorporate in my current research.

One is the knowledge acquisition bottleneck, and hand in hand with that, although we tend not to talk about it so much, I think is the software engineering bottleneck; that is, it's one thing to know what all the knowledge structures are that you need to incorporate in a system. It's another thing to make that all really work once you've passed a certain level of mass. We all have toy systems that work nicely under certain conditions, but if you really start pumping in all the stuff you need, you discover that the profile of the system alters. One of the problems that I've been perplexed by for years now is the problem of controlling multiple knowledge structures. If you believe in a heavily knowledge-based system, then you must believe in multiple knowledge structures, and in my mind no one has satisfactorily come up with a general architecture for the integration of multiple knowledge structures. I'm talking about everything from the level of plans, and goals, and scripts, and themes, and you name whatever your favorite knowledge structure is, down to the very simple age-old problem of integrating syntax and semantics. I just don't see any proposals for general architectures that can address all of that. But in eyeing the connectionist approaches to information processing, I chanced upon a fairly simple concept called network relaxation, and it seems to me that we should be able to exploit that within our symbolic systems. We don't have to get into sub-symbolic distributed representation to do this.

I think the term was first used by people who were doing numeric relaxation. If you had a curve of data that was very jagged, you could relax that curve into a smoother curve using an iterative process called numeric relaxation. In this context, network relaxation is similar. The idea is one of stabilizing a network, in terms of activation levels. If you have nodes with varying degrees of activation, you iterate over that network in order to spread the activation, and inhibit the activation. If the network has certain properties, it will stabilize into a hopefully useful pattern of activation. If the stable state is useful, then it will describe something like preferred word sense, or a syntactic parse, or a bunch of slot fillers for a case frame. You decide what you're interested in. So I've been able to utilize the general idea of network relaxation for the task orientation of sentence analysis, but I'm doing it in a very hybrid manner.

It does throw me into the connectionist camp, though, because as soon as you buy into this, what you're doing is you're tweaking numbers, right?

Eugene CHARNIAK: A little-known fact about me is that I actually got my bachelor's degree in physics, which gives me a slight edge-up in these things. An edge-down is an even less-known fact because I only got a B in statistical mechanics. However, my current work has nothing to do with that. My current work has to do with recognizing character motivation, or plan recognition in stories, so if you see "Jack went to the supermarket," you want to assume that he is going to shop there. This is, of course, very closely tied if not isomorphic or identical to the question of speaker intention, which is a well-known problem in computational linguistics. To show this, simply consider what would happen if your spouse called up and said "Please stop at the supermarket on the way home" and you went to the supermarket, stopped, and then continued on. In both cases, what has to happen is you want to recognize the plan which prompted the utterance in one case and the action in the other. In doing this, I have been using a marker-passing approach. The paradigmatic example is "Jack got a rope. He wanted to kill himself." And there what I'm doing is I'm trying to find a path between 'rope' and 'kill,' presumably through 'hang,' which would give you some clue as to the motivation for getting the rope. Because I've used a marker-passing approach, many people have thought of me as a connectionist. I don't consider myself one, mainly because at most I could be considered a localist-connectionist, and I must confess, the only kind of connectionism that to me seems worthwhile doing is distributed, because it is really different. If I'm going to do localist, I might as well do what I'm currently doing, it seems to me.

One of my research problems has been how to figure out, when you see "Jack went to the supermarket", why he's going to do it. One good clue is that supermarkets are only used for a limited number of things. So, in particular, what you could imagine yourself doing is going to the supermarket looking for what roles it plays in actions, and you might find supermarket-shopping, and that is of course what you want to do. Then, when you go upwards, you see "store," and of course you'll find something attached to "store," namely "shopping," and you'll think you have possibly two motivations, whereas you really only have one. One possibility would be to eliminate this and say, you can't go up, but that's not going to do because if you for example saw "Jack got some milk," you would presumably want to infer the most likely of the inferences that he's going to drink it, which is a connection not from "milk," but from "beverage," as opposed to, say, "He's going to make cereal," which would be a connection directly to "milk." Now, the point is that I have to be able to rule out one of these candidates, and I can think of myriads of ways of doing that. It's just one of those thousands of nitty-gritty problems that confront you every day, and very often when I see a problem like this I say, "Well, gee, what would happen if I were using some completely different way of thinking about things?" And lately, because of connectionism, I've been prone to think what would happen if I were using a connectionist model of all this? What would this problem look like? Would it still be there? And so, I went through the following gedanken experiment.

First, let me remind you of Rumelhart's work on rooms. You have various nodes corresponding to the various things that a room might have; your schema comes out as an activation pattern over the entire network. What's really important to remember in all this, and the term has been used before, is that what these things are really doing is filling out patterns. There are certain patterns that they really like, like the pattern for bedroom, the pattern for kitchen, etc., and given little pieces of these patterns, they're able to fill out the complete thing. Now, let's translate that over to my problem. Here's the obvious translation, so instead of having pieces of rooms, I have pieces of actions, or individual actions, and they're connected to one another positively or negatively. So "supermarket-shopping" would be connected up to "get basket, go to supermarket, get food." Then "get food" would be negatively connected to "sew, to tailor." Tailors do work in stores, so there'd be a good connection there, etc. You can imagine filling this whole thing out, and now we're going to put in things, and we're going to let the system fill out the pattern. I don't mean this seriously, by the way, this is pure imagination. Now, if you think about this, though, as far as it goes, it would work beautifully and it would completely eliminate all those issues about what to do in my problem case. Sure, "store" might get activated, "store-shopping" might get activated, but that's irrelevant. The point is that "supermarket-shopping" would get activated, and the meaning of what's going on is the meaning of the whole. So you say, "Okay, fine, why don't you become a connectionist?" And the reason is, Because lots of other problems hit you over the head with a sledgehammer, and now I'm going to talk about that.

Imagine the following story: "Jack went to the supermarket. Bill went to the tailor." And you want to answer Who got a basket, or Who's getting food. Notice that this thing can't do it. It doesn't say who went to the supermarket, just said "going to the supermarket." This is a network from the viewpoint that there's a single agent in the world who's doing everything. There's no way, given this particular representation, this particular network, of indicating who's doing what. Or, to put it more generally, these things aren't propositions in the sense of having symbols which relate to one another. "Jack" is the agent of this particular action. Well, can you do it in connectionism? The answer is yes: McClelland has three connectionist networks, one for argument, one for case, and one for action. So the arguments might be 'Jack' 'human,' 'male,' etc. The point is, 'human' is generally going to be consistent with 'agent,' whereas 'store' would not be consistent with 'agent,' whereas 'store' would be consistent with 'destination,' but 'human' wouldn't be, 'eat' would not be consistent with 'destination,' etc., etc. He relaxes his whole thing and he gets out who's doing what to whom. Now, all very nice. You say okay, fine, that does what you want, now you've got the agent. But notice, in getting the agent, we lost everything we had before. What we had before was a description in our network of the entire gestalt: what was going on. The entire network corresponds to one proposition. So, sure, you've got propositions, but you've lost everything else. Now, can anything be done about this? I can imagine all sorts of possibilities. The most obvious is to take every one of the nodes you had before and expand it into this pattern. It gets expensive, though. How many actions do we know about? Well, earlier, in lexicography, you might have a million items, so think of a million. That's not too bad, actually.

Again, think of a node roughly corresponding to a neuron, although I must say the connectionists are very good at not using the word neuron, but let me do it, because I'm not one. So, we've got about 10 to the 10th neurons, so a million isn't that much, right? It's a piddly fraction of the total. However, now when we start doing this we've got a minimum of, say, a hundred nodes to represent each one of those, so we had 10 to the 6th, now we're up to 10 to the 8th. Now we're beginning to get a bit twitchy. Of course, this only represents one argument, and for the average pattern we might have ten different arguments, its location, time, destination, origin, etc., so now you're up to 10 to the 9th. At that point, I'm sorry, maybe I'm old-fashioned, but when I start talking about a billion elements to do this sort of thing, I really get worried. If I did see how to do it, I might become a connectionist, but I don't. Thus, I think it's fair to say, at the moment, connectionism simply can't represent propositions. Perhaps a more fair way to say it is, to the degree they can represent propositions, it's like a horse walking on two legs. Sure, it can do it, but you lose all the grace and beauty that made you want to use a horse in the first place. If I want to gallop, I'm going to get a horse. If I have to walk, I'd rather do it in Lisp.

Martin KAY: My office phone number consists of a permutation of fours and threes, and there's another permutation of fours and threes very close to it which gets you an office supply house, and so I'm very, very used to picking up the phone and saying "Wrong number" almost before I've listened to what the person on the other end has to say. I guess I should have made that an excuse and used that response when Dave called me and said "Will you be on the panel on connectionism?" because it's perfectly clear to me that what I know about connectionism is very, very little, and I hadn't realized how much had been done with it in fact in our field. It was interesting to speculate about why I got asked in the first place. Two ideas came to mind. One was that I had something to do with inventing chart-parsing; and what chart- parsing was supposed to be was a way of dealing with nondeterminism in a very general way that didn't commit oneself to a particular set of algorithmic steps. So, for example, it enabled you to discuss the properties of nondeterministic processes in language parsing without specifying the Earley algorithm or any other particular algorithm. So, in a sense, it was an attempt to provide a general way of doing parallel processing in a world in which everybody knew that parallel processing wasn't and never would be possible. The other side of nondeterminism, of course, is one that we keep on being told about these days, namely that it's psychologically, hopelessly unrealistic because we are deterministic machines, and the sort of behavior that a general nondeterministic system would seem to predict is not the sort the kind of behavior that human beings seem to evince.

Now the nice thing about connection machines, is that they remove some of this embarrassment. I can go back to believing in nondeterminism as being a fundamental basis for linguistic processes, without having to subscribe to the necessity of hopeless computational complexity. With that in mind, on the order of ten years ago I built a little parallel machine of my own (which was something you could do in those days) by going around the halls in the evening, and inserting programs into all the free machines that you could find, because they had all been connected up at that time with an ethernet, but nobody could think of very much to do, either with the ethernet or with the nocturnal energies of those machines. So I set them to work parsing sentences in the following way. I assigned one word of each sentence to each machine.

This wasn't particularly fast, because you actually had to walk from one machine to the other in order to do this. Each machine was responsible for finding all the phrases in the sentence that began with that word, and the way it did that, of course, was to send messages to its friends further down the line, asking about the kinds of words they had that might be useful in building the kinds of phrases that began with its word. Each machine had a complete copy of the grammar, so it knew about the kinds of things that might be useful. If the next machine down the stream found a useful word, or better still, a useful phrase, and had had a request from somebody else for such a thing—it would usually be a co-operative sort of machine—it would send it back. And eventually, machine number one, if you were lucky, the machine who would have probably asked early in the game for the remainder of a noun phrase, would get the remainder of the noun phrase and send its successor a message saying, "I would like a verb phrase, please," and would get back a verb phrase, and would eventually say "Eureka! I've got a sentence." Now, this sort of scheme would not give you instantaneous parsing, so to speak, in the best of all possible words, but in the best of all possible worlds it would give you parsing in logarithmic time, which would be rather better than most of us expected to get for some time. But when I looked at the problem in connection with this panel, it seemed to me actually a little bit misleading, and if I had been able to find more machines without having to walk too far, I might have discovered this.

The reason for it is this: sentences in natural languages, although they might very well be organized as binary trees, syntactically, never are for some reason or another. They are always organized in the languages we know best as right-branching trees, and the languages we know less well as left-branching trees, but never as trees that branch in a sort of random or even fashion. What this means is that the parsing of the sentences in fact always is going to be dependent upon the length of the sentence so that one's attempt to sort of get the effect of sequentiality out of the business of sentence parsing is going to fail for that reason alone. There is an essential intrinsic dependence of the process that finds a phrase earlier in the sentence on processes that will find phrases later in the sentences, in a right-branching language like the one we speak, which no amount of computational cleverness or expenditure on expensive hardware can possibly overcome. It seems to me endemic.

All that I have said here is in the paper and I think it's all perfectly correct except for the final conclusion, which is that this means that a connectionist approach to parsing is wrong. That conclusion seems to me to be wrong because of one problem I didn't quite get around to looking at carefully enough, which is of course as we know the key problem. It's not something that comes from one individual structure of one individual sentence. It's something that comes from the fact that sentences in general have lots of competing structures, and worse still, they have lots of competing substructures for little pieces of the sentence, which we have to explore, even though they may never eventually contribute to a final structure of the sentence as a whole. So, it seems to me that I have written an absolutely correct seminal paper and the only thing that's wrong with it is the sign bit.

Dave WALTZ: I had the first word; What's good about connectionist models? Well, overall, what is important about connectionist models? The title of my paper is just this, that it's not just a notational variant, on the other hand not a panacea. I think something new really is happening, connectionist models really do present a new paradigm, something that hasn't existed before which represents an opportunity. Well, one really nice property is being able to deal with a nearest match, rather than an exact match. AI has only allowed for processes like exact match. And that can go away in connectionist models. They can learn. Learning is clearly important. If we want to scale up, hand coding isn't going to do. The systems are fault-tolerant, and they degrade gracefully. This is also rare in traditional AI, and a good property. If you were to take a connectionist network, a very large one, and knock out some of the nodes, especially in the distributed one, it will still work. They are scalable, and I don't think that the number of billion of things that Charniak mentioned is particulary scary. I've been doing some projections on systems that might involve 400 million individual entities, which I think is acheivable on a connection machine, even within a year. That's a pretty reasonable number. Now, how we'd actually fill those with interesting things is a much bigger question. Generating hardware that will carry this out is the easy part, and numbers of that size really are not frightening.

What's bad? Well, I think that a lot of the work that's been done has assumed we have networks starting from a random state. Some people, I think Rumelhart in particular, really do believe that you can start with a random system and have it learn everything, including overall organization. I don't think that's really true. Another problem is, especially for the distributed model, they're difficult to analyze, for a couple of reasons: Each node in a distributed model doesn't mean very much, and furthermore, the fault-tolerant and graceful degradation properties mean that the system can even be wrong in some places and it would be hard to detect. Another big difficulty is that variables have been difficult to force into such systems. This didn't come up very much here, but if you want to see how difficult it can be to fit variables into a system, read Touretzky's paper (Touretzky and Hinton, IJCAI 1985).

Why is this all important? Well, I will say this flatly and maybe will start some controversy, but I believe very strongly that an AI based purely on physical symbol systems, heuristic search, and logic isn't going to work, that those are not an adequate basis for building a smart machine. I would say they probably aren't a basis for building a natural language understanding system, either. I think, on the other hand, that perhaps adding something like associative memory could make the rest of the set tractable. Associative memory, I think, is extremely important, which is something that Schank's been saying for a long time, and other people as well, that memory is very important. A lot of things can be done by lookup, a lot of things in language can be done by lookup. A system as was suggested at the very beginning, which was able to do a sort of associative recovery of various lexical items or perhaps patterns, could do a lot of understanding without any parsing at all, or without much parsing. Ultimately, if we think about how the mind is organized, for me the proper organization is probably something like Society of Minds, which harks back to the old Pandemonium model. That says, that each module, unlike the connectionist modules, is really a lot smarter, more capable. Possibly we can construct a society of minds out of lots of little connectionist modules, but there isn't much work going on in the direction yet; I'm not sure how we get there from here.

A promising short-term direction, as a couple of people have suggested, may be to use connectionist models as adjuncts to other programs, and I'll give a very specific example. In artificial intelligence, in general, and natural language in particular, one of the real difficulties is deciding what to try next, what goal to try, or in natural language what linguistic entity or what meaning to put in for a word. In a heuristic planning system, the problem is what operators may apply, or what goal the system should solve overall, and there is a relevance to planning, as Wilensky has shown. Now, in general AI hasn't worried about that problem very much because they've worked with systems that have been so small in the number of operators they had, or so small in the number of goals they had, that you could essentially enumerate them all, try them all, and yet, really that's a memory problem. If we have a very large number of operators or goals, how do we decide in a given situation which of those we should even attempt? Well, I think that connectionist models present an opportunity to solve that problem, which AI badly needs.

Another big problem is learning from experience. Learning from supervised examples is one thing, but learning from real experience is another, an ultimately much harder problem. I think there have been interesting suggestions made on how to deal with images and vision, but people have been working hard on vision for a while, and I think it will take a lot more than that idea, a lot more structure built into a system in order for it to work. *A priori* structures are going to be essential for such systems to work. Without them I think we would learn nothing. As far as I can tell from the psychological literature, people never really learn to see. We are born in some sense knowing how to see. We may do some parameter adjustment in our visual systems, but we have a pretty good idea about what the important units are. A big problem in credit assignment is temporal credit assignment. In credit assignment, if you have a sample pattern and a reward or punishment or an error signal right afterwards, it's pretty easy, relatively easy to decide. But let's suppose some action you take or some decision you make has a consequence only substantially later on. And this could mean the next sentence or the next paragraph in natural language processing, or in acting, it could mean you make some policy decision about how you're going to run your life and only later on discover whether that's good or bad. How do we decide to assign credit? Where do we assign credit within the system when the punishment/reward may be separated a long distance from the actual actions or decisions that need to be rewarded? Learning language, I think, has this kind of associated problem. We don't get much feedback right away when we are learning language. We hear language and presumably do something with what we hear, but we don't get feedback on our decisions, good or bad, until much later.

Gary COTTRELL: First, in response to Kay there is a connectionist parser that uses chart parsing. It was done by Mark Fanty at the University of Rochester, and basically what it does is to build all possible chart nodes in advance for the particular grammar, and then it works in time proportional to the length of the sentence by going one pass up through the chart, which activates all possible constituents, and then a backwards pass activates all the ones that are actually constituents. It's not very believable in the number of nodes, and it does have the limitation that it only works for fixed-length sentences, but, on the other hand, regular parsing algorithms usually have some fixed stack size, too, so they're all finite state machines.

One response to Charniak: for us connectionists, 10 to the 9th isn't bad, considering you have 10 to the 11th units to worry about in the brain. That means we could have a hundred systems like this, And if the one for language is only one of those, I'm not too worried about what to do with the other 99. This distributed-localist argument is, I think, a red herring. It's a granularity argument in my system, for parsing was localist and, in the end, I had a distributed representation of the parse over a set of nodes. And on the opposite side, when is a feature a microfeature? I think that micro is a term that should go out with massive. Anyway, there are also some results that you can train a network to produce a distributed representation from a localist input, by Hinton. On the binding problem—that's Charniak's problem with who did the shopping and who did whatever the other thing was—part of the system I didn't show you was that there were actually a set of binding units between the senses and their possible roles, so this was a localist version of a binding network where we have concepts on this side and roles on the other. And then a winner-take-all net encodes the possible assignments of this concept to its roles, so that, if say, you're processing a sentence "John loves Mary," 'John' starts out, he could be the 'love agent' or 'love object,' then when 'Mary' comes along, and some constraints from syntax on these bindings, then the assignment for 'Mary' can be encoded here and the assignment for 'John' here as the 'agent.'

And then, back to Lehnert: I don't think what we're doing is Twitit. That's what I did for my thesis, and let me tell you, it's really bad. Setting weights is one of the worst possible jobs anyone could want, and that's exactly why people that are interested in this develop learning algorithms to let the networks set their own weights. So, the actual methodology involves two things: designing representations for the input and output of our nets, and what I've called connectionist plumbing: the architecture of the network. If you don't do it right, you end up with sewage. One more thing to Wendy: I think it's a good idea to use relaxation in symbolic systems, but you still have the problem [of] representational blindness. You're choosing the symbols, and as anyone who's tried to write a useful program knows, often the symbols or constructs you use turn out to break when someone else tries to use your system. And it's nice to have a system that can adapt its own representations.

Jay McCLELLAND: I'd like to make a brief comment about the binding issue, because it's one that I myself have been very sensitive to, also with respect to the general issue that Charniak was raising, and it also ties into the question of sequentiality that came up in Kay's paper earlier. The way I'm currently envisioning the process of taking in a sequentially unfolding utterance and building up a representation of it is kind of like this. The notion is that the individual constituents come in, one at a time, in sequence, and what we do is we build up gradually a representation of the whole of which this sequence of constituents is a part. Now obviously the constituents come at many levels: The noun phrases are embedded in the sentences, and so on. Let me set that problem to the side and just imagine a sequence of constituents, say, the constituents of a sentence at the level of the noun phrases and the prepositional phrases, and the verb, the idea being to build up a description of the action described by that sentence from them. The goal of this approach is to build a system that will do the following: which will take each constituent in as it comes, and use it as a set of clues that constrain the possible representation of the whole of which this is one constituent. So, when you hear "the boy" preceded by nothing, that produces few initial constraints on what this whole is going to be. Then "broke", and there's much more constraint suddenly. From just these two constituents, the notion is that you should now be able to construct a whole representation from which not only you can retrieve that it was the boy who did the breaking, so the constituents are encoded in this representation. But, you also, by virtue of the fact that this predicts a lot about what the following constituents will be, should be able to make guesses about subsequent constituents, just on the basis of these inputs.

Chapter 4

Discourse Theory, Goals, & Speech Acts

Chapter 4.1

TOWARDS A SEMANTIC THEORY OF DISCOURSE

C. Raymond Perrault

I don't feel comfortable trying to build reliable, well-understood NLP systems without providing a semantics for their "mental state," including the data structures they encode. One step in that direction is a semantics of sentences, for example that of Montague. However, to handle extended discourses, the methods of model-theoretic semantics need to be extended in (at least) three directions. First, anaphora and deixis require that the interpretation (of phrases, sentences, and entire discourses) should be made sensitive to context, both linguistic and physical. Second, non-declarative sentences must be treated uniformly with declarative ones. Finally, it should be possible to make room in the semantics for interpretation constraints based on the subject-matter of the discourse and on communication itself. I'm thinking particularly of the kind of inferences typically captured computationally by the use of scripts, plans, prototypes, etc. Typically these constraints on interpretations have been kept outside the realm of semantics, and might even be taken to be the distinguishing characteristics of a separate pragmatics component. I'd like to suggest that we already have available many of the necessary elements for a context-sensitive theory of discourse, although substantial work still needs to be done to bring the pieces together and to build implementations faithful to the semantics.

Several proposals have now been made to account for possible relations between anaphora and antecedents within and across sentences, including treatments of the interaction between quantifiers and anaphors (Webber, 1983; Kamp, 1981; Heim, 1982; Barwise, 1986). Kamp and Heim both introduce an intermediate level of representation of sentences and give a semantics to that level while Barwise's syntax-directed interpretation relation also takes as arguments input and output contexts which are partial assignments of values to variables. However, none of these treatments takes into consideration the domain constraints, perhaps better described as preferences, or those discussed by Grosz et al. (Grosz, Joshi, and Weinstein, 1983) under the name of centering.

I used to think of the interpretation of non-declarative sentences as being outside the domain of semantics; it wasn't clear how semantics was compatible with the attribution of illocutionary force (or speech act type) to utterances.

But a uniform semantics for different sentence types is possible if one takes the interpretation of an utterance (of any number of sentences) to be a relation, determined by mood, intonation, and propositional content, between the joint mental state of the participants before and after the utterance. The speech acts (illocutionary and perlocutionary) applicable to the utterance are then determinable as a function of the initial mental state of the speaker (in the case of illocutionary acts, such as assert and warn) or of both initial and final mental states of speaker and hearer (in the case of perlocutionary acts, such as convince and scare). The beginning of such an analysis can be found in (Perrault, in preparation). There are other good reasons for this move. It treats utterances as first-class actions, making it possible to use them in complex actions including non-linguistic acts. It also makes it easier to show the relation between illocutionary acts and the related intended perlocutionary effects. It also makes it possible to show what are the consequences of utterances which, intentionally or not, violate the normal conventions, as is the case with ironical, indirect, and insincere utterances. The key feature of the analysis is its dependence on default rules, formulated within Reiter's non-monotonic default logic (Reiter, 1980), to express the consequences of utterances, making clear that the conveyance of propositional attitudes constituting a speech act is based on the use of utterances with certain features in mental states appropriate to the attitudes being conveyed, but that, in general, the speaker need not be in the requisite mental state.

Several other discourse constraints have been studied in the framework of various non-monotonic logics (e.g., presupposition, Mercer and Reiter, 1982; anaphora resolution, Dunnin-Keplicz, 1984; conversational implicature, Joshi, Webber, and Weischedel, 1986). So have questions with obvious relation to discourse such as plan recognition (Kautz and Allen, 1986) and temporal reasoning (Shoham, 1986; Lifschitz, 1986). Script-based reasoning should allow the defeasible inference of the existence of various entities, including events, from the statement of the existence of related entities.

Although non-monotonic reasoning seems to hold the key to a wide range of discourse phenomena, the developments above appeal to a range of different systems: in fact, no two of the papers mentioned above use exactly the same system. One promising area of unification of the various systems is through their use of preferred models. It may be useful to start with a familiar case. In Montague grammar (based on intensional logic, a monotonic system), it is possible to specify constraints on lexical items (e.g. the fact that *seek* is equivalent to *try to find*, or that the subject of *seek* is extensional, or human) in a set of meaning postulates. These postulates are used to restrict the class of models considered: a sentence *s* is valid iff it is true in all models satisfying the meaning postulates. Similarly, various non-monotonic theories are given semantics by restricting the models in which they are interpreted. McCarthy's circumscription, for example, makes use of models in which certain predicates are restricted to their smallest extensions; Shoham's logic of chronological ignorance depends on what he calls chronologically maximally ignorant models, and Kautz's logic of plans minimises over several dimensions, including, e.g., the number of steps in a plan.

The whole area of non-monotonic reasoning is in a state of great flux, in part because of the diversity of systems and the technical difficulty of arguments within and between the various systems (Hanks and McDermott, 1986). Nevertheless, the simple fact that no other approach comes close to dealing with so many of the relevant problems suggests to me that three questions should be investigated on the way to a semantic theory of discourse:

• whether other "pragmatic" problems can be couched in the same terms (e.g., noun-noun modification, metonymy, word-sense selection),

• whether there is a general enough notion of preference to cover all these cases,

• whether a positive anwer to these questions can be translated into processing algorithms.

Maybe we'll know the answers at the next Tinlap.

Acknowledgment

This paper was made possible by a gift from the Systems Development Foundation.

Chapter 4.2

SOME COMPLEXITIES OF GOAL ANALYSIS

Robert Wilensky

Introduction

Hypothesizing the plans and goals of a speaker has been recognized as an important component of language understanding in general and discourse processing in particular. The general motivation of this approach may be characterized as follows: To some degree, the structure of a discourse mirrors the structure of one's plans and goals. Therefore, it is necessary to understand the plan/goal structure under which someone is operating in order to comprehend and respond reasonably to them.

Important as plan/goal structure is for understanding discourse, most theories presume a relatively impoverished notion of planning. An overly simple theory of plan/goal structure will produce an overly constrained model of discourse. Here I would like to sketch some of the reasons that a more complex notion of plan/goal structure is needed. I draw on examples from UC (UNIX Consultant), a program aimed at providing an intelligent natural language help facility to an operating system (Wilensky et al., 1988).

Goal Conflict and Background Goals

Most planners generally assume that a speaker's goal can be inferred from his statement, which is construed as some direct or indirect way of fulfilling his goal. Thus a speaker saying "How can I delete a file?" probably wants to know how to delete a file, and is asking this question as a way of finding out. However, in general it is necessary to interpret a speaker's statement with respect to unstated "background" goals. For example, a speaker who asked the question "How can I get more disk space?" should not be answered with the response "Delete all your files." Partly, this is a question of interpretation. The speaker presumably has background goals of preserving desirable file contents; therefore, the speaker's statement needs to be treated not as a request to fulfill a goal, but as an attempt to resolve the conflict between two goals, namely, the more obvious goal of getting more space, and the background goal of preserving previous file contents. This issue is elaborated in Wilensky (1983).

Improving Upon the Speaker's Goals

It is generally assumed that a cooperative, helpful participant will help the speaker achieve his stated goal. However, a good discourse participant may find it necessary to ignore or at least modify the goal he responds to. For example, imagine a conversation in which a participant asks "Who else is using the system?" Rather than respond to this request, it is reasonable to tell the user to use the "users" command, although this does not address his request directly. However, this response is motivated by the realization that the requester may not have known enough to ask the right question, and moreover, it is good for the user to learn how to do things on his own. Thus, an intelligent listener may substitute the goal attributed to the user with one the listener deems is more suitable.

Evaluating the Plausibility of a Speaker's Goal

Hypothesizing the goals a speaker is operating under involves some notion of plausibility. For example, suppose a person makes the following statement: "Can you tell me how to delete someone else's file?" Presumably, this is an indirect request for information about how to delete something. Often, this is analyzed as a kind of convention—namely, asking about ability (or some such) is a way of requesting an action. However, most likely, the notion of what is a plausible goal comes into play. In this case, it is unlikely someone would be interested in one's ability to tell you this fact per se. On the other hand, it is reasonable to assume that someone may have the goal of finding our how to delete someone else's file. This is plausible because it is plausible to have the goal of deleting someone else's file, and also, to not know how do so. The fact that this goal is plausible prevents additional interpretation. For example, we need not be concerned with why someone has such a goal. On the other hand, a goal not deemed plausible might signal the need for additional interpretation. For example, if someone asked "How can I prevent someone from reading my file?" we might like to respond by telling the person about encryption. However, encryption does not really prevent someone from reading one's file, but merely from coming to know its contents. If we knew that "preventing reading" is an unlikely goal, then, presumably, further analysis would produce the correct, less over-specified goal of "prevent coming to know contents". Then the desirable response could be generated. The issue of goal plausibility is discussed further in Mayfield (1986).

Concerns

We generally theorize about hypothesizing the speaker goals, or hypothesizing conflicts among these goals. However, in many situations, a speaker cannot be said to have a goal or goal conflict but must deal with the mere suspicion of such items. For example, it is inappropriate to respond to someone who asks "How do I delete someone else's file?" by saying "First, you have to have an account on the machine; then, your machine must be turned on; of course, you have to log in...." These are legitimate preconditions of a plan for deleting a file, but they are unlikely to be goals of the user. On the other hand, it may be pertinent to say that you must have write permission on the other person's directory. Similarly, it is not reasonable to say that the user has a goal conflict between wanting more disk space and preserving files. Rather, what is necessary is the recognition that such possibility is worthy of consideration.

A state that should be given consideration by a planner is called a *concern*. For example, we might say that there are some preconditions of a plan that are typically reasonable to worry about, and some that are not, even though we may not know whether any of these is met in a given situation. The former would constitute concerns, while the latter would not. Similarly, we know what goals might conflict with a given goal, even though we rarely know for sure whether a conflict actually exists.

The point is that most of the time we must compute a speaker's concerns rather than a speaker's goals. When the speaker above suggested that he wanted to delete someone's file, we inferred one goal, but all the other considerations involved concerns. Thus a reasonable conversationalist needs knowledge about the kinds of things that one is likely to consider, rather than information about what goals a speaker actually has. Concerns comprise one approach to extending plan/goal analysis to such situations. They are discussed further in Luria (1986).

Chapter 5

Why has Theoretical NLP

made so little Progress?

Chapter 5.1

THE RATE OF PROGRESS IN
NATURAL LANGUAGE PROCESSING

Norman K. Sondheimer

With all due respect, the rate of progress in natural language processing has been disappointing to many, including myself. It is not just that the popular press has had overblown expectations, but that the attendees of Tinlap have. The consequences of these errors could be severe. Hopefully, this short note will give an accurate evaluation of our rate of progress, identify what some of the problems have been, and present some reasonable suggestions on what can be done to improve the situation.

Where Are We?

The most obvious evidence of slow progress is found at the end of the chain from research through development to application. Practical natural language interfaces, writing aids, and machine translation systems all exist. But the public has not been quick to accept what we can produce. I know of no company that has "gotten rich" off natural language interfaces. More importantly, in my estimation the most technically successful natural language interface to database systems was introduced in the late 1970's. Although the research community has been quick to point out shortcomings with that system and other systems have been introduced, no clear rival has appeared. Commercial MT efforts follow the same pattern.[1]

Moving backwards along the chain, serious large-scale prototypes of the next generation of systems are hard to find. This is not due to lack of industrial interest. All major computer manufacturers seem to have been interested in natural language processing in recent years. Those systems which I have heard about generally appear to be severely limited and habitually delayed.

More common are the initial laboratory demonstrations of new understanders and generators, as well as their components. Finally, at the beginning of the chain, are the ideas for new systems that come from new frameworks, new perspectives on the problem, and new insights from related disciplines. These are the stuff of our conferences and journals. Here may be found the possibility of real progress at a good pace.

Yet, even though the years since the first Tinlap have seen a steady stream of new ideas, I find no special reason to believe that these will be better able to scale up and still solve the difficult problems that have always faced us.

These problems include lexical ambiguity, ill-formed input, metonomy, and even the fundamental problem presented by the size of a realistic knowledge base. Without greater proof of the ideas' usefulness, they serve at best as better insights into the problems natural language presents to us. Although these may be useful to us and others who study language, they cannot be accepted as ends in themselves for a field that is defined in terms of machine processing.

If my analyses are correct, it is unreasonable to expect the broad base of support we have thus far been provided to continue.

What is Wrong Here?

I can only guess where the problems lie and I can only do that from my personal perspective. You can assume that I have seen every one of these mistakes in my own behavior.

A fundamental problem is that I and, probably, most researchers are not truly realistic about the difficulty of the problem. Most of us do try hard to understand our situation, promise only what we think we can deliver, and do our best to develop appropriate public expectations. Even so, the problem is that we probably still underestimate the difficulties. It is likely that there is still much more to natural language than we now realize. How can we really say what we need to allow for to achieve truly human-level performance? The mere fact that we take the problem to be formalizing one of the most complex human abilities may well make complete success impossible.

It is also likely that we can't hope to unambiguously identify progress. We can get neither the type of experimental evidence that physics or chemistry requires or the rigorous proofs that mathematics can produce. Given the nature of language, we must settle for carefully reasoned arguments for our proposals based on limited and challengeable insights and many explicit and implicit assumptions. In this respect, we resemble the "soft" social sciences. Fortunately, we are also like engineering in that we should be able to measure our results in terms of a body of useful techniques of limited utility characterized by appropriate case studies. That doesn't sound half bad to me; if only we were doing a good job of it!

But I think we have some serious sociological problems that keep us from making faster progress. We seem to value the most theoretically ambitious research far out of proportion to its proven worth. Such work has the best possibilities for publication and gets the most respect from our colleagues. In addition, jobs and funding aimed at achieving such results come with the least commitments. All of these are natural and good things—in limited amounts.

Consider, however, what often results. Sometimes we resemble a school of fish. When our leaders turn, many of us turn with them. Unification and connectionism are only the latest turning. We do it all the time. Heck, I do it.

It's fun to work on new things; for the first few years there are lots of easy problems to solve. This schooling behavior probably happens in every field. However, it is especially bad in our case because we rarely get the old technology worked out in enough detail to really evaluate its usefulness.

A related error on our part finds us acting like "fish out of water" when we enter the worlds of the philosopher, linguist, or psychologist. Naturally, we want the respect of the older disciplines that are concerned with language. However, their values cannot possibly match ours very well. Unfortunately, we have often ended up adopting theirs and abandoning our own. When this happens the results of our research have less and less likelihood of contributing to the progress of our computational discipline. Concluding the fish metaphor, it is clear that in order to communicate with them, we are going to have to ask our friends in other disciplines to learn to swim with us.

I could explore some of the other problems that impede progress, such as our awful tendency to focus on solutions to particular problems without thinking through their compatibility with solutions to other problems, our studied ignorance of earlier work, our willingness to accept unproven ideas as the basis for further work, and our tradition of not warning readers of known shortcomings of our results. However, before you give up on me completely, let me suggest some future directions.

What Can We Do?

Am I ready to give up on natural language processing? Certainly not. If I were, I would not be in my office on a perfectly gorgeous Southern California Sunday writing this. In fact, I'm more ready than ever to push on. Besides, the situation is not hopeless. I'll refrain from pushing my favorite technology; instead, I'll try the trickier tactic of addressing our field's values.

Our field exists because of one natural phenomenon, human language, and one technology, the computer. Our values must come from these two roots. It is easy to see that we have to value the meanings and uses of human language in building our systems. Clearly, the ultimate goal must be to understand or generate language in a way that matches what we see humans do.

More important to point out are the values from our computational root. We have shown some concern for computational complexity, but usually of the worst case sort, not the more important average performance. But there are other concerns as well: the ease of coding an algorithm, the ease of maintaining and enhancing a system, the portability of the system, the way in which the system responds to output beyond its basic coverage, how it responds to ambiguity and vagueness, the facilities available to tailor a system to an application, site, or user, and so on. Probably, the most confusing pressure from computation comes to natural language interfaces from the fact that people end up communicating with the machine in ways that they would never communicate with other people. We must value these realities as much as we value the demands of natural human communication. Such topics should be discussed as often as anaphora, metaphor, conjunction, et al. are in our panels and papers.

Values of another sort have to come from the society that supports us. It is not just the ethics of accepting a salary; it is a matter of self-preservation. We simply have to pay more attention to pushing our own ideas down the chain from theoretical research. The outside world is not going to believe we are making progress unless they see something come of our ideas in terms they can understand. And if the people at this conference do not see to it that this happens, who will? And if we do not do it now, when will we have the chance again?

Given that we want to take our ideas down the chain from theoretical research to empirical study and beyond AND that natural language is an extremely difficult task, how can we proceed? There is only one answer: Work within our current limits. Let's treat our work as that of successive approximations. Let us forget about the unexplored problems for the time being. Let us see what we can really do with the proposals we have that seem to work. Basically, let us emphasize building systems and full-scale components for a while.

For example, why don't a group of us take the best parser, the best semantic interpreter, the best generator, the best inference system, etc., and tie them together? Then let's pick a domain of discourse and make them work for more than a few sentences. Let's beat on them until they work for as much of language as they appear capable. While we are at it, let's make the system as fast, as robust, as portable, as maintainable, etc., as we possibly can. Similarly, let's beat on individual components in the same way.

I know there is no guarantee this approach will produce a useful system or component. But even if we fail to produce something worth going further with, we will have learned a lot about what works and what doesn't. If those results are not allowed to be lost, the next effort can do better.

Of course, a problem with this approach lies in the source of our funds. Rare is the company or funding organization that is not asking for new ideas and encouraging us to move on. So we have to convince them that stability is necessary for systems building and the overall well-being of the field.

Our field arose out of a perceived need for language processing systems. The basic problem we have is that we have not been able to produce these systems at the rate we had thought possible. Unless we turn our primary attention to increasing the speed our theoretical ideas move out to initial demonstrations, initial demonstrations move out to prototype systems, and so on, we will face a serious crisis. To bring the point home, if we do not remember why the field of natural language processing exists and accept the necessary values, I venture to guess that there will be little external support for a TINLAP in the not too distant future.

Acknowledgments

This work is supported by the Defense Advanced Research Projects Agency under Contract No MDA903 81 C 0335 and by the Air Office of Scientific Research under FQ8671-84-01007. Views and conclusions contained in this report are the author's and should not be interpreted as representing the official opinion or policy of DARPA, AFOSR, the U.S. Government, or any person or agency connected with them.

I am delighted to thank my colleagues: Ralph Weischedel, Ray Perrault, Tom Galloway, Ron Ohlander, Ed Hovy, Bob Neches, Larry Miller, Bob Kasper, Mitch Marcus, Larry Birnbaum, and Bill Mann, for taking the time to set me straight.

1.   In fact, since this was written in January 1987, two microcomputer products with natural languages interfaces have seen significant commercial acceptance. In addition, two new commercial natural language interfaces have been announced that appear to significantly advance the commercial state-of-the-art. Still microcomputer products appear to be based on comparatively unsophisticated technology and the two new products still lag six years behind the latest research.

Chapter 5.2

LET'S PUT THE AI BACK IN NLP

Lawrence Birnbaum

Artificial intelligence is, or should be, at the heart of natural language processing research. After all, it is AI more than any other cognitive science that has made *processing* a central issue in the study of the mind. Yet, it seems to me that there has been a tendency recently on the part of many natural language researchers to view AI as playing a secondary role in the study of language, at best as a useful engineering adjunct to the more important "theoretical" studies carried out elsewhere. One need not reach as far back as the blunderbuss attack of Dresher and Hornstein—an attack whose ferocity in fact reflected a certain amount of healthy respect for AI, or at least anxiety about its success—to find signs of this tendency. Consider, for example, the title of a recently published book, *Natural Language Parsing: Psychological, Computational, and Theoretical Perspectives* (1985). It seems reasonably clear what the "computational" and "psychological" perspectives mentioned in the title are intended to refer to, but what does "theoretical" mean in this context? That becomes clearer, perhaps, when we observe that the book was edited by several linguists. The use by them of "theoretical" in place of "linguistic" reflects, I suspect, not only a desire to rhyme but also an unconscious assumption on the part of the editors that they amount to the same thing when it comes to the study of parsing.

Such an assumption may be pardonable as reflecting a natural pride in their field on the part of some linguists. What is much more surprising is evidence that this attitude exists within AI as well. For example, a recent monograph on natural language processing begins by propounding the following historical views: When NLP research first began, linguists were preoccupied with syntax, so AI researchers had no choice but to cobble together semantic theories as best they could. But now that the linguists (and philosophers) have turned their attention to semantics in a serious way, these *ad hoc* AI theories can and should be replaced by implementations of the far more rigorous products of our brethren sciences. This is only a slight exaggeration of an argument which seems quite seriously intended.

It should be obvious that in my view this attitude is detrimental to progress in NLP research. AI's unique contribution to the study of the mind stems from its dedication to the proposition that functional considerations arising from the need to perform realistic tasks, rather than considerations of parsimonious empirical description, should be the primary constraints on cognitive theories. To take the view that AI's job is to "implement" the theories produced by other cognitive sciences is therefore to abandon what makes AI worth doing in the first place. Natural language processing may include computational linguistics, but there is a lot more to it than that.

One unfortunate consequence of the tendency to ignore what AI can genuinely contribute is that a great deal of effort gets devoted to implementing theories (primarily linguistic theories) that were never intended to be process models in the first place, while somewhat paradoxically attempting to stick as close to the original conception as possible. The results are generally uninteresting both from the perspective of linguistics—since such an implementation is likely to be, at best, only a somewhat more rigorous reformulation of the original theory—and from the view of AI—since the original theory was not formulated with a view towards making any interesting functional claims.

To return to an old controversy, consider the case of AI models which draw their inspiration from linguistic theories of syntactic competence—that is, theories which attempt to capture the content of our knowledge of language structures—which are based on the assumption of syntactic autonomy. I do not question the substantial *empirical* contributions made in pursuit of these linguistic theories themselves. The question is what additional contributions are made by the AI theories based on them?

The majority of the parsing models which are inspired by these linguistics theories, such as ATN and Prolog-based parsers, depend quite explicitly on nondeterminism. The rules that they employ, and the representations that they build, seem for the most part taken over from pre-existing linguistic theory. Very few of these models seem to have anything to say about how the space of hypotheses generated by the grammars that they implement is to be searched, or how they are to be integrated into the understanding process as a whole, or how these factors might impinge on the rules and representations employed. None of them, that is, has much to say about the most specifically *AI* issues involved. The indiscriminate reliance on nondeterminism is particularly troubling in this respect. As process models, these theories simply fall back on a general model of symbolic computation—namely, backward chaining with back-up.

On the other hand, Marcus's theory of deterministic syntactic analysis is a far more profound attempt to build an AI model of parsing based on linguistic theory. Marcus (1980) tries to provide a genuinely computational explanation for certain putative properties of English syntax, by arguing that they are a natural consequence of functionally motivated aspects of his model. I happen to think he fails—largely because his overall claim that autonomous, deterministic syntactic analysis is possible is seriously undercut by failure to address such issues as lexical ambiguity or genuine structural ambiguity, particularly prepositional phrase attachment—but at least some genuine claims are being made. Unfortunately, the more recent work of Marcus, Hindle, and Fleck (1983) marks a step backwards in this regard. In order to maintain the position of autonomous syntactic processing, Marcus *et al.* propose that the output of the parser be a somewhat vague description of the syntactic structure of the input sentence, capturing whatever structural information can be gleaned without semantics or nondeterminism. What claim is being made here? It is tautological that autonomous deterministic syntactic analysis is possible if the output is defined to be whatever can be yielded in such a fashion. In order to support a meaningful claim of syntactic autonomy, certain *functional* criteria must be met: It is necessary to show that such an output will be useful, and that it can be used without violating the assumption of syntactic autonomy— i.e., that the rest of the language processing system will not need to employ syntactic knowledge. There is good reason to believe that this is not the case.

In the case of generation, the attempt to maintain syntactic autonomy is equally counterproductive. A generator must be able to relate semantic representations and pragmatic goals to the syntactic constructions that can be used to express the appropriate meanings and achieve those goals. If a model of generation deals only with purely syntactic rules and representations then it cannot, by definition, deal with such relations, and therefore it cannot address the interesting planning issues raised by generation—that is, the specifically AI issues. Thus, for example, MacDonald's model of autonomous syntactic generation makes virtually no decisions itself—everything from what to say to which word to use has already been decided. If this theory is to make any meaningful processing claims, therefore, it must at least be shown that the rest of the language processing system can make all of these decisions without any recourse to knowledge of the syntactic options offered by the Language. Particularly in the case of lexical selection, there is good reason to doubt this.

The real tragedy in all of this, of course, is that many genuine, and genuinely important, AI problems get lost in the shuffle. NLP is desperate for good methods whereby contextual constraints can be brought to bear in a timely fashion to help resolve such problems as lexical and structural ambiguity in language analysis. Lexical selection has received far too little attention in generation research. The problem of controlling search in conversational planning remains virtually untouched. Aside from Charniak's recent work and a few other attempts, the problem of controlling explanatory inference in understanding has largely been put aside since the heyday of script/frame theory, despite its centrality. What are the criteria (e.g., parsimony, completeness, etc.) by which explanations are judged, compared, chosen? What kinds of constraints do they impose on knowledge representations? All of these issues are crucial to natural language processing, and AI is crucial to their solution. Let's put the AI back in NLP. We might even put some of the fun back in at the same time.

Acknowledgment

This work was supported in part by the Defense Advanced Research Projects Agency, monitored by the Office of Naval Research under Contract N00014-85-K-0108.

Chapter 6

Formal versus Common Sense Semantics

Chapter 6.1
ON FORMAL VERSUS COMMONSENSE SEMANTICS

David Israel

There is semantics and, on the other hand, there is *semantics*. And then there is the theory of meaning or content. I shall speak of *pure mathematical* semantics and *real* semantics. I have very little idea what "formal" means in "formal semantics"—unless it simply means semantics done rigorously and systematically.[1]

I have even less idea what is meant by "commonsense semantics." I shall not speak much of the theory of meaning. The distinction between these two modes of semantics, the mathematical and the real, is not meant to be a hard and fast distinction—nor, most assuredly, is it intended to be rigorous or systematic. As I see it, the distinction has primarily to do with purposes or goals, derivatively, with constraints on the tools or conceptual resources considered available to realize those goals. In particular, real semantics is simply pure mathematical semantics with certain goals in mind and thus operating under certain additional constraints. Another way to put the point: some work in pure mathematical semantics is in fact a contribution to real semantics; however, it does not have to be such to make a genuine contribution to pure mathematical semantics.[2] Hence, since real semantics *can* be executed with the same degree of rigor and systematicity as must all of pure mathematical semantics, it *should* be.

Have I made myself clear? Not *entirely*, perhaps. Let's try a more systematic approach. Pure mathematical semantics is either a part of or an application of mathematical logic. Real semantics, even though an application of mathematical logic, is a part of the theory of meaning or content. Contributions to real semantics had better cast some light on naturally occurring phenomena within the purview of a theory of meaning—on such properties and relations as truth analyticity, necessity, implication.

Traditionally (indeed, until Montague, almost undeviatingly), the techniques of pure mathematical semantics were deployed for formal or artificial languages. But this by itself is of no importance. These languages were invented, and are of interest only because, or insofar as, they are plausible and illuminating models, in the intuitive sense, of real phenomena in thought and in informal language. Consequently, the nature of the languages studied need not make an essential difference.[3] What does make a difference is the purpose or *end* of the study and the fact that the end imposes constraints on the choice of means.

In doing work in semantics, the logician has a range of tools available and certain criteria for choosing among them. In pure mathematical semantics, the only criteria are, in a suitably broad sense, technical. There are no nontechnical constraints; **anything** goes. That is, even if the development of a class of logics was inspired by an attempt to model various pretheoretic notions, work on the pure mathematical semantics of the languages can still diverge quite far from the original motivation. The objective is to provide a systematic way of assigning mathematically describable entities to the nonlogical expressions and mathematically characterizable operations to [or correlating them with] the logical constants so that the best proofs of the strongest and most general results may be achieved. Not so for work in real semantics. There the choice of tools and conceptual resources should be grounded somehow in the nature of the phenomena to be analyzed or, to put it differently, problems in real semantics generate not-purely-technical criteria for choosing among technical means.

This, I realize, is all rather vague and airy—so let's get down to cases. The first illustration is from work on higher order logics, in particular Henkin's proof of completeness in the theory of finite types (Henkin, 1950). The intended interpretation of the relevant language is that the individual variables—those of type 0—range over some domain of elements T_0, and that for each n, T_{n+1} is the power set of T_n, that is, the set of all subsets of T_n. Monadic predicate variables of type $n + 1$ range over all elements of the power set of T_n, m-place predicate variables of that type range over the entire power set of the mth Cartesian product of T_n. The theory of finite types can therefore be regarded as a [perhaps noncumulative] version of a part of impure set theory, that is, it formulates a conception of an "initial segment"— up to rank w of the set-theoretic universe over some domain of individuals. Now it is a fairly immediate corollary of Gödel's proof that second-order logic—let alone w-order logic, which is what we are now concerned with—is incomplete relative to this intended interpretation. Yet Henkin proved completeness for a system of w-order logic. How?

By ingenious hook and ingenious crook is how. He introduced a wider class of models (interpretations) according to which the sole requirement was that each T_n be nonempty; otherwise, the interpretation of the T_n's was arbitrary. In particular, it is not required that each T_n be the power set of the immediately preceding type. This approach made it possible for Henkin to reduce w-order logic to a many-sorted first-order logic, thereby allowing him to obtain soundness, completeness, compactness, and Löwenheim-Skolem results. Henkin's work was an exercise in pure mathematical semantics. The task before him was to provide a class of models for an axiomatic system in such a way as to provide soundness, completeness, and other results—and to do so in whatever way worked, without any thought being given to the interpretation on which the real significance of the system was based.[4]

Now let's move on to the treatment of languages for propositional modal logics.[5] Modal logics have been studied as axiomatizations of different conceptions of necessity or possibility—or to put it somewhat differently, as axiomatizations of different conceptions of modal facts. The current standard semantical account is in terms of Kripke structures. For our purposes, let us think of these as ordered pairs <K, R>, with K a nonempty set and R a binary relation on K. (Kripke structures are now usually thought of as triples, the third element of which is a distinguished element of K. I'll return to this briefly later.)

Roughly speaking, what happens is that the elements of **K** are used to index classical propositional models or interpretations—that is, assignments of **T** or **F** to the sentence letters—and the relation **R** which is correlated with the modal operator is a relation among such indices. (There may be more than one modal operator in which case there will be more than one binary relation.) Now if one thinks of the models as representing ways the world might be or as alternative possibilities (or some such), it is not really such a bizarre exercise to follow Kripke's heuristic; the set **K** of indices of models is a set of possible worlds and **R** is a relation of accessibility or relative possibility among worlds. This heuristic results in a version of an old idea due to Leibniz: *Necessity is truth in all possible worlds.*

The work on model-theoretic semantics for modal languages and logics using Kripke structures is a bit of pure mathematical semantics that is arguably also a real contribution to real semantics. Moreover, the techniques involved have shown themselves to be widely applicable. Thus, besides work on temporal logics, in which the set **K** is understood to be a set of times or time slices and **R** the relation, say, of temporal precedence, we have work on provability interpretations in which, for example, **K** is the set of consistent recursively axiomatized extensions of Peano arithmetic and T_1 **R** T_2 if and only if the consistency of T_2 within T_1. There is also, of course, a good deal of purely technical, mathematical work on the Kripke-style semantics for modal languages. As Kripke asks, "What is wrong with the purely technical pursuit of mathematically natural questions even if the original motivation is philosophical?"

Still, the philosophical questions, questions from metaphysics and the theory of meaning, keep insinuating themselves, as they must. If the work on Kripke structures is to be taken seriously as a piece of real semantics, something must be said about these entities called possible worlds and about the relation between them and the classical models they index.[6] It will not do simply to say, as we can when doing pure mathematical semantics, that **K** is just some nonempty set and **R** is just some binary relation on **K**, that meets such and such conditions. You've got to put up about possible worlds or shut up. I would argue that when you do put up, the best net result is to postulate a family of structures like those to be found in the situation-theoretic universe. But that's an argument for another occasion.

I want to make one more point about propositional modal logics. Oddly enough, structures that yielded models for propositional modal logics had been made available as a result of research in Boolean algebra by Jonsson and Tarski. This work had nothing to do with the issues of necessity and possibility; the research was not in the least concerned with modal facts, nor, in fact, with modal languages. As a result of this work (and thanks to the perspicacity of hindsight), structures for modal languages can be seen to be /proper/ relation algebras. Proper relation algebras are a special case of Boolean algebras with operators; work on them is directly related to results in universal algebra, the metamathematics of algebra, and category theory. For my purposes, though, the crucial aspect of this work is precisely its austere abstractness and generality. This is work in mathematical semantics at its purest. In this framework, even the set **K** rather disappears into the background—to be replaced by binary relations on **K**, those being the elements of the algebra.[7] Once again the Kripke heuristic is available; it's just farther removed from the mathematical action.[8]

The point to stress is a simple, but an important, one: the "readings" of the set **K** as a set of possible worlds, and of **R** as a relation of accessibility among possible worlds play no part in the technical development. That heuristic enters precisely when claims of a real semantical nature are to be made for, or on the basis of, the technical results in pure mathematical semantics. And those claims cannot be extricated from more general issues in the theory of meaning.[9]

Earlier I suggested that I had just about no idea what is meant by *commonsense semantics*. Alas, this too was disingenuous of me. Sad to say, my guess is that most adherents of *commonsense semantics* are convinced that rigorous, systematic accounts of the semantics of natural languages are unattainable. In this regard, Schank and Chomsky are bedfellows, however strange. I know of no good arguments for the Schank-Chomsky view.[10] Rather than canvass the various bad arguments that have been trotted out, let me conclude by citing four crucial sources of confusion that may have led many astray. They all have to do with the scope and limits of semantics.

The first is to think that a semantic account of a natural language has to say everything there is to say about the *meanings* or *interpretations* of expressions of the language, with *meaning* and *interpretation* understood very *broadly and informally*. A theory of the semantics of a natural language, e.g., English, is not (nor is it intended to be) the whole story of that language, minus its syntax (phonology, morphology, etc.). A semantic account *may be* the whole story about a formal language, minus the account of *its* syntax. But that is because formal languages are studied, *not used*.[11] A semantic account of [the declarative fragment of] English should be one that, in a systematic and rigorous manner, relates various facts about (or aspects of) the circumstances in which sentences of English are used to various facts about (or aspects of) the truth conditions of those uses—that is, to various facts about the states of the world those utterances are intended to describe. This is a central aspect of meaning or interpretation—where again, these are pretheoretical notions—but it does not exhaust the subject.

The phenomenon to be studied is the use of language or, if you like, the phenomena to be studied are kinds of uses of English sentences. Each such use is a complex event with many aspects. Those aspects enter into many different kinds of regularities or systematic connections. There are syntactic facts, morphological facts, phonological facts, facts about the surrounding discourse, facts about the nonlinguistic circumstances of the utterance, facts about the connections between states of mind of the participants, and facts relating such states to various objects, properties, and relations in the environment. These facts are related to one another in a wide variety of ways, some of which are the province of semantics and some not. For instance, any theory of language use had better make room for a distinction between the semantically determined information content of an utterance and the total information imparted by the utterance. The former is not the latter; the latter includes information imparted by the utterance in virtue of the interplay of [broadly speaking] pragmatic factors. In short, acknowledging the possibility of real mathematical semantics for natural languages does not imply acceptance of *semantic imperialism*.

Second, semantics, even construed as part of a theory of language use, is not directly a theory of processing. Any real semantics for natural language should comport with good theories about the cognitive capacities and activities of users of such languages. But no theory of semantics can constitute or be directly a part of such a psychological theory. That a semantic theory does not attempt to be a processing theory, or more generally, a part of a psychological theory, is thus no cause for complaint.

The third point is largely about the scope and limits of lexical semantics. The point is that there are limits. Lexical semantics does not yield an encyclopedia. Any semantic account worth its salt will yield a set of [analogues of] analytic truths, sentences such that the truth of utterances of them is guaranteed by the meanings of the words occurring in the sentence (plus, of course, their modes of combination), together with what might be called "the demonstrative conventions of the language."[12] Any such semantic account, then, will have to distinguish between analytic truths and *world-knowledge*. Consequently, no such semantic account will say everything there is to say about the objects which are the denotations of lexical items. A brief point about the connection between the current and the previous points is *well worth making*. A good theory of natural language processing will have to explain how relevant *world-knowledge* is accessed, and how it is used in processing. *GOOD LUCK to such theorists!* In any event, their job is not the semanticist's job.

Fourth, and last: any real semantics for natural language should be a part of or be accommodable within a general theory of meaning—indeed a general theory of mind and meaning. Nevertheless no theory of the semantics of natural language can itself constitute such a general theory. Return with me now to the example of the mathematical, in particular, model-theoretic semantics of modal languages. As remarked earlier, the classical Lewis systems of modal logic *might* be said to express different conceptions of modality, but they don't express them in the sense that they constitute theories of modal facts. *Nor do Kripke-style, model-theoretic treatments of those logics constitute theories of modality.* The latter constitute ways of thinking about modal facts expressible in the former—that is, they provide *models*, in the intuitive sense, of the phenomena of modality. Kripke, for example, has presented bits and pieces of a *theory* of modal facts in *Naming and Necessity*, a piece which contains no mathematical semantics. David Lewis presents another conception of modal facts in his recent *A Plurality of Worlds*; that book, too, is devoid of the machinery of model-theoretic semantics. Those different theories may lead to the adoption of different mathematical treatments of modal languages. They will do this precisely by motivating choices among alternative pure mathematical semantic treatments-that is, by providing criteria of choice of a real semantics for modal constructions.[13]

Notes

1.   This is mildly disingenuous; talk of 'formal semantics' is usually grounded in one or another idea of 'logical (or, more generally syntactic) form'. But one should beware the overly eager application of such notions to the semantics of natural languages.

2.   Of course, problems pursued for purely technical, mathematical reasons often turn out to be related to important questions and issues in real semantics.

3.   Indeed, the two examples I shall consider concern the semantics of formal languages.

4.   Of course, quite independent of Henkin's motivations, it could have worked out that the class of models he focused on was indeed of real semantical interest. It just didn't work out that way.

5.   There is an interesting twist as regards motivation in this case. C.I. Lewis, the founding father of modern modal logic, was interested in different conceptions of implications (or the conditional), not in differing conceptions of contingency and necessity. Of course, on the conventional view, implication simply is validity or necessity of the conditional.

6.   For instance, the distinction between models and indices is crucial, but that very distinction leaves room for the following possibility; there can be distinct possible worlds which are exactly alike as ways the world might be; that is, one and the same model can be paired with more than one index. Is this just an artifact or is it supposed actually to represent something? If so, what? There are things to be said here, things about representing contingent relations to propositions. Never mind what they

are though; the point is that when taking work in the model-theoretic tradition seriously, one has to keep in mind that what is being done is, precisely, *modeling*. One must think seriously about what aspects of the proposed model are merely artifacts and what not.

7. Very nice work exists on relating Kripke-structures for modal logics to relational algebras-or, more specifically, to modal algebras.

8. As Professor Scott reminded us all at TINLAP, the prehistory of the model-theoretic semantics of modal logic is quite rich and complex. It starts (more or less) with Tarski's work on topological interpretations of intuitionist logic (1938, repr. 1956), continued by Tarski and McKinsey (McKinsey and Tarski 1944, 1946, 1948) in a more general algebraic setting in which they could draw illuminating connections to one of Lewis's systems (S4). But a more complete telling of this tale deserves both a more proper occasion and a better story-teller.

9. All these questions arise much more sharply in the case of quantified modal logics. Many of these have been canvassed in an important series of papers by Kit Fine (1978, 1978, 1981). In any event, work in quantified modal logic simply has not developed in the robust way as has work in propositional modal logic.

10. That's not to say, though, that the naysayers might not, in the end, be right. There are no guarantees of success in this business.

11. Still, we should remember what was said earlier about the purposes for which these languages are devised.

12. If we have picked out a small set of lexical items as *logical constants*, then those analytic truths will be *logical truths*. Of course, we can make that set as large and as heterogeneous as we want.

13. The research reported in this paper has been made possible by a gift from the System Development Foundation.

Chapter 6.2

ON KEEPING LOGIC IN ITS PLACE

Yorick Wilks

There need be no real dispute here about what is meant, in the broadest terms, by formal semantics (FS) when opposed to commonsense semantics (CSS): after registering his complaints and worries, the opposition David Israel opts for in his paper is broadly the one adopted here, and the model-theoretic semanticists he mentions will do just fine for me and I suspect for Karen Sparck-Jones in her characterization of a "logicist" approach to natural language processing. As will appear in a moment, though, I want to survey a range of strengths of FS commitment, not all of which are model-theoretic.

Formal semantics (henceforth FS), at least as it relates to computational language understanding, is in one way rather like connectionism, though without the crucial prop Sejnowski's work (1986) is widely believed to give to the latter: both are old doctrines returned, like the Bourbons, having learned nothing and forgotten nothing. But FS has nothing to show as a showpiece of success after all the intellectual groaning and effort. Here, I must register a small historical protest at Israel's claim (this volume) that "until Montague, undeviatingly, the techniques of pure mathematical semantics were deployed for formal or artificial languages". It all depends what you mean by techniques, but Carnap in his *Meaning and Necessity* (1947) certainly thought he was applying Tarskian insights to natural language analysis. And the arguments surrounding that work, and others, were very like those we are having now. I need that point if the Bourbon analogy is to stick: FS applied to natural languages is anything but new.

But there have been recent changes in style and presentation in computation as a result of the return: many of those working in the computational semantics of natural language now choose to express their notations in ways more acceptable to FS than they would have bothered to do, say, ten years ago. That may be a gain for perspicuity or may be a waste of time in individual cases, but there are no clear examples, I suggest, of computational systems where a FS theory offers anything integral or fundamental to the success of the program that could not have been achieved by those same processes described at a more commonsense level (what I am calling commonsense semantics, or CSS). However, I do not at all intend to define CSS by any particular type, or level, of notational description: all I mean by it is a primary commitment to the solution of the major problems of language processing, those problems that have obstructed progress in the field for thirty years. That I take to include: large scale lexical ambiguity (i.e. against realistically large ranges of sense ambiguity for lexical items of English), the problems of phrase, and other constituent, attachment, where those require considerations of meaning to determine, as well as the mass of problems that collect around the notions of expertise, plans, intentions, goals, common knowledge, reference and its relationship to topic, etc.

On these descriptions of FS and CSS they are not necessarily exclusive: it would be quite conceivable for an FS system to aid with the solution of a problem important to CSS. And it will always be possible for a successful CSS theory to be subsequently axiomatized. But that does not equate CSS and FS any more than axiomatizing physics does away with experiments: theories come first, axiomatizations follow. That has not in fact happened in natural language processing and there is no reason to believe it will, because the origins and ultimate preoccupations of FS are always elsewhere. The examples Israel chooses to discuss in detail (Henkin and Kripke) make my point exactly. He (ibid) notes that he could have taken others when defending FS and that "the nature of the languages studied makes no essential difference". But, as he seems to concede elsewhere in the paper, those are the very areas where the techniques can be shown to work and that is why they are always chosen ("the choice of tools . . . should be grounded somehow in the nature of the phenomena to be analysed"). My case, to be set out in a little more detail below, is that the kind of the language chosen for analysis (natural versus artificial) makes as much difference as any choice could make, and that in the last quotation Israel is dead right, though not in the way he intended.

A small concrete example may help: the choice between generating "a" and "the" is notoriously difficult in English, one that non-native speakers continually get wrong. Examples are sometimes hard to grasp in one's own language, and the choice between "des" and "les" in French is similarly crucial and notorious, though it is not the same distinction as the English one, yet it rests on the same kind of semantic criteria. It is not a problem with an arbitrary solution: French grammar books claim to offer principles that underlie the choice.

It also seems, on the surface, to be a problem that FS, or any logical approach to language structure, ought to help with: it is certainly some form of idiosyncratic quantification. Those particles are exactly the kind that Montague grammar, say, offers large, complex structures for (just as, as Sparck-Jones notes in her paper in this volume, such systems offer such minimal, vacuous, codings for content words. This is probably the clearest quantitative distinction between FS and CSS). As far as I am aware no FS solutions have ever been offered for these problems, nor would seem remotely plausible if they were; at best they would simply be a recoding in an alternative language of criteria satisfactorily expressed in other ways. Yet this is exactly the sort of place where FS should offer help with a concrete problem if it is to be of assistance to the NLP task at all, for it is to such items that its representational ingenuity has been devoted.

The historical and intellectual sources of FS lie in an alternative approach to what constitutes a proof: to meta-logical methods for the establishment of properties of whole systems, such as complete, consistent, etc., and the employment of properties such as decidability to establish the validity of theorems independently of normal proof-theoretic methods, i.e., by "semantic" methods, in that special sense. The applicability of this methodology has been perfectly clear in the case of programming languages, and to proofs of correctness of programs (even if the scope of the applications is still depressingly small), but in the application to natural language understanding its original aims have simply got lost.

From time to time, an application within the original methodology surfaces, such as Heidrich's proof (1975) of the equivalence of the methods of generative semantics and Montague grammar, but the result proved is then seen to be vacuous, in the terms of CSS at least, in that nothing was established whose absence had constituted any pre-existing problem. The usefulness or (in)adequacy of generative semantics was not anything that could be established or questioned by the sort of guaranteed equivalences that the proof offered. The problems with generative semantics, whatever they were, lay elsewhere and were not alleviated by any such proof.

The heart of the issue is good old decidability, or whether or not the sentences of a language form a recursive set in any interesting sense. It is clear to me that they do not and I contrasted various senses in which they might back in 1971 (Wilks, 1971). Contributions like Israel's only make sense on the assumption that sentences do form some such set, unless he is adopting only a "descriptive logical language position" (see below position #1), and his whole position paper suggests he is doing far more than that.

The alternative position is that natural language is not a phenomenon of the sort required and assumed by the various systems of logic under discussion; and that the interpretation of a sentence in a context is an approximative matter (including whether or not it has a plausible interpretation at all, and hence whether or not it is a sentence at all), one computed by taking a best-fit interpretation from among a number of competing candidates. That is not a process reducible to a decidable one in any non-trivial manner. Indeed, I recall going further in (Wilks, 1971) and arguing that that process of assigning an interpretation to a string, from among competing candidates, could be taken as a criterion of having a meaning: namely, having one from among a set of possible meanings. I mention this point for purely self-serving reasons: I do not want Israel to get away with identifying CSS with Schank and Chomsky as he does in his paper. I do not object to him joining them as bedfellows: that has been done before, and all serious opponents are said to share premisses. In the case of those two, the similarities become clearer as time goes on: and include a certain commitment to genetic claims, but above all a commitment to representations rather than procedures. My self-servingness is to point out that my own approach, preference semantics, was not about commitment to representations of a particular kind at all, but only to certain procedures (based on coherence and connectedness of representations) as the right way to select interpretations from among competitors, for competitors there will always be. CSS can be about procedures as much as representations (Winograd has made a similar point in his (1985)). In his own commitment to representations, and dismissal of procedures ("semantics, even construed as a theory of language use, is not directly a theory of processing"), Israel is actually in the same bed with that distinguished company. But not to worry, it is a big bed.

Preference semantics was, in a clear sense, procedural and had the advantage of declaring strings that did not admit the assignment of a single interpretation (i.e., remained ambiguous with respect to interpretation) as meaningless. Meaninglessness on that view was not having no meaning but having too many. I found, and still find that a satisfying position, one true to the process of language interpretation. Moreover, it also offers an opportunity, for computation, processing, artificial intelligence, or what you will, to have something to say about fundamental questions like meaning. It is clearly an assumption of Israel, and all who think like him, that that cannot be: "real semantics", as he puts it, is being done elsewhere.

It is one of the advantages of connectionist fun and games, from my point of view, that it has, against FS, brought implementation back to center stage from the wings; thus the new movement can be of enormous political interest and importance, whether or not one is a believer in it.

Let me try to separate levels (or perhaps just a continuum of positions, or aspects) that the claims of FS make about natural language processing:

1) There must be a certain style of formal description as the basis of any system of natural language description or processing. That this claim can be pretty weak can be seen clearly if we remember McCarthy's insistence on first-order forms of expression combined with his advocacy of heuristics and, indeed, his claim that heuristics constitute the essence of AI. One can accede to this demand without giving any support to the central part of the FS claim about decidability.

2) The assumption of compositionality has been central to FS since Frege. From a computational point of view that doctrine is almost certainly trivial or false. I am sure this has been said many times; but I discovered it in (1984), and it has been argued strongly by Schiffer (1987).

3) An emphasis on the particular role of quantifiers and the need of a field of distinguishable entities to quantify over (this is quite independent of #1, and more central to FS). The set of distinguishable entities is easily provided with labels like Lisp Gensyms and doing that in no way concedes the FS

claim. It must be admitted that it was a notable weakness in some early CSS systems (e.g., Conceptual dependency or Preference Semantics) that they did not offer a clear identification of individual entities, independent of intensional codings of concepts. But that lack was easily remedied. The first demand can always be met by special quantifier procedures (e.g., Woods, in his 1981 paper on procedural semantics). Nothing more is needed and demonstrations like Montague's stock example of radical quantifier ambiguity ("Every nice girl likes a sailor") are effectively quantificational garden paths and no plausible natural language processing system is under any obligation to treat them. How could any system for the representation of natural language depend upon such cases, for they have no relation at all to crucial experiments in the sciences?

4) The relation of reference to the world. The claim of FS to capture this relation is its weakest one, yet practitioners return to it repeatedly. If you do not adopt our methods, the claim is, you are trading in mere symbols, unrelated to the real world we, as plain men, know we share. I never cease to be amazed at the barefacedness of this: the classic statement of the position is David Lewis' attack on Fodor and Katz as peddlers of markerese (1972). But what else did he, or anyone else in FS, offer but symbol-to-symbol transformations? What else could they, in principle, ever offer by any conceivable formal methods? For symbols, and only symbols, are as much the trade and language of the denotational semanticist as of any computer modeller. Whatever the mysterious nature of the relation of symbols to things, it is not one on which FS could possibly throw light. Their solipsism is CSS's solipsism, and their position is metaphysically identical to ours.

Of course, arbitrarily named nodes identifying individuals are a handy, not to say essential, device, but no monopoly of FS. Worse yet, the proof procedures of FS demand such sets of entities to quantifier over, but there is no formal way of guaranteeing that the entities established (so as to provide the guarantees that the proved theorems are true within the model that such entities form) are appropriate, in the sense of corresponding to any plausible real entities in the world. Any model set whatever that allows proved theorems to be true would suffice for the purposes of FS, a point that Potts (1975) among others has pointed out repeatedly. Proofs of program correctness have faced this problem, but FS applied to natural languages and commonsense reasoning has not and cannot. Any claims to give access by such means to a plausible and appropriate world are not only false but utterly misleading as to the nature of FS.

What we reach by any formal or computational methods is always other symbols, and a "theory of meaning" for computational processes over natural language should recognize this fact (a suggestion along these lines was made in Wilks, 1974).

An important additional claim of FS, certainly made in Israel's paper, is that semantics, whatever it is, must be separated off from knowledge of the world: "Lexical semantics does not yield an encyclopedia" and "Any plausible semantic account, then, will have to distinguish between analytic truths and world-knowledge." It is interesting to see that baldly and forthrightly stated without qualification, as if Quine were not still alive and well, but had never been. Practical experience with natural language processing always suggests the opposite: Sparck Jones shows in her paper (this volume) how this borderline has to be fudged by peculiar means in certain FS approachs to practical problems. Real lexicons are such that information about meanings and the world are inextricably mixed, or are simply alternative formulations (at least Carnap, in opposing his "formal" and "material" modes of expression, got that right in 1947)

We should notice the repeated offer, to our sloppy and heuristic discipline, of a Real Serious Theory for the field (remember Chomsky's similar offer in 1957 to machine translation and language well formedness; and more recently FS's for the semantics of selected AI systems). The chances always are that this prescription is unrelated to the disease; has Chomsky really helped compute language processing? We do indeed need a good theory but these are quack cures trading chiefly on the fears and inadequacies of practitioners and patients in the field.

One other consistent position is possible (I suspect it may be Dijkstra's, 1986): one can point out frequently, as he likes to do, the gap between the the interpretations normally given to logical entities (e.g., propositional implication or conjunction) and the interpretations given to apparently corresponding language items. One can also, at the same time, advocate the most stringent formal methods in computational applications to areas whose underlying structure or properties will support such methods. By such standards, natural language is not such an area and therefore one should not attempt this form of computational activity. That is a consistent position, but not one that those commited to the computer understanding of natural language can take. It poses no problem for CSSers but does, I believe, put a serious choice before FSers who want to remain in some way relevant to language processing.

Chapter 6.3

THEY SAY IT'S A NEW SORT OF ENGINE: BUT THE SUMP'S STILL THERE

Karen Sparck Jones

I shall lump the specific semantic formalisms currently touted together as manifestations of logicism, because the issue is whether the logicist approach to language processing is the right one, not whether one particular formalism is better than another.

The logicist model of language processing is essentially as follows. We use a phrase structure grammar, heavily laced with features, for syntactic parsing; in analysis syntactic processing drives semantic interpretation strictly compositionally, to build a logical form representing the literal meaning of a sentence. This logical form is further processed, both in discourse operations of a larger scale linguistic character, as in (some) pronoun resolution, and, more importantly, in inference on global and local world knowledge, to obtain a filled-out utterance interpretation. Logical form plays a key role, motivated as much by the need for reasoning to complete interpretation as by the need to supply an appropriate input to further reactive problem solving. The use of a logical form to represent the meaning of an input naturally fits the use of a logical formalism to characterize general and specific knowledge of the world to which a discourse refers and in which it occurs.

Whether the logicist position is psychologically plausible is not an issue here: it can be adopted as a base for language processing without a commitment to, say, FOPC as a vehicle for human thought, and indeed can be adopted in a psychologically implausible form, for example with complete syntactic processing followed by semantic processing. The fact that a good deal of development work is being done using a case frame approach is no problem for the logicist either: case frames are either an alternative notation or can only work for the discourse of very restricted applications.

The logicists' problems are those of getting an expressive and tractable enough logic: What sort of logic is powerful enough to capture linguistic constructs, characterize the world, and support commonsense reasoning; and is this logic computationally practical? Determining and representing the knowledge required for a particular system application is not necessarily more of a problem for the logicist than for anyone else. The threat to the logicist's moral, or at least mental, purity is whether a logic which will do the job is really a logic at all. If the world is heterogeneous, our thinking sloppy, and our language uncertain, whatever closely reflects these may be barely worthy of the label "logic."

This is not to rake up the old semantic nets versus predicate logic controversy, or its analogues. We may have a formalism with axioms, rules of inference, and so forth which is quite kosher as far as the manifest criteria for logics go, but which is a logic only in the letter, not the spirit. This is because, to do its job, it has to absorb the *ad hoc* miscellaneity that makes language only approximately systematic. Broadly speaking, it can do this in two ways. It can achieve its results through some proliferation of rules, weakening the idea of inference. Or it can achieve them essentially by following the expert system path, retaining a single rule of inference at the cost of very many specific, individual axioms. It is at least arguable that if the stock of initial propositions is a vast heap of particulars defining idiosyncratic local relationships, the fact that one is technically applying some plain rule of inference to follow a chain of argument is not that impressive: conciseness and generality, which at least some expect a logic to have, are not much in evidence. Precision and clarity may be equally unattainable, at any rate in practice.

I believe the second possibility is already with us, masquerading in the respectable guise of meaning postulates, and that whatever precise view is taken of meaning postulates, they sell the logicists' pass.

This is well illustrated by following through the implications of the processor design adumbrated in a recent SRI report. (As I am one of the authors of this report, I should make it clear that I am using this design as a vehicle for discussion, and not in a particularist critical spirit.) The report proposal adopts the logicist approach outlined earlier, for the purpose of building language processing interfaces to, for example, advisor systems. The design is for two processors. The first, the linguistic processor proper, is a general-purpose, application- independent component for syntactic analysis and the correlated construction of logical forms. The output of the linguistic processor is then fully interpreted (progressing from a representation of a sentence to that of an utterance) in relation to a discourse and domain context. The semantic operations of the linguistic processor proper deal, respectively, with the logical correlates of linguistic terms and expressions, and with the application of selection restrictions. The logical structures for linguistic expressions are determined by the domain-independent properties of items like articles and modals and of syntactic constructs like verb phrases, and by the formal characterization of domain lexical items primarily as predicates of so many arguments. The lexical information about sorts, which supports the selection restrictions, is functionally distinct, as its role is simply to eliminate interpretations.

In this scheme of things the semantic information given for lexical items, and especially for "content words," in the processor's output sentence representation, is fairly minimal. It is sparse, abstract, and opaque. The assumption is that predicates corresponding to substantive words are primarily given meaning by the domain description, and hence by the world which models this. Within the linguistic processor one sense of "supply", call it "supply1", just means SUPPLY, where SUPPLY is an undefined predicate label. The sortal information bearing on predicate arguments which is exploited via selection restrictions does not appear in the linguistic processor's output meaning representation.

The domain description gives meaning to the predicates through the link provided by meaning postulates. These establish relations between predicates of the domain description language. But they are in a material sense part of the domain description, since these names are also used in the description of the properties of the domain world. Broadly speaking, the meaning postulates form part of the axiomatic apparatus of the domain description. Thus from a conventional point of view the lexicon says rather little about meaning: it merely points into a store of information about the world about which the system reasons, both to understand what is being said and to react to this both in task appropriate actions and more specifically in linguistic response. The system structure is thus a particular manifestation of AI's emphasis on world knowledge and inference on this. The fact that meaning postulates are also the source of the sortal information applied through selection restrictions underlines the somewhat ambiguous character that meaning postulates have; but as noted, this sortal information does not figure as part of the information supplied in the representation of input text items in the output of the strictly linguistic processor. However the predicate labels of the meaning postulates may be word sense names so, e.g., "supply1" is directly mapped onto "provide3": this suggests that the boundary between semantic information3 in some narrow linguistic sense which refers to the content of the lexicon that is transmitted by the first processor, and semantic or conceptual information in the broader sense of the knowledge about the world that is incorporated in the non-linguistic domain description, has no theoretical but only operational status.

The immediate motivation for the system design just outlined is a very practical one, that of maximizing system portability. Given our current inability to handle more than a very small universe of discourse computationally, we have to allow for the fact that some of the particular domain information appropriate to one specific application may be unhelpful or even confusing for another, and that the system design should therefore clearly separate the body of information which is general to language use and so should be transportable from that which is not. In the scheme presented the domain dependent information is confined to the lexical entries for the application vocabulary, and to the domain description.

But logicists also appear to advocate this form of processor as a matter of principle. Setting aside the question of whether the control structure of the processor is psychologically plausible (because it would be perfectly possible to apply syntactic and semantic, and linguistic and non-linguistic, operations concurrently), there is still the question of whether a viable general-purpose computational language processing system can be built with a strategy that treats meaning in the way the design described does, with so little information about it in the lexicon and so much in the knowledge base. The strategy implies both that there are no particular processing problems which would stem from the need to include both common and specialized knowledge, and perhaps several areas of specialized knowledge, in the knowledge base and, more importantly that none follow from the comparative lack of semantic information of the conventional kind found in ordinary dictionary definitions in the lexicon used for the purely linguistic processes, i.e., that there is only sortal information for selection restriction purposes. The first problem is not unique to the logicist position: any attempt to use information about the world, as all systems must, has to tackle the problem of arbitrarily related subworlds. The second problem seems to be more narrowly one for the logicist. The point here is not so much that, in staged processing, the attempt to avoid duplicating information means that information is unhelpfully withheld from earlier processes in favor of later ones. The point is rather whether, even in a situation where concurrent processing is done, providing much of the information germane to word meanings via domain descriptions is the right way to do semantics. It may be a mistake to regard linguistic meaning and world reference as the same; it is possible that some information about meaning has to be supplied, for representational use, in a form exclusively designed for strictly linguistic processing.

But all this is speculation. What is clear, on the other hand, is that the meaning postulates strategy, even if it does not involve the problems just mentioned, will, when applied to a non-trivial universe of discourse, imply vast amounts of very miscellaneous stuff. If language is intrinsically complex, simplicity at one point simply pushes all the complexity (or mess) somewhere else. In more exclusively linguistic approaches to processing this tends to take the form of putting all the detail in the lexicon: then the grammar can be nice and straightforward. Maybe one can get away with a simple syntactic analyzer and semantic interpreter; but only by supplying all the specialized matter they need to work effectively on the various texts they will encounter, through lexical entries. And if simplicity in one place is found at the expense of complexity in another, it does not obviously follow that the system as a whole has the elegance of its simpler part. In the same way, in the logicist approach, the set of meaning postulates required may turn out to be such a huge heterogenous mass as to suggest, to the disinterested observer, that the purity the use of logic might imply has been compromised. From this point of view, indeed, whether the kind of information captured by meaning postulates is deemed to be part of the domain description, or is deemed part of the lexicon and is even expressed in the representation delivered by the linguistic processor, is irrelevant. Either way, the logicist approach suffers from the Same UnManageable Problem of miscellaneous linguistically-relevant detail as every other approach to language processing.

This is without considering the proposition that there is a much larger problem for which the logicists have so far offered us no real solutions: how to capture language use, as this is a matter of salience, plausibility, metaphor, and the like. But whether or not the logicists can solve this, the real problem, we should not assume that they have got more mundane, literal matters of language taped.

Chapter 6.4

DISCUSSION
FORMAL VERSUS COMMON SENSE SEMANTICS

Discussion

Dana SCOTT: I would like to try to get an answer on why the logical approach has very great difficulties, because it is something that has made me feel very discouraged for a long time. I want to tie it in a bit to the historical remarks that people make but also to try somehow to catch a point here that seems very strange about the attitudes expressed earlier toward model theory.

Model theory is a theory of context. Tarski's definition of truth was truth in a model. The question, of course, is the appropriate choice of the context to get the right kind of properties that you want and it's certainly not at all obvious that you'll always be able to see how to choose those properly.

David Israel has Richard Montague described as some kind of amazing event in the history of natural language semantics. But it seems to me that he hasn't put him in any historical context at all. Montague and I were very close friends; we were students together. Tarski was his advisor. He was fully steeped in the Tarskian semantics, but Carnap and Church both had a very strong influence on Montague's development, and the use of higher order logic certainly was strongly influenced by Carnap's whole logical construction of the world. It was the advent of Kripke's semantics that gave a new slant to the way of doing these kinds of constructions, and one of the things that Montague did do was put Kripke together with Carnap in this highly logical version using higher order logic. And a great deal of the success that he had in showing how this semantics would work was to find immediate appropriate translations from the constructs of fragments of natural language very directly into higher order logic.

The Tarski paper Israel referred to is certainly a strong anticipation of Kripke semantics and all the formal tools for doing Kripke semantics are contained in the Tarski notes. In the thirties Tarski already had interpretations of intuitionistic logic by means of topological interpretation. He thought in terms of connections with Boolean algebras and topological concepts like closure. The early days of set-theoretic topology suggested that analogy very strongly. The point is that closure operators and the Kripke semantics were motivated by modal logic, so, I don't think Israel's main point holds up.

Here now is the main point that I want to make about the formal semantics, and the difficulty that I see with it.

You want to get an interpretation in a model and you want to construct a model that is going to have the right kind of structural relationships that will make the interpretation work out. Now, mathematics gives us too many successful examples of that. If you think of geometry, at first it was very hard to understand non-Euclidean geometry and then people realized you could make a model in which, for example, the world non-Euclidean geometry could be interpreted within the interior of a circle, and then lines were arcs of circles within that, so you found that kind of model could reinterpret things.

Mathematicians do this by model building, cutting away inessential things to get just the right kind of properties. The attempt is not always successful. But when we look at natural language semantics, I think we have seen very little success in building models. If you want to make up models of things for natural language, you are immediately faced by all the problems of abstractions: Is a virus alive or not? You can add in all the chemistry of viruses, but then is it going to fit into everything else you have in your model? Or consider events: many people in modal logic talk about events. There is a terrible problem of knowing when an event begins or ends, of knowing whether two events are equal or not. And when you start trying to do axiomatization and build models, one thing keeps leading to another, so that the kinds of properties that the individuals should have, become more and more and more baroque. You don't have the advantages that Euclid and Lobachevsky did in axiomatizing very pure worlds because all these impurities keep messing up everything you want to do.

Kripke semantics, it seems to me, is a failure. It does not tell you what individuals should be, nor how we discover theories of individuals. In fact I think we have made very little progress on that. We have good examples in physics, but physics also operates at a pretty high level of abstraction and doesn't give the kind of philosophical natural language interpretations we want to have. So I think it is this failure of Montague semantics, a failure of being able to get any kind of axiomatizable theory of individuals, that is the place where formal semantics does not do the job it was said to do.

Yorick WILKS: Would you, could you, accept your position as what I said in my paper satirized Dijkstra's position, namely that natural language is not up to formal semantics, so forget it?

Dana SCOTT: Well, you put me in a very difficult situation here, because I hate being classed together with Dijkstra!

Yorick WILKS: What I mean is, are you saying that natural language is not up to standards because it can't be axiomatized?

Dana SCOTT: Well, I think situational semantics made a step there. What we need is to have a great deal of partiality in the construction of the models, but I don't think that situational semantics found the magic philosopher's stone for model building either. But I have a hope also, from work that I've done in programming languages semantics, that there is the notion of approximation to part of the structure that individuals and objects should have. I suppose that is rather platonist, and at heart I hate to admit to it. But there are many different kinds of worlds in which you can live with a platonist philosophy.

And I do have some hope that partial descriptions of things could help with the model building. But I'm not ready to write a DARPA contract proposal on it yet.

Timothy POTTS: I think that there has been a confusion in the discussions so far, and I think it would help to clarify this. The choice of the term formal semantics was extremely unfortunate because both of the words in it are ambiguous and they are ambiguous in a way which has misled a lot of people. As Wilks pointed out, when logicians talk about semantics, they are talking about producing models which will allow them to prove certain properties of formal systems.

The models may be, and usually are, mathematical models, numbers or something like that. And therefore you can give a semantics to a formal system which in no way at all gives any clue at all as to its meaning. So semantics as it is used by the logicians has nothing to do with the meaning of semantics as it is used by the linguists to mean the theory of meaning.

I find constantly that people get in a muddle because there are two completely different senses and they think that when someone, a logician, is offering model theoretic semantics, he is offering a theory of meaning. He might be, but not necessarily. That depends on what the model is.

The second thing is to clarify the use of the term **formal**, which simply means something which is an appeal to structure, and not necessarily an appeal to models.

Now an appeal to formal structure, it seems to me, is going to present something that is essential to your enterprise, which I take to be the representation of language content.

So it might be much better if those who usually use the term formal semantics just called this **model theory**. If you want to keep the term **semantics** in the theory of meaning, just call the Montague stuff model theory.

The other term that I think is confusing is **logicism**. I hope people won't go on using that term, because it has been used, historically, as was pointed out earlier in Frege's program of formal semantics to refer to logic alone, and that program is dead and has been for years.

To the extent that people are opposed to model theory, they need not necessarily be opposed to the use of logic. There are strong objections to the application of model theory to natural language. And the problems have been stated in the literature, and have not, as far as I know, been satisfactorily answered.

To mention just two of the central ones: Richard Montague thought that everyday language constituted a formal system, and as far as I can tell from his papers, this was an act of faith on his part. He gave no proof of this at all. It seems to me highly dubious that everyday language is a formal system. Also, in this method, there is a central appeal to the notion of every possible world, and it is therefore used to characterize tautologies in the system. But the notion of every possible world, taken absolutely, is quite clearly an incoherent one.

Our language was devised for us to live in this world and therefore, if the very general facts of nature which underlie this world were changed, our concepts would change with it. Therefore, what would be tautologies in this world would not necessarily be tautologies in every possible world.

There is perhaps one way round this: in certain versions of this theory, such as Kripke's there are restrictions on the possible worlds and there are various accessibility relations defined, relating the real world to the possible worlds. If the accessibility relation was defined so that the very facts of nature were not allowed to be altered in the possible worlds, it might have some future. But I know of no one who has attempted this.

So there are very serious objections to the use of model theory. But on the contrary, it seems to me that logic is essential for your enterprise, and by logic, I understand what has always been understood by logic, namely, the study of arguments and that includes arguments that occur in everyday language with a view to determine whether or not they are valid. If we want to process natural language, we want to be able to determine what inferences are valid.

And if you're going to do that, you're going to have to be able to determine patterns of inference. And you're going to have to consider the connection between truth and validity. And you're going have to look at the circumstances under which propositions are true and you're going to have to look at them in terms of their structures. So you're going to have to posit certain structures, and that makes your work formal. And you're going to have to look at things which are connected with truth and so you're inevitably going to be involved in doing quite a lot of logic.

But that doesn't have to stop with the sort of logic that is available at the moment, such as Frege's logic which was developed for mathematics. We've got to develop logic and we're going to have to take it further. We've got to devise structures that will give us a correct account of inferences for a whole range of topics in everyday language: things to do with, let us say, with time, with place, with mass terms, with adverbs, with things that Frege's logic cannot handle at all. It is a great challenge to develop logic and that, it seems to me, is really quite central to your enterprise.

David ISRAEL: Professor Scott depicts me as describing Montague's application of model theoretical techniques to natural languages as something quite new under the sun. But, of course, there is nothing really new under the sun. But, of course, there is nothing really new under the sun. (No Heraclitean, I.) Still, change is real. (No Parmenidean, either.)

It is certainly true that I made no attempt in my little piece to put Montague's work into its historical context. Part of the technical background is hinted at in the two case studies I included: higher-order logic, in particular the theory of finite types, and the semantics of modal logic. With respect to the point at issue, namely the history of model theoretic semantics of natural languages, I said just about nothing—arguably, nothing would have been better.

What, after all, goes on in model theoretic semantics? In the simplest case of interest, that of standard first-order languages, one starts with an *uninterpreted* language, L, with a certain sort of vocabulary and a collection of models (set theoretic constructs) of a certain sort. One then defines the crucial relation of *satisfaction-in-a-model* between models, variable assignments and formulae of L. In terms of this relation, one next defines *truth-in-a-model* for closed formulae, etc.

Scott says that "model theory is a theory of context. . . . The question is the appropriate choice of context . . . ." A full response to this would be a long story. Here, I abbreviate: models have been asked to play two roles: that of representing alternative meanings for the nonlogical vocabulary and that of representing alternative ways the facts might have gone, relative to some way of talking about the facts—the structure of latter fixed by the structure of the nonlogical vocabulary. When ordinary folk think of variations in context, they are thinking about the second kind of variation, not the first. Tarski himself, though, had the first notion in mind. The (re)birth of modern modal and intensional logic waited on getting clear about this distinction: getting clear, that is, that models, by themselves, were not adequate to model the kind of variation in context such logics were meant to treat.

To return to the main theme: Mathematics aside, model theoretic treatments of artificial languages are of interest only because, and to the extent that, the whole apparatus adequately, illuminatingly, models some interesting and problematic range of phenomena involving *languages in use*.

For certain purposes, it is all right to identify languages actually used, such as English, with *interpreted languages*. These last are identified as ordered pairs ($< L , M >$), where M is one of the collection of models—the *intended* model, or real model. But it should be borne in mind that this way of talking, e.g., of English as an interpreted language, is a little bizarre. Remember, the contrast between interpreted and uninterpreted languages is not like that between, e.g., French and some nut tougher to crack than Linear B, as might be the language that Martians use.

Note the double use of the word 'model' in the last paragraph but one. Formal, artificial languages and their models are precisely *models*, in the intuitive sense, of various naturally occurring semantic phenomena. The same, then, is true of interpreted languages—understood in the technical sense sketched above. The judgment of the extent to which a rigorously described interpreted language constitutes a good model of a given range of phenomena (relative to some more or less specific analytic purpose) is not a purely mathematical exercise.

Given this conception of model theoretic semantics, it is quite clear at the outset that there is something a little odd about the very idea of providing model theoretic semantics directly for natural languages, and this, quite independently of the "linguistic plausibility" of the grammar posited in the presentation of the language or the nature of the models. Yet this is how Montague's work is often described; indeed, this is how I spoke of it above. Did Montague attempt to apply model theoretic techniques to English? Or should we rather think of Montague as applying model theoretic techniques to a formal uninterpreted language, call it *Loglish*, often written "English," with a string set devilishly like (a fragment of) English in some respects.

I fully realize that there is something weird, something inappropriately definite-sounding, about the alternatives. Still, having asked the question, I shall go ahead and answer it. The whole model theoretic setup argues that Montague was doing the latter, that is, was creating an artificial uninterpreted language meant to look a lot like English. The goal was to analyze certain semantic phenomena of English; the means, to posit a collection of models for the language and to define a satisfaction relation between formulae of the language and models from that collection.

This, of course, is not how Montague described his project, what with his talk of "fragments of English", although he could be cagey on this score. Perhaps one can think of Loglish as (a fragment of) *disinterpreted* English; but disinterpreted English isn't English. The idea of disinterpretation—(roughly) of abstracting from the meaning, though not the "type" of all nonlogical constants—comes from Hilbert; but in his case what is disinterpreted is an interpreted artificial, language, modeling some bit of language in use, say the "informal" language, of geometry.

To sum up this point, there is something of a pun involved in Montague's actual procedure and in his talk of 'fragments of English'. I think we should recognize that Loglish ≠ English.

Professor Scott ends by addressing the failures of formal semantics, including 'Kripke semantics' for natural languages. He focuses his complaints on the problem of finding an appropriate ontology for natural language, or, more accurately perhaps, on coming up with an appropriate metaphysics of e.g., English—more particularly still, on the question of the structure of the collection of individuals and the structure(s) of the individuals in that collection. There are many failures of formal semantics of natural languages, but Professor Scott has certainly fingered a very central one.

Chapter 7

Reference:

The Interaction of Language & the World

Chapter 7.1

REFERENCE AND PRAGMATIC IDENTIFICATION

Douglas E. Appelt

Identification constraints

Kronfeld (1987) has presented the outline of a theory of referring that provides an excellent framework for explaining how referring actions operate in various contexts. However, it also raises some important questions, one of which I will examine in greater detail in this paper. This question is "Where do identification constraints come from?"

According to Kronfeld's model, the literal goal of a referring action is to make it mutually believed that "identification" of some entity is required. This idea is similar to that advanced by Cohen (Cohen, 1981; Cohen, 1984), who argues in favor of analyzing referring as the illocutionary act of requesting as opposed to a propositional act, whereas Kronfeld's model retains aspects of the propositional act analysis. Regardless of the details of the proposal adopted, it does little good to say merely that a referring action requires identification of the referent, because the precise facts that must be known for a hearer to say that he has identified a referent are different in practically every case.

In the model under consideration, an individual is represented to an agent by an individuating set of terms, each believed to denote the individual. The ultimate goal of a referring action is to induce the hearer to identify a subset of one of his individuating sets that satisfies a number of identification constraints. The speaker and hearer must mutually know what the relevant identification constraints are in the current situation. Given this general theory of referring, the key problem becomes the explanation of how the speaker and hearer can agree on what identification constraints are currently applicable.

The point of this paper is that identification constraints come from a variety of sources, including knowledge about actions, general world knowledge, particular facts about the situation at hand, the semantic content of the referring expression, and principles of discourse. Each of these is an important area of analysis in its own right. I shall suggest how the various aspects of reference addressed by the members of the TINLAP-3 reference panel fit together under this general framework.

Constraints from World Knowledge

Goodman (1986) states that "Reference identification is a search process where a listener looks for something in the world that satisfies a speaker's uttered description." One can argue that this definition is too restrictive because it does not apply to situations in which an epistemological notion of identification is inappropriate. However, for task-oriented dialogues such as those of Goodman's protocols, it is correct. The speaker and hearer are cooperating on a task that involves physical manipulation of assorted parts and tools. A reasonable theory of action would imply that physical manipulation of objects requires perception of the objects by the agent, and such a theory would be mutually believed by all agents. Therefore, the requirement that the individuating set contain a term resulting from some perceptual action would apply to nearly every reference to material objects in this domain.

Goodman's research is centered primarily on the problem of satisfying the referring request by carrying out the identification plan. Some of the bizarre referring expressions obtained from Goodman's protocols (1985) are quite reasonable from the standpoint of achieving the literal referring goals. When the speaker used the referring expression "the champagne top sort of looking bottom" to refer to the tube base of the water pump, it is clear that (1) he intended the hearer to perceive the part, because he was asking the hearer to manipulate it, and (2) the referring description, consisting of perceptual descriptors, suggests a plan of visually observing objects in the domain and comparing their characteristics to those indicated by the description. The hearer in Goodman's protocol was unable to identify the intended object given this odd description, which demonstrates the need for the speaker to take both the satisfaction plan as well as the literal goals into account when planning a referring expression.

Constraints from Definiteness

The use of a definite determiner in a referring expression introduces an additional constraint on the hearer's individuating set: the individuating set must exist at the time of the utterance, or it must be implicitly associated (Dahl, 1987) with an existing individuating set, i.e., its existence can be inferred from its association with an existing entity. This constraint prevents the hearer from creating an individuating set containing only the speaker's referring expression, which would amount to hypothesizing an entirely new entity. There is no such constraint associated with the indefinite determiner, which leaves the hearer free to hypothesize new individuating sets in the absence of any other prohibitive constraints.

Other constraints may be brought to bear on the individuating set as well. For example, if the speaker is requesting the hearer to manipulate the entity introduced with the indefinite article, a perceptual term must be part of the individuating set. For example, if the speaker says "There is *a phillips screwdriver in the toolbox* that you can use to fix the pump,'' the hearer's individuating set must contain a perceptual term denoting some existing object that he can perceive. Contextual information can sometimes be strong enough to imply a very strict criterion for referent identification. For example, at a testimonial dinner honoring John, a speaker says ''We are gathered here to honor a gentleman and a scholar.'' The hearer must know there is only one person honored at the banquet, and that is John. Therefore, the individuating set specified must be the same as his individuating set for John, except that it must contain the descriptors ''gentleman'' and ''scholar.'' The speaker has exploited the overwhelming contextual influence to produce an expression that performs both informing and referring functions. This strategy has been called action subsumption (Appelt, 1985b). Dahl (1987) discusses several more complex situations in which the use of an indefinite noun phrase is not permitted to introduce new individuals.

Constraints from Discourse

A particularly interesting set of referring expressions is those that also have anaphoric connection to the preceding discourse. Not all anaphoric expressions are referring expressions. For example, in the sentence *"No AI researcher* will admit that *he* is wrong.'' neither the pronoun ''he'' nor its antecedent is a referring expression. However, pronouns and anaphoric definite noun phrases are frequently referring expressions. Because pronouns must refer anaphorically (or to some very salient object in the context), the identification constraints that apply to a pronominal referring expression are simple to state: The active individuating set must contain a term from the individuating set intended by a previous reference to the same individual, with gender and number providing additional constraints on the possible referent.

It is not so simple, however, to state how the satisfaction of the anaphoric identification request takes place. Much research in recent years has been devoted to this problem, including (to mention only a few instances) recent work on discourse context and centering by Grosz, Joshi, Sidner, and Weinstein (Grosz et al., 1983, Grosz and Sidner, 1985), and Webber (Webber, 1978; Webber, 1987). It is far beyond the scope of this paper to discuss this work, or to add anything to it. The reader should bear in mind that the principles of centering and the construction of discourse models, event/situation structures, etc. are all mutually known to the speaker and hearer in a dialogue. The speaker takes these principles into account when reasoning about how the hearer can formulate a plan to identify the referent of an anaphoric referring expression.

Identification constraints from multiple sources are necessary to explain changes that may take place in the identification constraints applicable to different instances of coreferential expressions. Consider the following sequence of utterances:

I am looking for *a screwdriver*.

It has a green handle.
Have you seen *it* recently?

In the first sentence, no constraints apply to the identification of the referent of "a screwdriver." The hearer therefore constructs a new individuating set to represent it. In understanding the second sentence, the hearer uses the centering algorithm to determine that the intended individuating set for the pronoun is the same as the one intended in the first sentence. The fact that the hearer intends the same individuating set for the pronoun in the third sentence can also be determined from the centering algorithm. However, the fact that the hearer is asked if he has seen the object implies that an additional identification constraint must be imposed on the individuating set at that time: the referent must be perceptually identified. A cooperative speaker must reason that the hearer has enough knowledge to satisfy the identification request before deciding that "it" constitutes an appropriate referring expression.

Conclusion

If referring is to be regarded as an action that requires the hearer to pragmatically identify the referent of a description, then it is important to describe how it is that the speaker and hearer know what pragmatic identification means in a given situation. This paper suggests that the situation-dependent meaning of identification follows from general world knowledge, the syntactic and semantic structure of the referring expression itself, and principles of discourse anaphora resolution. This is by no means an exhaustive analysis of the ways in which identification conditions are recognized, but is rather intended to provide the first steps toward the analysis of reference in a framework that links the results several diverse research programs.

Acknowledgments

This research was supported by the National Science Foundation under grant DCR-8407238. The author is grateful to Amichai Kronfeld for comments on the draft of this article, and for stimulating discussion of these and related issues.

Chapter 7.2

DETERMINERS, ENTITIES, AND CONTEXTS

Deborah A. Dahl

I am concerned with the relationship between the forms of linguistic expressions, noun phrases in particular, and the discourse entities to which they refer;[1] that is, when does a noun phrase introduce a new referent into the discourse? My concern in particular is to specify the role that the discourse context plays in answering this question. A simple first approach to the relationship between noun phrases and discourse entities might suggest that definite noun phrases refer to entities which are assumed to be mutually known to the speaker and hearer, and indefinite noun phrases refer to entities which are not mutually known, and thus, that discourse context plays no role at all. This discussion will point out problems with this approach for both definite and indefinite noun phrases. I will describe examples where definite noun phrases are used to introduce new referents, and, conversely, where indefinite noun phrases do not introduce new referents. In the first case, the local focus structure provides a guide to recognizing that a new entity is involved, and in the second case, the recognition that no new entity is introduced is based on the given/new status of propositions in the discourse. I will begin by describing certain definite descriptions that introduce new entities. I will then describe some examples where indefinite descriptions do not introduce new entities. In each case, I will discuss some related processing issues. I will restrict the current discussion to deal with cases where the mutual knowledge is based on the discourse context, rather than on knowledge that the speaker and hearer bring to an interaction. In the cases of indefinites, I will also restrict my discussion to sentential contexts where an indefinite could introduce a new entity; in other words, to specific contexts, as distinguished from non-specific contexts as discussed in (Prince, 1981).

The case of definite noun phrases that are intended to introduce new discourse entities has been relatively well researched, in particular by Hawkins (1978; 1984). Hawkins points out that entities that have a slot/frame relationship with previously introduced entities often have a definite determiner. For example, in

(1)   There were loud noises coming from a starting air compressor. The drive shaft was sheared.

it is possible to refer to the drive shaft with a definite noun phrase because of its relationship with the previously mentioned starting air compressor, even though the drive shaft has not been mentioned. This same relationship is described by Prince (1981) as inferrable, and is also discussed in Heim (1982). Because we understand the drive shaft mentioned in (1) to be not just any drive shaft but the drive shaft that is part of the air compressor mentioned in the previous sentence, a full understanding of this noun phrase must capture this relationship. The new noun phrase is implicitly associated with the local focus as described in Dahl (1986), and Sidner (1979). In (2d) below, for example, the referent for the paper seems to be the paper associated with the new package even though there is a previously mentioned entity which matches the noun phrase; that is, the paper in (2b).

(2)   a. A package arrived yesterday.

       b. The wrapping paper was beautiful.

       c. While I was admiring it, another package arrived.

       d. I removed the paper.

After the focus change to my package, the associates of the new package seem to be preferred as referents over previously mentioned items, even if the old items had been in focus at one time. This is consistent with Sidner's algorithm.[2]

The second main point to be dealt with in this paper is that of indefinite noun phrases in specific contexts, which nevertheless fail to introduce new discourse entities. Most of those who have discussed indefinites seem to have assumed that an indefinite reference in a specific context invariably introduces a new discourse entity. This includes the discussions in Clark and Clark (1977) and Heim (1982). However, there is a class of indefinites, which I have called specific attributives (Dahl, 1984b), which I claim do not have this function. Consider the example,

(3)   a. Dr. Smith told me that exercise helps.

       b. Since I heard it from a doctor, I'm inclined to believe it.

An entity, Dr. Smith, is introduced in (3a), and an indefinite noun phrase, a doctor, is used in (3b). It is clear that this noun phrase is not intended to introduce a second doctor into the discussion. This is an example of a specific attributive. I use the term in the sense that a specific reference means that the speaker has a particular individual in mind when s/he uses the indefinite description. It is clear in (3), for example, that the speaker did not hear that exercise from some unspecified doctor, but from Dr. Smith. The term as used by Donnellan (1971) can also be applied to these indefinites, although it was originally suggested only for definites, because the specific identity of Dr. Smith is not relevant to the predication, only Dr. Smith's attribute of being a doctor. (See Dahl (1984a) for detailed arguments about the applicability of this term.) There are two important issues that must be dealt with in a treatment of specific attributives. First, there is the issue of recognizing that the noun phrase in fact is not being used to introduce a new entity. Second, it is necessary to recognize the speaker's purpose in using an indefinite noun phrase, when a definite noun phrase would have been possible. Both of these issues have implications for language generation as well as understanding. For example, in the first case a language generator will have to decide when it is possible to use a specific attributive, and in the second case, it will have to decide whether a specific attributive would be useful in accomplishing its communicative goals. I have previously suggested (Dahl, 1984b) that a specific attributive can be recognized by its occurrence in a proposition that is given as in (3), is related to a given proposition by simple entailment as in (4), or is related to a given proposition by a plausible inference, as in (5).

(4) Mary and Bill both volunteered to walk the dog. Since at least one is willing to walk the dog, we don't have a problem.

(5) A: I'm afraid I miscalculated Jones's insulin dosage.

     B: What happened?

     A: He died.

     B: So, a patient has finally died due to your carelessness.
     (Inference: "Jones is a patient".)

Thus, in order to determine when an indefinite introduces a new entity, it is necessary to know whether the proposition in which it occurs is given or new. For this, we need a representation of the events and situations described in the discourse, which can then be examined in order to determine when a proposition is given or new. Such a representation, of course, will be needed in any case for pronouns or full noun phrases that refer to events and situations. For example, in the PUNDIT text processing system, (described in Palmer, et al. 1986), a representation is built for each event or situation mentioned. A noun phrase like the failure in (6) or it in (7) can then be recognized as a reference to something previously mentioned.

(6) The starting air compressor failed when the oil pressure dropped below 60 psig. The failure occurred during the engine start.

(7) The starting air compressor failed when the oil pressure dropped below 60 psig. It occurred during the engine start.

The difference in processing between (6) and (7) on the one hand and specific attributives on the other is that for the specific attributives we are saying that something analogous to reference resolution should be performed on clauses, as well as on noun phrases. That is, we want to ask whether this event has been mentioned before, or can be inferred from something that has been mentioned. If so, we can match corresponding participants so that it is possible to recognize that no new entity is being introduced.[3]

(8)   a. Dr. Smith told me that exercise helps.

       b. Since I did hear it from the doctor, I'm inclined to believe it.

(8) suggests that there is something special about Dr. Smith in particular that makes this advice reliable, while (3) does not. To sum up, I have discussed two categories of noun phrases which demonstrate the effects of discourse context on determining whether a new entity is introduced. Implicit associate definites introduce new entities which are related to the local focus. Specific attributives refer to previously introduced entities in given propositions. Minimally, specific attributes have to be recognized, in order to prevent the creation of an extra discourse entity, and this requires a representation of given propositions. In addition, a complete understanding of specific attributes requires a recognition of the speaker's reason for choosing an indefinite when a definite would have been possible.

Notes

1.   The research described in this paper was supported in part by DARPA under contract N000014-85-C-0012, administered by the Office of Naval Research, and by a post-doctoral fellowship in Cognitive Science from the Sloan Foundation. I have received helpful comments on this paper from John Dowding, Lynette Hirschman, Marcia Linebarger, Martha Palmer, Rebecca Schiffman, and Bonnie Webber.

2.   A discussion by Heim (1982) suggests that introduction of a new entity with a definite noun phrase is a violation of a felicity condition, and is therefore to be handled by a repair or accomodation mechanism. Since accommodation mechanisms are typically triggered by the failure of normal processing, Heim's approach suggests that a failure of normal processing would have to occur before a system could recognize that a new referent was being introduced. If normal processing means searching through the discourse context for a referent matching the new description, then the example in (2) provides evidence against this position, since the correct processing cannot have been invoked by the failure to find a matching referent in the previous discourse.

3.   This raises the issue of what discourse goals would be served by repeating something that is already given. There are probably a number of reasons to do this. Investigating them would be an interesting topic for future research. The second issue raised by specific attributives is the speaker's purpose in selecting an indefinite when a definite would have been possible. This seems to be related to the use of indefinites in general to serve to deemphasize the particular individual referred to while emphasizing its general class. In (3), for example, it is not the fact that this doctor told me that exercise would help that is relevant, but rather that the person has the property of being a doctor. Notice the contrast between (3) and (8).

Chapter 7.3

GOALS OF REFERRING ACTS

Amichai Kronfeld

Motivation

A pragmatic theory of reference is a theory that specifies and explains the human competence to use referring expressions in order to achieve certain goals. Since the relation between referring expressions and speaker's goals is what needs explaining, it is natural to consider referring as planned action (Appelt, 1985a; Cohen, 1978; Cohen and Perrault, 1979). This, in turn, requires showing how the use of referring expressions is systematically related to changes in the hearer's mental state. For that purpose, we need to know the speaker's goals concerning the hearer's mental state, and therefore, a pragmatic theory of referring must first of all specify and describe the goals that typically motivate the use of referring expressions. It is with such goals that this paper is concerned.

The view that the referring act is a planned effort to achieve certain goals through linguistic means simply follows from the fact that referring is a speech act: all speech acts are attempts to achieve certain goals through linguistic means. However, referring acts (and in general, propositional acts) are significantly different from illocutionary acts such as asserting and requesting:

Literal Goals. In performing one and the same speech act, a speaker may have many distinct goals. For example, by saying "The house's on fire!", a speaker may intend to inform the hearer that the house is on fire, scare the hearer half to death, as well as make the hearer leave. Only the first goal, however, is what I call a literal one. The term is taken from Kasher (Kasher, 1977), where literal purposes are introduced. My use of the term, though, is slightly different.

Literal goals are the goals of Gricean communication intentions, i.e., they are intended to be achieved partly through the recognition of the intention to achieve them. Thanks to Austin, Grice, Searle, and others, we have a fairly clear notion of what the literal goals of illocutionary acts are. For example, the literal goal of a promise is to let the hearer know that the speaker places himself under an obligation to do something. But it is not clear at all what the literal goal of a referring act is.

Conditions of Satisfaction. Illocutionary acts have propositional content, but referring acts do not. The propositional content of an illocutionary act determines what Searle (Searle, 1983) calls its conditions of satisfaction: a request that the door be opened is satisfied iff someone opens the door, and an assertion that the door is closed is satisfied (true) iff the door is indeed closed. But since a referring act lacks propositional content, it is not clear what its conditions of satisfaction are.

Note that specifying the conditions of satisfaction of a referring act is not the same as specifying its literal goal. The literal goal of a speech act and its conditions of satisfaction are usually distinct: If I tell you that I want the door closed and you understand me, the literal goal of my request is achieved. But it is still up to you whether or not to satisfy my request.

Syntax and Semantics. In (direct) illocutionary acts, we have a fairly precise correlation between syntax and semantics on the one hand, and illocutionary point on the other. Assertions and commands, for example, have their syntactic counterparts in indicative and imperative sentences, and illocutionary points are represented by performative verbs. But while a serious utterance of an imperative sentence is almost always taken as a directive type of speech act, the serious utterance of a noun phrase—even a definite noun phrase—is not necessarily an act of referring. Similarly, one can promise, say, to pay one's debt by stating "I hereby promise to pay my debt," but merely uttering "I hereby refer to a friend of mine" is hardly satisfactory. Thus, the semantic and syntactic clues that enable the hearer to recognize an illocutionary act do not help much as far as referring is concerned.

Compositionality. The major difference between propositional acts and illocutionary ones is that the latter are constructed out of the former and not vice versa. Referring and predicating are related to illocutionary acts as the form and meaning of NP's and VP's are related to the form and meaning of a full sentence. In pragmatics, as in syntax and semantics, it must be shown how the whole is a function of its parts. One way of stating the problem is in terms of pragmatic presuppositions. The pragmatic presuppositions of a speech act can roughly be described as the class of propositions that is characteristically associated with felicitous performances of that speech act. The truth of these propositions is mutually believed to be taken for granted by the participants (Kasher, 1985). Now, it would be difficult to see how such a class of pragmatic presuppositions is generated, unless the pragmatic presuppositions associated with illocutionary acts are to a large extent a function of the pragmatic presuppositions associated with parts of the illocutionary acts, namely, propositional acts. For example, a pragmatic presupposition of the command "Show me the letter!" is that it is mutually believed that a certain letter exists and both speaker and hearer know which one it is. This pragmatic presupposition is generated through other presuppositions that are associated with the propositional act of referring: for example, that it is mutually believed that the use of the definite article in this case signals an anaphoric link with a referring expression mentioned earlier.

To sum up, we have four problems with respect to referring acts which seem harder to resolve than their corresponding problems in a theory of illocutionary acts:

1) What is the literal goal of a referring act?

2) What are its conditions of satisfaction?

3) When is an NP a referring expression, and what role does its meaning play in the referring act?

4) How does referring contribute to the success of illocutionary acts?

In this paper I concentrate on the first two questions. I argue that in order to answer them, we must develop a pragmatic (as opposed to an epistemological) concept of referent identification. I then sketch a model of referring that is capable of representing such a concept.

Literal and Identification Goals

The Literal Goal of Referring. The literal goals of all speech acts are to affect the hearer's propositional attitudes in a particular way. Intuitively, the point of referring is to let the hearer know what is being talked about. The literal goal of the referring act must be, therefore, to make the hearer believe that it is mutually believed by all participants that a noun phrase is being used as a referring expression, and that "identification" of a particular object is required.

Rules for Identification. What counts as "proper identification" changes from discourse to discourse. For example, in "Replace this 300-ohm-resistor," the hearer is asked to "identify" the referent in the sense of locating it in his visual field. But in "Tell me what other plays were written by the author of Hamlet," visual identification is clearly not required, although the hearer is still expected to identify the author of Hamlet in another way. If the point of the referring act is the establishment of mutual agreement as to which object is being talked about, then a necessary condition for successful referring is that the hearer understand the ground rules for establishing such mutual agreement. These ground rules, which change from discourse to discourse, should be arrived at by the analysis of what we call the pragmatic notion of referent identification.

Identification Goals. Understanding the ground rules for referent identification is not the same as following these rules. While the literal goal of a referring act is that the hearer recognize the speaker's intentions that the hearer identify an object in a particular way, the condition of satisfaction of the referring act is that the hearer actually identify the referent as required. Under typical circumstances, understanding the utterance "Replace the 300-ohm resistor" entails understanding that visual identification of the resistor is required. Another question entirely is whether actual identification eventually takes place. Let us call the goal that actual identification takes place as required the identification goal.

To sum up, we have defined the literal goal and the conditions of satisfaction of referring in terms of what the hearer is supposed to believe and do respectively. The literal goal is divided into two parts: first, making the hearer believe that identification of a particular object is required, and second, making him realize what kind of identification is appropriate. The referring act is satisfied when the hearer successfully follows the rules for correct identification.

A Model of Referent Identification

How can literal and identification goals be represented in a model of referring? We need two concepts, individuating sets and identification constraints.

Individuating Sets. Any model of referring must include representations of objects in the agent's model of the world. Such representations must be grouped into individuating sets. An individuating set S of an agent A is a maximal set of terms, all believed by A to denote the same object. The terms that constitute an individuating set can be either perceptual or descriptive. Perceptual terms are obtained by perceptual acts (e.g. looking at an object), while descriptive terms are obtained through the use of referring expressions in discourse. For a more detailed discussion of individuating sets and their terms see (Appelt, 1986; and Kronfeld, 1986).

A speaker intends to invoke or activate an individuating set when he intends a particular individuating set to be used in the interpretation of the current utterance. The notion of an individuating set being invoked or activated is closely related to the idea of an item being in focus during a discourse segment (Grosz, 1980; Grosz, 1985). One can imagine a dynamic stack of active individuating sets representing the objects under discussion.

Do we really need individuating sets? The answer is yes, for two important reasons. First, individuating sets provide elegant solutions for several problems that are raised by the Referential/Attributive distinction (Kronfeld, 1981; Kronfeld, 1985; Kronfeld, 1986). Second, as we have seen, a major problem for a referring model is specifying the conditions under which a hearer can be said to have identified the intended referent. Some authors have required that for identification to take place, the agent must possess a standard name or a rigid designator that denotes the referent. But very few objects are endowed with standard names, and it can be easily shown that a rigid designator is neither sufficient nor necessary for successful referent identification (Kronfeld, 1986). Moreover, requiring agents to know standard names or rigid designators for individuals that they refer to makes some undesirably strong predictions about what a speaker must know in order to refer to something (Appelt, 1985b). Using individuating sets we can solve these problems.

Identification Constraints. As noted earlier, "identification" should be interpreted pragmatically. Referent identification does not mean knowing who (or what) the referent is, but rather knowing who or what is being talked about. In general, the requirements for referent identification can be characterized in terms of constraints that the speaker places on the activated individuating set. I call these constraints identification constraints.

Let S be the activated individuating set. The following examples illustrate different identification constraints on S:

1)   Take THIS CHAIR to my office.

In Example (1), the hearer should "identify" the chair in the sense of locating it in his visual field. We can express this requirement as a constraint on S that it contain a new perceptual term.

2)   Do you remember THE BROWN DESK I used to have in my office?

In Example (2), the identification constraint is that the S should contain an old perceptual term, i.e., "identification" consists of connecting a definite description with an image in memory.

3)   A friend of mine has just won 10,000 in a sweepstakes, but THE LUCKY BASTARD will probably gamble it all away.

Identification constraint: that S activated by the description "The lucky bastard" be augmented to include a term that has already been introduced into the discourse. "Identification" here is simply making an anaphoric connection.

4)   My sister has just got married. THE LUCKY MAN met her only three weeks ago.

Identification constraint: the S should contain the description "the husband of the speaker's sister". Note the difference between this case and Example (3): the description "my sister's husband" was never mentioned, and had to be deduced by the hearer. The deduction, of course, is a necessary condition for successful identification.

5)   THE MAN WHOSE FINGERPRINTS THESE ARE, whoever he is, must be insane.

Assume that the context of Example (5) is as follows: the speaker is investigating the horrible murder of Smith, and he has just found clear fingerprints on what he believes to be the murder weapon. The speaker, of course, wishes to assert that whoever murdered poor Smith in such a terrible way must be insane. Hence the identification constraint is that the S should contain the description "Smith's murderer". This example illustrates why we insist that identification as the goal of the referring act is a pragmatic rather than an epistemological concept. Neither speaker, nor hearer in this case, have any idea who murdered Smith, and thus, they cannot identify him in any epistemological sense of the term. But from a pragmatic point of view, there is a clear dichotomy: if the hearer makes the connection between "The man whose fingerprints these are," and "Smith's murderer," he has identified who the speaker is talking about. Otherwise, he has not.

6)   I met AN OLD FRIEND OF MINE yesterday.

This is the case of the null set of identification constraints. S contains a single term, and this is sufficient for pragmatic identification.

These examples show that the requirements for referent identification can be very diverse indeed. They all can be represented, however, as constraints on relations among individuating sets.

The Referring Act. Armed with the concepts of individuating sets and identification constraints, we can characterize the act of referring as an act of conveying an ordered pair: an individuating set (which becomes the active one), and a set of identification constraints. The literal goal of the referring act is that it is mutually known by all participants which individuating set is active, and what the identification constraints are. The referring act is satisfied if the hearer is able to manipulate the active individuating set in such a way that all identification constraints are met.

Acknowledgments

This research was supported by the National Science Foundation under grant DCR-8407238. I am grateful to Doug Appelt for comments on earlier drafts, and for lots of stimulating discussions on the problem of constructing a computational model of referring.

Chapter 7.4

REFERENCE AND REFERENCE FAILURES

Bradley A. Goodman

Introduction

Reference in the real world differs greatly from the reference processes modelled in current natural language systems. A speaker in the real world is a rational agent who must make a decision about his description in a limited time, with limited resources, knowledge, and abilities. In particular, the speaker's perceptual and communicative skills are imperfect or his model of the listener is erroneous or incomplete. Additionally, a speaker can also be sloppy in his description. Since the speaker's goal in the reference process is to construct a description that "works" for the listener, the listener, from his viewpoint, must take these imperfections into account when trying to interpret the speaker's utterances. Yet, listeners, too, have imperfect perceptual or communicative skills and can be sloppy. Hence, they must be prepared to deal with their own imperfections when performing reference identification. In real reference, listeners often recover from initial misunderstandings with or without help from the speaker. Natural language understanding systems must do this, too. Therefore, in performing the reference process, a system should assume and expect problems.

The focus of my work (in Goodman, 1986, 1985, 1984) was to study how one could build robust natural language processing systems that can detect and recover from miscommunication. I investigated how people communicate and how they recover from problems in communication. That investigation centered on reference problems, problems a listener has determining whom or what a speaker is talking about. A collection of protocols of a speaker explaining to a listener how to assemble a toy water pump were studied and the common errors in speakers' descriptions were categorized. The study led to the development of techniques for avoiding failures of reference that were employed in the reference identification component of a natural language understanding program.

The traditional approaches to reference identification in natural language systems were found to be less flexible than people's real behavior. In particular, listeners often find the correct referent even when the speaker's description does not describe any object in the world. To model a listener's behavior, a new component was added to the traditional reference identification mechanism to resolve difficulties in a speaker's description. This new component uses knowledge about linguistic and physical context in a negotiation process that determines the most likely places for error in the speaker's utterance. The actual repair of the speaker's description is achieved by using the knowledge sources to guide relaxation techniques that delete or replace portions of the description. The algorithm developed more closely approximates people's behavior than reference algorithms designed in the past. The next section describes in more detail my work on reference.

Reference

Communication involves a series of utterances from a speaker to a hearer. The hearer uses these utterances to access his own knowledge and the world around him. Some of these utterances are noun phrases that refer to objects, places, ideas, and people that exist in the real world or in some imaginary world. They cannot be considered in isolation. For example, consider the utterance "Give me that thing." It can be uttered in many different situations and can result in different referents of "that thing". Understanding such referring expressions requires the hearer to take into account the speaker's intention, the speaker's overall goal, the beliefs of the speaker and hearer, the linguistic context, the physical context, and the syntax and semantics of the current utterance. The hearer could misinterpret the speaker's information in any one of these parts of communication. Such misunderstandings constitute miscommunication. In my research I focused primarily on effects of the linguistic context and the physical context.

To explore such reference problems, the following method was devised and followed. First, protocols of subjects communicating about a task were analyzed. Knowledge that people used to recover from reference miscommunications (knowledge about the world and about language) was then isolated. Algorithms were designed to apply a person's knowledge about linguistic and physical context to determine the most likely places for error in the speaker's utterance. Then, computer programs were written: (1) to represent a spatially complex physical world, (2) to manipulate the structure of that representation to reflect the changes caused by the listener's interpretation of the speaker's utterances and by physical actions to the world, (3) to perform referent identification on noun phrases, and, when referent identification failed, (4) to search the physical world for reasonable candidates for the referent. These programs form one component of a natural language system. One goal in this summary of my research is to illustrate how my views on reference identification departed from views held by other researchers in artificial intelligence. Another goal is to show where my research fits in the scheme of natural language understanding by computers. My last goal is to summarize the approach of my research.

A New Reference Paradigm from a Computational Viewpoint

Reference identification is a search process where a listener looks for something in the world that satisfies a speaker's uttered description. A computational scheme for performing such reference identifications has evolved from work by other artificial intelligence researchers (e.g., see Grosz, 1977). That traditional approach succeeds if a referent is found, or fails if no referent is found (see Figure 1(a)). However, a reference identification component must be more versatile than those previously constructed. The excerpts provided in Goodman (1984) show that the traditional approach is inadequate because people's real behavior is much more elaborate. In particular, listeners often find the correct referent even when the speaker's description does not describe any object in the world. For example, a speaker could describe a turquoise block as the "blue block". Most listeners would go ahead and assume that the turquoise block was the one the speaker meant since turquoise and blue are similar colors.

A key feature to reference identification is "negotiation." Negotiation in reference identification comes in two forms. First, it can occur between the listener and the speaker. The listener can step back, expand greatly on the speaker's description of a plausible referent, and ask for confirmation that he has indeed found the correct referent. For example, a listener could initiate negotiation with "I'm confused. Are you talking about the thing that is kind of flared at the top? Couple inches long. It's kind of blue." Second, negotiation can be with oneself. This self-negotiation is the one that I was most concerned with in this research. The listener considers aspects of the speaker's description, the context of the communication, the listener's own abilities, and other relevant sources of knowledge. He then applies that deliberation to determine whether one referent candidate is better than another or, if no candidate is found, what are the most likely places for error or confusion. Such negotiation can result in the listener testing whether or not a particular referent works. For example, linguistic descriptions can influence a listener's perception of the world. The listener must ask himself whether he can perceive one of the objects in the world the way the speaker described it. In some cases, the listener's perception may overrule parts of the description because the listener can't perceive it the way the speaker described it.

To repair the traditional approach I developed an algorithm that captures for certain cases the listener's ability to negotiate with himself for a referent. It can search for a referent and, if it doesn't find one, it can try to find possible referent candidates that might work, and then loosen the speaker's description using knowledge about the speaker, the conversation, and the listener himself. Thus, the reference process becomes multi-step and resumable. This computational model, which I call "FWIM" for "Find What I Mean," is more faithful to the data than the traditional model (see Figure 1(b)).

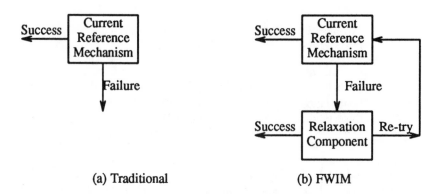

(a) Traditional   (b) FWIM

Figure 1: Approaches to reference identification

One means of making sense of a failed description is to delete or replace the portions that cause it not to match objects in the hearer's world. In my program I am using "relaxation" techniques to capture this behavior. My reference identification module treats descriptions as approximate. It relaxes a description in order to find a referent when the literal content of the description fails to provide the needed information. Relaxation, however, is not performed blindly on the description. I try to model a person's behavior by drawing on sources of knowledge used by people. I have developed a computational model that can relax aspects of a description using many of these sources of knowledge. Relaxation then becomes a form of communication repair (in the style of the work on repair theory found in Brown and VanLehn, 1980). A goal in my model is to use the knowledge sources to reduce the number of referent candidates that must be considered while making sure that a particular relaxation makes sense. A brief description of it follows.

The component works by first selecting with a partial matcher a set of reasonable referent candidates for the speaker's description (see also Joshi, 1978). The candidates are selected by searching the knowledge base, scoring partial matches of each candidate to the speaker's description, and selecting those with higher scores. The component then generates, using information from the knowledge sources, a relaxation ordering graph that describes the order to relax features in the speaker's description. Finally, it combines the candidates with the ordering to yield the most likely referent. An ordered relaxation of parts of the speaker's description can be provided by consulting knowledge known about linguistics (the actual form of the speaker's utterance), perception (physical aspects of the world and the listener's ability to distinguish different feature values in that world), specificity (hierarchical knowledge to judge how vague or specific a particular feature value is), and others. In other words, the algorithm attempts to show how a listener might judge the importance of the features specified in a speaker's description using knowledge

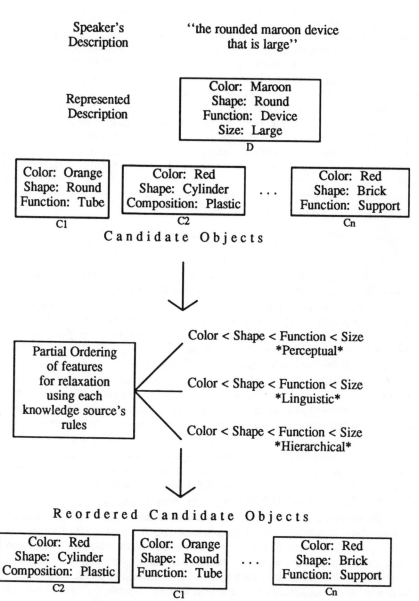

Figure 2: Reordering referent candidates

about linguistic and physical context. Figure 2 illustrates this process. The speaker's description is represented at the top of the figure. The set of specified features and their assigned feature value (e.g., the pair Color: Maroon) are also shown there. A set of objects in the real world are selected by the partial matcher as potential candidates for the referent. These candidates are shown near the top of the figure (C_1, C_2, ..., C_n). Inside each box is a set of features and feature values that describe that object. A set of partial orderings are generated that suggest which features in the speaker's description should be relaxed first—one ordering for each knowledge source (shown as "Linguistic," "Perceptual," and "Hierarchical" in the figure). For example, linguistic knowledge recommends relaxing Color or Shape before Function, and relaxing Function before Size. A control structure was designed that takes the speaker's description, puts all the (partial) orders together, and then attempts to satisfy them as best it can. This is illustrated at the bottom of the diagram by the reordered referent candidates.

Summary

My goal in this work is to build robust natural language understanding systems, allowing them to detect and avoid miscommunication. The goal is not to make a perfect listener but a more tolerant one that could avoid many mistakes, though it may still be wrong on occasion. In this summary of my research, I indicated that problems can occur during communication. I showed that reference mistakes are one kind of obstacle to robust communication. To tackle reference errors, I described how to extend the succeed/fail paradigm followed by previous natural language researchers.

I represented real-world objects hierarchically in a knowledge base using a representation language, NIKL, that follows in the tradition of semantic networks and frames. In such a representation framework, the reference identification task looks for a referent by comparing the representation of the speaker's input to elements in the knowledge base by using a matching procedure. Failure to find a referent in previous reference identification systems resulted in the unsuccessful termination of the reference task. I claim that people behave better than this and explicitly illustrated such cases in an expert-apprentice domain about toy water pumps (Goodman, 1984).

I developed a theory of relaxation for recovering from reference failures that provides a much better model for human performance. When people are asked to identify objects, they appear to behave in a particular way: find candidates, adjust as necessary, re-try, and, if necessary, give up and ask for help. I claim that relaxation is an integral part of this process and that the particular parameters of relaxation differ from task to task and person to person. My work models the relaxation process and provides a computational model for experimenting with the different parameters. The theory incorporates the same language and physical knowledge that people use in performing reference identification to guide the relaxation process. This knowledge is represented as a set of rules and as data in a hierarchical knowledge base. Rule-based relaxation provided a methodical way to use knowledge about language and the world to find a referent. The hierarchical representation made it possible to tackle issues of imprecision and over-specification in a speaker's description. It allows one to check the position of a description in the hierarchy and to use that position to judge imprecision and over-specification and to suggest possible repairs to the description.

Interestingly, one would expect that "closest" match would suffice to solve the problem of finding a referent. I showed, however, that it doesn't usually provide you with the correct referent. Closest match isn't sufficient because there are many features associated with an object and, thus, determining which of those features to keep and which to drop is a difficult problem due to the combinatorics and the effects of context. The relaxation method described circumvents the problem by using the knowledge that people have about language and the physical world to prune down the search space.

Future directions

The FWIM reference identification system I developed models the reference process by the classification operation of NIKL. I need a more complicated model for reference. That model might need a complete identification plan that requires making inferences beyond those provided by classification. The model could also require the execution of a physical action by the listener before determining the proper referent. Cohen gives two excellent examples of such reference plans (pg. 101, Cohen, 1984). The first, "the magnetic screwdriver, please," requires the listener to place various screwdrivers against metal to determine which is magnetic. The second, "the three two-inch long salted green noodles", requires the listener to count, examine, measure, and taste to discover the proper referent.

Acknowledgments

This research was supported in part by the Center for the Study of Reading under Contract No. 400-81-0030 of the National Institute of Education and by the Advanced Research Projects Agency of the Department of Defense under Contract No. N00014-85-C-0079.

I want to thank especially Candy Sidner for her insightful comments and suggestions during the course of this work. I'd also like to acknowledge the helpful comments of Marie Macaisa and Marc Vilain on this paper. Special thanks also to Phil Cohen, Scott Fertig, and Kathy Starr for providing me with their water pump dialogues and for their invaluable observations on them.

Chapter 8

Metaphor

Chapter 8.1

VIEWING METAPHOR AS ANALOGY: THE GOOD, THE BAD, AND THE UGLY[1]

Dedre Gentner, Brian Falkenhainer and Janice Skorstad

Metaphor is a pervasive and important phenomenon, both in literature and in ordinary language. It is also an immensely variable phenomenon. The term **metaphor** is often used to refer to nonliteral comparisons that are novel and vivid and that convey ideas that might otherwise be difficult to express (Ortony, 1975). But the term has also been used to refer to systems of extended meanings that are so familiar as to be almost invisible, such as the spatial metaphors "soaring spirits" or "falling GNP" (Lakoff & Johnson, 1979; Nagy, 1974). Even if we restrict ourselves to literary metaphors, there is still an enormous range of metaphor types, as shown in the following list:

(1) She allowed life to waste like a tap left running. (Virginia Wolfe)

(2)   *I have ventured,*
   Like little wanton boys that swim on bladders,
   This many summers in a sea of glory;
   But far beyond my depth: my high-blown pride
   At length broke under me; and now has left me,
   Weary and old with service, to the mercy
   Of a rude stream, that must forever hide me. (William Shakespeare)

(3) For the black bat, night, has flown. (Alfred Lord Tennyson)

(4) The glorious lamp of heaven, the sun. (Robert Herrick)

(5) On a star of faith pure as the drifting bread,
   As the food and flames of the snow. (Dylan Thomas)

(6) The voice of your eyes is deeper than all roses. (E. E. Cummings)

Perhaps because of this staggering variety, there is little consensus on how metaphor should be defined and analyzed. Most would agree that metaphors are nonliteral similarity comparisons (though not everyone would agree on how literality should be defined), and that they are typically used for expressive-affective as opposed to explanatory-predictive purposes. But beyond this, metaphor has remained elusive of analysis. In this chapter we offer a partial solution. We use Gentner's (1980, 1982, 1983) structure-mapping framework to distinguish three classes of metaphors—two that are computationally tractable within the framework and one that is not. Then we demonstrate how the analysis works, using the Structure-mapping Engine, a simulation written by Brian Falkenhainer and Ken Forbus (Falkenhainer, Forbus, & Gentner, 1986).

The basic intuition of structure-mapping theory is that an analogy is a mapping of knowledge from one domain (the base) into another (the target), which conveys that a system of relations that holds among the base objects also holds among the target objects. Thus an analogy is a way of noticing relational commonalties independently of the objects in which those relations are embedded. In interpreting an analogy, people seek to put the objects of the base in 1-to-1 correspondence with the objects of the target so as to obtain maximum structurally consistent match. The corresponding objects in the base and target don't have to resemble each other at all; object correspondences are determined by roles in the matching relational structures. Central to the mapping process is the principle of systematicity: people prefer to map systems of predicates that contain higher-order relations with inferential import, rather than to map isolated predicates. The systematicity principle is a structural expression of our tacit preference for coherence and deductive power in interpreting analogy.

Besides analogy, other kinds of similarity matches can be distinguished in this framework, according to whether the match is one of relational structure, object descriptions, or both. Recall that analogies discard object descriptions and map relational structure. Mere-appearance matches are the opposite: they map aspects of object descriptions and discard relational structure. Literal similarity matches map both relational structure and object-descriptions.

Kinds of Metaphors

Now let us apply this framework to metaphor. We can distinguish three rough categories of metaphors: relational metaphors, attributional metaphors, and complex metaphors that cannot be simply analyzed. Relational metaphors—e.g., metaphors (1) and (2)—are mappings of relational structure. They can be analyzed like analogies. Attributional metaphors—e.g., metaphors (3) and (4)—are mere-appearance matches: their focus is on common object attributes. Among these two classes, adults (but not children) seem to prefer relational metaphors (Gentner and Clement, in press). So far both these classes can readily be described in structure-mapping terms: both utilize 1-to-1 object mappings and are characterizable by their distribution of relational and attributional predicates. The third class, which we will not attempt to analyze, is exemplified by metaphors (5) and (6). These metaphors lack clear 1-to-1 mappings; they are characterized by many cross-weaving connections with no clear way of deciding exactly how the base predicates should attach in the target (see Gentner, 1982).

To illustrate the way in which relational metaphors can be analyzed, we now describe the operation of SME on metaphor (1):

> *She allowed life to waste like a tap left running.*

The representations for base and target are shown in Figure 1. We assume the reader starts off with some notion of water flowing through a tap into a drain, and with the idea that waste occurs if an agent allows such a flow to occur with no purpose. In the target domain of life it is less clear exactly what to assume as initial knowledge. In this example we have chosen a rather sparse description. We assume that the reader has the idea that life flows from present to past. Since the information that the protagonist's life is being wasted is given directly, we also include that knowledge in the initial life representation.

SME starts by finding local matches—potential matches between single items in the base and target. For each entity and predicate in the base, it finds the set of entities or predicates in the target that could plausibly match that item. These potential correspondences (match hypotheses) are determined by a set of simple rules:[2]

(1)   If two relations have the same name, create a match hypothesis:

(2)   For every match hypothesis between relations, check their corresponding arguments: if both are entities, or if both are functions, then create a match hypothesis between them.

Here, rule (1) creates match hypotheses between the FLOW relations which occur in base and target. Then rule (2) creates match hypotheses between their arguments: water-life, tap-present, drain-past. At this stage the program may have a large number of local matches, possibly mutually inconsistent. Another set of rules assigns evidence scores to these local matches:

(1)   Increase the evidence for a match if the base and target predicate have the same name.

(2)   Increase the evidence for a given match if there is evidence for a match among the parent relations—i.e., the immediately governing higher-order relations.

Rule (1) reflects a preference for relational identity and rule (2) reflects a preference for systematicity. Here, the match between the FLOW predicates discussed above gains evidence from the identicality of the FLOW predicates themselves (by evidence rule (1)) and also from the identicality of the parent CAUSE relations (by evidence rule (2)).

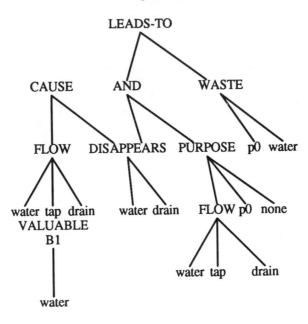

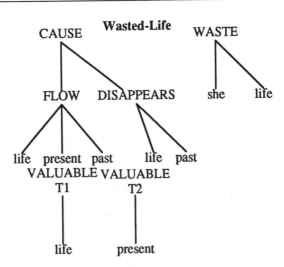

Figure 1: Wasted-Tap-Water and Wasted-Life Descriptions

The next stage is to collect these local matches into global matches—systems of matches that use consistent entity-pairings. SME propagates entity-correspondences upward and finds the largest possible systems of matched predicates with consistent object-mappings. These global matches, called Gmaps, are the possible interpretations of the analogy. Figure 2a shows the Gmap for the life/water example.[3] Associated with each Gmap is a (possibly empty) set of candidate inferences—predicates that are part of the base system but were not initially present in the corresponding target system. These will be hypothesized to be true in the target system. In this case, the system brings across the inference that the protagonist is letting her life pass with no purpose, and that this purposeless flow is causing her life to be wasted. Finally, each Gmap is given a structural evaluation, which depends on its local match evidence.[4]

(a) *Gmap #1:*
{ (WASTE ←→ WASTE) (FLOW ←→ FLOW)
(DISAPPEARS ←→ DISAPPEARS) (CAUSE → CAUSE)
(p0 ←→ she) (tap ←→ present) (water ←→ life)
(drain ←→ past) }

Weight: 6.7018
Candidate Inferences:
{ (LEADS-TO (AND   (DISAPPEARS life past)
(PURPOSE (FLOW life present past) she none))
(WASTE she life)) }

(b)   *Gmap #1:*
{ (VALUABLE$_{B1}$ ←→ VALUABLE$_{T2}$) (water ←→ present) }

Weight: 0.9500
Candidate Inferences: { }

(b)   *Gmap #2:*
{ (VALUABLE$_{B1}$ ←→ VALUABLE$_{T1}$) (water ←→ life) }

Weight: 0.9500
Candidate Inferences: { }

Figure 2. (a) Analogy Match Rules, (b) Mere Appearance Match Rules

SME can also operate in mere-appearance mode to process attributional metaphors. Figure 2b shows the interpretation that metaphor (1) receives under these matching rules. Clearly the relational interpretation is preferable in this case.

Comments

A few points about the simulation model should be noted. First, SME's interpretations are extremely sensitive to the knowledge representations of base and target. We think this roughly reflects the state of affairs in human processing of analogy and metaphor. Second, SME's matching process is entirely structural. SME arrives at its interpretation by finding the most systematic mappable structure consistent with the 1-to-1 mapping rule. The reason that relatively interesting interpretations are found is that the systematicity principle operates to promote predicates that participate in causal chains and in other constraining relations. Unlike some current models of analogy (e.g., Holyoak, 1985), structure-mapping does not need to use a prior goal-structure to select its interpretation.[5] This makes it particularly apt for the interpretation of novel metaphors, in which we may have no advance knowledge of the content of the interpretation.

At this point, it appears that structure-mapping can handle the good and the bad—ie., either relational or attributional mappings that are 1-to-1. Whether it can handle the (computationally) ugly—the complex n-to-1 mappings—remains to be seen.

Acknowledgments

This research was supported by the Office of Naval Research under Contract No. N00014-85-K-0559, NR667-551. During preparation of this paper, Brian Falkenhainer was supported by an IBM Graduate Fellowship and Janice Skorstad was supported by a University of Illinois Cognitive Science/AI Fellowship. We thank Ken Forbus for his invaluable assistance.

Notes

1. A version of this paper appears in D.H. Helman (Ed.), *Analogical Reasoning: Perspectives of Artificial Intelligence, Cognitive Science and Philosophy*, ("Viewing Metaphor as Analogy: The Good, The Bad and The Ugly", by Dedre Gentner, Brian Falkenhainer and Janice Skorstad), pp. 171-177, Copyright (c) 1988 Kluwer Academic Publishers, Dordrecht, The Netherlands.

    We mean "ugly" here in the sense of "computationally difficult." Clearly many of these metaphors are aesthetically pleasing. We use "metaphor" here to refer to both metaphor and simile.

2. This description is for analogy. SME can also be run with different match rules to simulate mere-appearance matches and literal similarity matches.

3. Because of the sparseness of the representations, only one Gmap is discovered. When we run this example with richer representations, adding such potentially confusing information as "Life consumes water," in the life domain, we find more Gmaps, although the highest evaluation still goes to the Gmap shown here.

4. The system also has the capability to consider the number of candidate inferences and the graph-theoretic structure in determining the evaluation, but their ramifications need to be explored. It is interesting that the simple version of systematicity embodied in the local evidence rules seems to lead to very reasonable interpretations.

5. Of course, if there were a specified contextual goal, then the output of the Structure-Mapping engine would have to be evaluated with respect to that goal by a further processor (see Burstein, 1983; Carbonell, 1983).

Chapter 8.2

THE ROLE OF METAPHORS
IN DESCRIPTIONS OF EMOTIONS

Andrew Ortony and Lynn Fainsilber

Why do we use metaphors? For nearly 2,000 years, the most generally accepted answer was that people only use metaphors for rhetorical purposes. Metaphorical language was thought to be merely ornamental—the seasoning of language, exploited for effect by poets and politicians,[1] as compared with the cold factual language of the scientist. This view, however, is now no longer accepted (see, for example, Gentner, 1982; Boyd, 1979). It is now assumed, at least by psychologists and linguists, that metaphors, and their close cousins, analogies, are important tools of cognition and communication, providing us with unfamiliar ways of conceptualizing familiar things, and familiar ways of conceptualizing unfamiliar things (Lakoff & Johnson, 1980; Ortony, 1979; Vosniadou & Ortony, in preparation). Yet, what is still *assumed,* rather than demonstrated, is that nonliteral uses of language are sometimes *necessary* for accomplishing such goals, rather than merely convenient or elegant ways of doing so. In this paper we present a sort of empirical existence proof that there are some things whose descriptions appear to invoke much more use of metaphorical language than others. This, while not establishing the necessity of metaphors, certainly is a first step.

In theory, there are at least three communicative functions that metaphor might serve (Ortony, 1975). First, they might allow one to express that which is difficult or impossible to express if one is restricted to literal uses of language. Evidence for this 'inexpressibility' claim would constitute encouraging support for the necessity-of-metaphors view. A second possible function of metaphors is that they may constitute a particularly compact means of communication. Although conscious experience is continuous in form, the linguistic system we use to talk about is comprised of discrete elements (lexical items). Unlike more literal forms of language, metaphor may enable us to convey a great deal of information in a succinct manner by obviating the need to isolate the predicates to be expressed into their corresponding lexical representations. Finally, metaphors may help capture the vividness of phenomenal experience. If metaphors convey chunks of information rather than discrete units, they can paint a richer and more detailed picture of our subjective experience than might be expressed by literal language. This we call the 'vividness' claim.

In this paper we shall concentrate on the first and last of these possible functions. In order to do so, we need to examine a discourse domain for which a prima facie case can be made for supposing that literal language will often be inadequate and which lends itself to variations in vividness. These doubtless are many such domains. The one that we selected was that of internal states, in particular, emotional states. The literature on the linguistic expression of emotions suggests a relatively high incidence of figurative language use (e.g., Davitz, 1969), providing pragmatic reasons for believing that the context of (linguistic) emotional expression may be a profitable one within which to study metaphor production. Emotional states seemed well-suited for our purposes because they tend to have an elusive, transient quality that is difficult to describe using literal language, although, of course they can usually be *labeled* using literal language. Thus, while it might be easy for a person to label an emotional state as, for example, 'fear,' it is difficult to provide a literal description of the *quality* of some particular experience of fear. Furthermore, because emotions vary in intensity, one might expect differential levels of vividness.

There seem to be two possible ways in which people might try to communicate the quality of an emotional state. First, a speaker might use literal language to describe the events that triggered the emotional state and hope that the hearer correctly infers how he or she felt. For example, a person might describe the details of being mugged, hoping that a listener would recognize the emotional experience as the type one would have if one were attacked by a mugger. In such a case, the literal description would not describe the *quality* of the subjective state itself but would merely identify its eliciting conditions (Ortony, Clore, & Collins, in preparation). Alternatively, a speaker might use a metaphor in an attempt to describe the quality of an emotional state. For example, one might say that one felt as though one's insides were a butter churn. Here, the metaphorical description does represent an attempt to characterize the quality of a subjective state.

Although we think that emotions constitute a good domain for studying metaphor production, it does not follow that the use of metaphorical description will be equally prevalent for different facets of emotions. Emotion theorists frequently attribute differential significance to the subjective experience of emotion (De Rivera, 1977) or to their associated actions or action tendencies (Frijda, in press). It may be that the subjective experience of an emotion can benefit more from a metaphorical description than the associated action or action tendency. Consider the subjective experience of some specific case of anger. The *quality* of such a subjective state cannot be publicly observed. In contrast, the actions to which an anger experience might give rise, for example, pounding one's fist on the table, *are* publicly observable. Thus, one might expect people to employ more metaphorical descriptions when trying to characterize the subjective experiential quality of emotional states than when trying to characterize the overt behaviors associated with such states. The intensity of emotions that might also be expected to influence the use of metaphorical language. It is possible that relatively mild emotional states are sufficiently unremarkable that speakers are more willing to settle for simply labeling them, whereas the vividness of intense emotional states might sometimes generate a more pressing need for detailed description.

To investigate some of these issues we ran a simple experiment in order to examine the production of metaphors during descriptions of emotional states and events. We predicted that people would be more likely to use metaphors and metaphorical comparisons when describing how they *felt* when they were experiencing an emotion than when describing what they *did* when they experienced it. We also thought it possible that more metaphorical language would be used in descriptions of intense as compared to mild emotional states. The two hypotheses combined could be construed as predicting an interaction of description type (feelings vs actions) and intensity, with the intensity factor having a greater effect on feeling descriptions than on action descriptions. Descriptions of feeling states, which may already make use of metaphorical language, may be especially likely to use metaphors when the states are intense. On other hand, it could be argued that although intense emotions are more vivid than less intense ones, the associated actions do not necessarily enjoy a corresponding increase in vividness. This is admittedly a tenuous argument, so the prediction of an interaction between description type and intensity is made with less confidence than the predictions of main effects for these variables. Finally, in the experiment to test these hypotheses, the valence of the emotions was manipulated to determine whether this factor has any systematic effect on metaphor use.

Subjects were asked to describe either how they *felt* when they experienced certain emotions, or what they *did* when they experienced them. The emotions used included four positive ones (happiness, pride, gratitude, and relief) and four negative ones (sadness, fear, resentment, and shame). Note that the particular hypotheses to be tested do not depend in any important way on exactly which emotions are used. In addition to providing descriptions involving emotions of different valence, subjects were required to describe situations involving either very intense experiences of them or very mild ones.

Metaphors were identified in the transcripts of interview sessions. Protocols were scored in terms of idea units (Johnson, 1970) because metaphors are generally better conceptualized as single ideas than as individual words. Metaphor production was then measured in terms of the proportion of all distinct idea units that were metaphorical in nature. In other words, the measure of metaphor production was the ratio of metaphor types to the total number of idea unit types appearing in a protocol.[2] A variety of considerations led us to operationalize metaphor production in this manner. We were concerned that possible systematic differences in the amount of verbal output produced during descriptions of the different emotion-inducing events might contaminate the measure of metaphor production, such that high verbal output might lead to high production of metaphor, and low verbal output might be associated with little metaphor use. If so, metaphor production would be a consequence of verbal output per se and this effect might conceal any differential use of metaphor during descriptions of feelings and actions. By looking at the ratio of metaphor types to the sum of both metaphorical and non-metaphorical idea units, the potential confounding of metaphor production and amount of linguistic output was partially avoided. A second concern was that subjects' tendency to repeat words and phrases during an oral account might artificially inflate the measurement if metaphorical tokens as opposed to types were used.

The results showed that a significantly greater proportion of metaphors occurred in descriptions of feeling states (17%) than in descriptions of actions (4%).[3] Furthermore, the mean percentage of metaphor types used in descriptions of intense emotions (12%) was significantly greater than in descriptions of mild ones (9%). Two factors (intensity and valence) interacted with the type of description (feelings vs. actions). first, there was a significantly greater increase in metaphor production when describing the feelings associated with intense emotions than when describing the actions associated with intense emotions. Second, although of less theoretical interest, while in the description of actions there was a tendency for more metaphors to be produced for negative than for positive emotions, this trend was reversed for descriptions of feelings. The patterns of these interactions are shown in the Tables below which show the percentage of idea unit types that were metaphor types.

Intensity			Valence		
Description Type	Mild	Intense	Description Type	Positive	Negative
Feelings	14.7	19.6	Feelings	18.7	15.6
Actions	3.5	4.5	Actions	3.2	4.9

The results also revealed that there were eight times as many frozen, or dead, metaphors as there were novel ones. More interesting, however, is the fact the ratio of novel to frozen metaphors was greater for intense emotions (12%) than for mild ones (8%), suggesting perhaps that when people are experiencing intense feeling states, they are more likely to generate striking and complex metaphors to explain how they feel. To the extent that novel metaphors are more metaphorical than frozen ones, and assuming that intense emotional states are more vivid than mild ones, this finding of more novel metaphors for intense emotions adds support to the vividness claim because it suggests a qualitative as well as quantitative increment in metaphor use.

To summarize, we have offered evidence that metaphorical language may make it possible for people to convey what would otherwise be difficult or impossible to express. This seems to be the case with the quality of unobservable internal states like emotions, as evidenced by our results showing the predominance of metaphorical language during descriptions of feeling states as opposed to actions, especially when those states are intense. So, for example, when one of our subjects reported that he felt like 'a storm was brewing inside,' he succeeded in conveying a particular quality of his subjective experience that is richer, more vivid, and more specific than could have been conveyed had he merely labeled the experience as 'resentment.' For the most part, the types of metaphors that people used to describe their emotions were figurative forms that have become conventionalized in the English language. When novel metaphors were used, they seemed to be particularly evident in descriptions of intense feeling states. Taken together, our results suggest that the inclination of psychologists and linguists to reject the classical Aristotelian view of metaphor as merely linguistic decoration, in favor of a view that accords it an indispensable communicative function is empirically, as well as theoretically, supportable.

Notes:

1.   Winston Churchill once remarked: 'How infinite is the debt owed to metaphors by politicians who want to speak strongly but are not sure what they are going to say'!

2.   Other indices were also used, such as the absolute number of metaphor types and the proportion of the total number of idea units that were metaphorical. The choice of measure made little difference to the pattern of results.

3.   I.e., the percentage of metaphor types averaged across emotions and subjects.

Chapter 8.3

MENTAL MODELS AND METAPHOR

Edwin Plantinga

Introduction

This paper investigates the significance of the mental models (MM) hypothesis for computational linguistics in general and for metaphor comprehension in particular. The MM hypothesis is the claim "that people understand the world by forming mental models" (Sowa, 1984) The general form of this hypothesis is not new: Immanuel Kant and neo-Kantians such as Hans Vaihinger and Ernst Cassirer have argued that there is no direct access to the *things-in-themselves.* Concepts and conceptualizations mediate between the person and the world.

Although the general contours of the MM hypothesis have been around for some time, the emphasis on models and domains which one finds in the literature is a more recent phenomenon. Let us consider a definition of an MM:

> A mental model is a cognitive construct that describes a person's understanding of a particular content domain in the world. This contrasts sharply with much other work in cognitive psychology, which attempts to be domain-independent (Carroll, 1985). Donald Norman, for example, investigated calculator usage and found that the models constructed by individuals varied considerably from user to user (Norman, 1983). If we take the time to to find out, we see that individuals do differ in the conceptualizations which they form.

In Search of Homo Loquens

An emphasis on individual differences does not mesh very well with the current linguistic paradigm. The individual has been banished from contemporary linguistics. Linguistics studies language but not *homo loquens.* There are a number of reasons for this.

First, linguistics wants the prestige and status that we bestow on disciplines which are sciences. To achieve this, linguists tend to the abstract and to the universal while ignoring much of the idiosyncratic nature of language use.

Second, the Saussurean distinction between *langue* and *parole* became a cornerstone of Chomskian linguistics. Competence, the abstract linguistic system, became the major interest of linguists; performance, the actual output of language users, was only of passing interest.

Third, much of our thinking about language is shaped by a very powerful metaphor which Michael Reddy has named the "conduit metaphor" (Reddy, 1979). According to Reddy, our model of human communication is based on the following:

1. Ideas (or meanings) are objects.
2. Linguistic expressions are containers.
3. Communication is sending.

A speaker puts ideas (objects) into words (containers) and then sends them (along a conduit) to a hearer who takes the ideas/objects out of the word/containers. What an expression means depends on what meaning the speaker inserted into the container. Since the meaning is *in* the expression, the recipient need only retrieve the meaning. In this model, the individual hearer contributes nothing—he merely receives.

But the hearer does not receive meanings—he receives words. To the hearer falls the task of generating meaning in response to these words. In short, meaning is response (Plantinga, 1986). What is manufactured depends on the architecture of the meaning generator. Abandoning the *conduit metaphor* forces us to bring the individual into linguistics so that the discipline focuses on both language and the individual language processor. Mental models give us a way of bringing the architecture of the individual language processor into linguistics.

Modeling Mental Models

A common strategy for software development is to precede the implementation phase with a problem definition phase. Normally, the implementation does not commence until the problem definition is complete. This strategy will not work in constructing models of MMs. Philip Johnson-Laird, who has written a major book on the subject, argues that mental models cannot be defined currently:

> At present, no complete account can be given—one may as well ask for an inventory of the entire products of the human imagination—and indeed such an account would be premature, since mental models are supposed to be in people's heads, and their exact constitution is an empirical question (Johnson-Laird, 1983).

An alternative strategy is to use an iterative software development methodology. We learn by building so that the problem definition is refined during the development process. The computer-based modelling of mental models should shed light on their nature.

Assume the existence of some domain d.[1] An agent, agent_1, constructs a MM of that domain which we call MM_agent_1(d). It is tempting to claim that another agent, agent_2, forms a second MM of "that same domain." But that assumes that agent_1 and agent_2 participated in "exactly the same discourse." The domain of agent_1 may be similar to the domain of agent_2, but they are not the same.

MMs are not restricted to "domains in the world". First, an agent can construct a MM of some imaginary domain. Second, an agent can construct a MM of some other agent's MM. Let MM_i(MM_j(d)) represent one agent_i's MM of some other agent_j's MM of some domain.

In order to model a MM on a computer, we must select some individual, perform knowledge acquisition operations with the individual, and then build a model of the informant's MM. What we are constructing is not a model of the informant's MM (i.e., MM_informant(d)) but a model of the analyst's MM of the informant's MM (i.e., MM_analyst(MM_informant(d))). If the development involves a number of individuals, then the model constructed may not correspond to any particular agent's model.

John Sowa has defined a notation called conceptual graphs (CGs) which is ideal for modelling MMs. CGs are suitable for both knowledge representation and also for the knowledge acquisition phase which must precede the representation phase.[2]

Sowa suggests that concepts are the atomic components of mental models:

> Concepts are inventions of the human mind used to construct a model of the world. They package reality into discrete units for further processing, they support powerful mechanisms for doing logic, and they are indispensable for precise, extended chains of reasoning (Sowa, 1984).

MMs have a structure which can be modelled using CGs. Each conceptual graph consists of nodes which either represent concepts or conceptual relations. In their linear notation, conceptual graphs are directly machine representable. Operations on MMs can be modelled using operations on conceptual graphs. Since Sowa has defined the algorithms necessary to implement a conceptual processor,[3] CGs form a basis for modelling both MMs and operations on MMs.

Natural Language Processing and Mental Models

Although our vocabularies overlap considerably, the concepts which each of us hold have our own personal stamp upon them. George Steiner has stated this most elegantly:

> Each living person draws, deliberately or in immediate habit, on two sources of linguistic supply: the current vulgate corresponding

to his level of literacy, and a private thesaurus. The latter is inextricably a part of his subconscious, of his memories so far as they may be verbalized, and of his singular, irreducibly specific ensemble of his somatic and psychological identity. Part of the answer to the notorious logical conundrum as to whether or not there can be a private language is that aspects of every language-act are unique and individual. They form what linguists call an idiolect. Each communicatory gesture has a private residue. The "personal lexicon" in everyone of us inevitably qualifies the definitions, connotations, semantic moves current in public discourse (Steiner, 1975).

Is this "personal lexicon" a blessing or a curse? It is this "personal lexicon" which makes language understanding idiosyncratic. While there is some overlap in the concepts each of us possess, there is considerable non-overlap; while there is room for understanding, there is also considerable room for non-understanding or misunderstanding.

If this "personal lexicon" is a deficiency, why should we build this into computers? Why should computers misunderstand? So far, attempts have concentrated on making computers understand. Understanding in this case means translating linguistic input into the meaning representation. For example, if the representational system is CGs, then the translation maps words into concepts. But which concepts should the machine have?

The temptation is to say, "Only those which are true." But this poses two problems. First, as Lakoff and Johnson have pointed out, our conceptual systems are metaphorical. To lock the door on concepts which do not "correspond to reality" will exclude the machines from modelling a large part of our mental life. Second, who decides what is true? This is a pragmatic issue which must be faced in the knowledge acquisition phase. Should the analyst claim that the informant's concepts are wrong?

During the knowledge acquisition phase which precedes construction of a natural language processing system, the analyst should attempt to acquire the concepts of the informant without judging the concepts to be acceptable or unacceptable. In practice, this is difficult to achieve. Once acquired and represented in a machine usable form, the words which act as input to the system are mapped to concepts.

Sowa has suggested a mechanism for connecting words and concepts: the lexicon lists the concepts into which a word can be mapped. If a word has multiple senses, multiple concepts are stored in the lexicon. In Sowa's lexicon, for example, the word "occupy" is associated with three different concepts: [OCCUPY-ACT], [OCCUPY-STATE], and [OCCUPY-ATTENTION]. The following sentences illustrate the three concepts:

The enemy occupied the island with marines.
Debbie occupied the office for the afternoon.
Baird occupied the baby with computer games.

Metaphor Processing Without Mental Models

Metaphor and analogy have always been very closely associated in AI research. Consider a sentence such as (1).

(1) Peter's argument is full of holes.

If this sentence means anything, it does not mean what it says. The conventional way of producing a "metaphorical" meaning is to assume that there is an underlying analogy which must be computed. What it means to compute an analogy depends on which knowledge representation scheme you are using but generally means something like analogical reasoning, inferencing, or transfering information from one domain to another. Since computing analogies is computationally expensive, metaphorical interpretions should not be generated for gibberish. Hence the emphasis in the work of computational linguists such as Jerry Hobbs (1979) and Jaime Carbonell (1981) has been twofold.

1. Find criteria whereby ill-formed input is rejected and metaphors are accepted.[4]

2. Define the rules that govern which inferences may be drawn.

Metaphors are expensive to process and hence it is crucial that NLP systems are able to label input as metaphoric or non-metaphoric. Now, some metaphors signal their presence by violating semantic constraints. A sentence such as

(2) John hit the nail with a hammer.

fails to violate semantic constraints whereas a sentence such as (1) does since arguments do not "literally" have holes. But a sentence such as (3) does not violate semantic constraints.

(3) Zeke's father is an accountant.

By most definitions of "literal", (3) has a literal reading. But a metaphorical reading can also be generated, a reading in which attributes such as meticulous, finicky, boring, dull, and mousey are predicated of Zeke's father.[5] On the basis of the sentence alone, it is not possible to tell which reading of (3) is preferred. While the violation of semantic constraints may be used to detect some metaphors, it will not reveal them all. When multiple readings or interpretations are available, we say that a sentence is ambiguous and that disambiguation requires "context."

Mental Models and Metaphor

Mental models provide some conceptual clarity to some aspects of metaphor processing. I will examine three such aspects.

First, it is incorrect to appeal to "context" as an aid in disambiguation. A user has no access to "context" although he (potentially) has access to his mental model of the context.

Second, it has become common to distinguish between "dead" metaphors and "live" metaphors. This distinction is made purely on the basis of the linguistic expression. A "dead" metaphor, so the explanation goes, has acquired a fixed meaning through repeated use. Retrieving the meaning is simple: it only requires a table lookup. Since there seem to be no interesting research issues here, "dead" metaphors have received little attention from computational linguists.

But a "dead" metaphor is not dead for everyone. Children, for example, are frequently puzzled by a "dead" metaphor such as "out to lunch."

(4) Charles is permanently out to lunch.

What is "dead" and what is "live" does not depend on the linguistic expression, but upon the mental model of the language processor. Since MMs are evolving models, we can use them to model this kind of change.

Third, it appears that some "metaphors" can be processed without relying on analogical reasoning. Since each agent participates in multiple discourses, he possesses multiple mental models. An agent might even have a number of inconsistent models of the "same domain." Depending upon which model is running, there may or may not be a mapping from word to concept. Hence what was not a metaphor at time t may be a metaphor at time $t + n$ simply because another model is running.[6]

MMs allow us to make distinctions which cannot be made reliably otherwise. What is and is not a metaphor and what is a "live" and what is a "dead" metaphor cannot be decided by looking at the linguistic expression. Nor can it be decided by looking at the expression and the agent. These determinations can only be made with respect to a particular mental model at a particular point in time.

Conclusion

Mental models have been used as explanatory models for investigating the conceptualizations which individuals form of fairly structured domains. Little research has been done in using MMs in linguistics. Since CGs provide a basis for modelling MMs, it is now feasible to use MMs in computational linguistics. A linguistics based on mental models is in its infancy and many open questions remain. But MMs do offer a promising approach.

Notes

1. As Stephen Regoczei and I have argued, the domain of discourse is created by the discourse. This idea is consistent with the Whorfian hypothesis and much of post-structuralist thinking. See, Stephen Regoczei and Edwin Plantinga, "Ontology and Inventory: A Foundation for a Knowledge Acquisition Methodology", *Proceedings of the Workshop on Knowledge Acquisition*, Banff, Alberta, November 1986.

2. The merits of Sowa's approach are outlined in more detail in Regoczei and Plantinga.

3. At least one conceptual processor has been implemented. See Fargues, Landau, Dugourd, & Catach (1986).

4. George Lakoff and Mark Johnson's *Metaphors We Live By* has been helpful on this score and its popularity among computational linguists is undoubtedly due to Lakoff and Johnson's suggestion that metaphors are systematic and not *ad hoc*.

5. Such a metaphorical reading should be easy to generate for fans of Monty Python's Flying Circus who are familiar with their caricatures of accountants and bank clerks.

6. It may be helpful to think of Lakoff and Johnson's conceptual metaphors as inconsistent MMs of this type. Each one of their conceptual metaphors would have a different ontology. What is permissible in one ontology may be forbidden in another. The alternative to multiple ontologies is what we have now: one 'pure' ontology and lots of computation.

Chapter 9

Natural Language Generation

Chapter 9.1

GENERATION — A NEW FRONTIER OF NATURAL LANGUAGE PROCESSING?

Aravind K. Joshi

Comprehension and generation are the two complementary aspects of natural language processing (NLP). However, much of the research in NLP until recently has focussed on comprehension. Some of the reasons for this almost exclusive emphasis on comprehension are (1) the belief that comprehension is harder than generation, (2) problems in comprehension could be formulated in the AI paradigm developed for problems in perception, (3) the potential areas of applications seemed to call for comprehension more than generation, e.g., question-answer systems, where the answers can be presented in some fixed format or even in some non-linguistic fashion (such as tables), etc. Now there is a flurry of activity in generation, and we are definitely going to see a significant part of future NLP research devoted to generation. A key motivation for this interest in generation is the realization that many applications of NLP require that the response produced by a system must be flexible (i.e., not produced by filling in a fixed set of templates) and must often consist of a sequence of sentences (i.e., a text) which must have a textual structure (and not just an arbitrary sequence of sentences containing the necessary information). As the research in generation is taking roots, a number of interesting theoretical issues have become very important, and these are likely to determine the paradigm of research in this "new" area.

Some of the key issues discussed in addition to those listed in the introduction are as follows. Appelt has explored the notion of bidirectional grammars, i.e., grammars that can be used by processors of approximately equal computational complexity to parse and generate sentences of language. In this sense, he wants to treat comprehension and generation as strict inverses of each other. He suggests that by using bidirectional grammars the problems of maintaining consistency between comprehension and generation components when one of them changes can be eliminated. Kroch (1987) is concerned with the limits on the capacity of the human language generation mechanism, which translates preverbal messages into sentences of a natural language. His main point is that there are limits to the competence the generation mechanism is trying to model. He suggests some theoretical characterizations of these limits that should help in circumscribing the problem of generation. McDonald points out that although one could have a common representation of linguistic knowledge, the processes that draw on this knowledge for comprehension and generation cannot be the same because of the radical differences in information flow. He also points out that in generation it is difficult to ignore syntax and control of variation of linguistic form. Mann considers various aspects of lexicon, grammar, and discourse from the point of view of comprehension and generation. Although both comprehension and generation have to deal with all these problems, there are differences with respect to particular problems addressed in generation. He suggests that these differences arise because the technical problems that limit the quality of generated text are very different from the corresponding set of problems that limits the quality of comprehension. Marcus focusses on the problem of lexical choice, which has not received much attention in the work on generation so far. He suggests that if the generation systems are to be both fluent and portable, they must know about both words and meanings. He is concerned about the fact that much of the current research on generation has focussed on subtle and difficult matters such as responding appropriately to the user's intentions, correctly utilizing rhetorical structures, etc., but it has avoided the issue of what would make such systems mean the literal content of the words they use.

Comprehension and generation, when viewed as functions mapping from utterances to meanings and intentions and vice versa, can certainly be regarded as inverses of each other. However, these functions are enormously complex and therefore, although at the global level they are inverses of each other, the inverse transformation (i.e, computation of one function from the other) is not likely to be so direct. So, in this sense, there may be an asymmetry between comprehension and generation even at the theoretical level. There is an asymmetry certainly at the practical level. In comprehension, under certain circumstances, some of the linguistic knowledge may be ignored (of course, at some cost) by utilizing some higher levels of knowledge, which is required in any case. However, under the same circumstances, one cannot avoid the use of the very same linguistic knowledge in generation, the quality of the output becomes quite unacceptable to a human user very rapidly, otherwise. It is this asymmetry that, I think, will force us to examine in detail the relationship between grammar, lexicon, and message planning and may elucidate the relationship between linguistic knowledge and conceptual knowledge. All these questions are equally relevant to comprehension. However, work on generation seems to require us to be more sensitive to these relationships than we may have been in the past, when the focus was on comprehension only.

Comprehension and generation are not just inverses, they are also related to each other in another manner. The human generation mechanism also involves some monitoring of the output, presumably by the comprehension mechanism. Computer generation systems so far have not been concerned with this issue (as far as I know). The generation and comprehension components work independently, even if they share some procedures and data structures, they have no knowledge of each other. Whether or not comprehension and generation should be related to each other in this sense in a computer system is an open question and needs considerable attention. The panelists have not paid much attention to this question (one of them has declared it as a non-problem). Perhaps, the audience will make some contributions here.

Acknowledgments

This work is partially supported by DARPA grants NO0014-85-K-0018 and NO0014-85-K-0807, NSF grants MCS8219196-CER, MCS-82-07294, 1 RO1-HL-29985-01, U.S. Army grants DAA6-29-84-K-0061, DAAB07-84-K-F077, U.S. Air Force grant 82-NM-299, AI Center grants NSF-MCS-83-05221.

Chapter 9.2

NO BETTER, BUT NO WORSE, THAN PEOPLE

David D. McDonald

Generation versus Understanding

Natural language understanding and natural language generation systems could have the same knowledge of language.[1] They could even represent their knowledge in the same way, provided that it was a nonprocedural encoding.[2] However, the two processes that draw on the knowledge cannot be the same because of the radical differences in information flow: Decision making is a radically different kind of process than hypothesis maintenance. Understanding proceeds from a sequentially scanned text to content and intentions; generation does just the opposite. Understanding processes must cope with ambiguity and underspecification, problems that do not arise in generation (i.e., an audience receives more information from situationally controlled inferences than from the literal text). Generators on the other hand must on some basis choose from an oversupply of syntactic and lexical mechanisms all the while remaining consistent with the constraints imposed by grammaticality, linear order, and stylistic convention—a classic planning problem that now invites careful solutions closely tuned to the special demands of natural language.

Neither process is particularly more heuristic in its judgments than the other. If generation appears more algorithmic, it is because of the weakness of the present models of intentionality, situation, lexical sources, and especially audience reactions. People have no assurance that their choice of what to say will be effective; when programs have richer models they won't be certain either. For all but the most mundane tasks, the complexity of the circumstances will preclude fixed procedures. Instead, our programs will have to do what we appear to: make their choices heuristically, anticipating how the rest of the discourse will go if their assumptions are correct, and being prepared to adjust if it turns out that they are not. Any conclusion other than that the same knowledge structures underlie both understanding and generation would be a drastic philosophic jump from our common view of language as an interpersonal medium and an interface to thought. Any difficulties we presently have in making the same structures "go both ways" reflect weaknesses in our conceptual designs rather than facts about people.

In particular, present target representations for understanding are impoverished: inverting them leads to badly underspecified messages since they contain no information about deliberately adopted perspectives or connotated information (such as newness or value judgments), and very little about what the original speaker's goals were.

Generation is Special

To do good work in generation one is forced to come to grips with problems that other tasks are today able to ignore. Three examples: One cannot work on generation and ignore syntax. One cannot avoid accounting for the control of variation in linguistic form by making appeals to synonomy or cannonical form. One cannot passively accept the semantic representations of one's colleagues' knowledge-based reasoning systems without first determining that they are notationally and epistemologically able to support the distinctions that language makes. It is not clear to me that these are the sorts of issues that will draw the otherwise reluctant linguist to consider AI, but without question they draw the AI people who work on them to linguistics. Proficiency in the technicalities of syntax and morphology is obligatory in generation research.

More importantly, generation people must have a linguist's skill at arguing the consequences of alternative theoretical decisions: Working as we do from empirically unestablished models of intention and knowedge out to text, we have to justify our designs using indirect evidence and comparative reasoning, something that linguists are well trained for. This difficulty is in other respects a great advantage (one that linguists in my experience well appreciate) when we are working on today's cutting-edge problems in computational linguistics, such as the structure of discourse or the signaling of intended inferences and their relationship to underlying knowledge of the world and social behavior.

Our established tools such as example-driven comparative analysis do not fare well on these problems because of the enormous number of factors that contribute to them. Descriptive theories of underlying abstract structure are unsatisfying because the abstractions are slippery to evaluate. What they need is the synthetic approach provided by generation. The generation process converts abstract structures into concrete texts whose properties we can evaluate empirically. Theories of discourse now can stand or fall on whether they lead to effective conversations, theories of inferencing on whether texts based on them do evoke the intended conclusions.

Two Non-problems

The possibility of a program somehow generating things that no human could understand is a red herring.[3] People say things all the time that other people don't understand, yet we don't think anything unusual is happening. Usually the audience fails to make an expected inference rather than misunderstand some literal part of the utterance, a problem that can happen quite easily when the speaker misjudges what the audience already knows, or the speaker thinks that they share some judgment or context when they do not. Another source of the problem comes from the speaker thinking that a certain turn of phrase should signal a certain inference but the audience is opaque to that signal. The very same mistake could be made by a program—we cannot program them to be superhumanly aware of their audience. The only protection is incorporating into language interfaces the same kind of sensitivity to later audience reactions that we have ourselves. We know what the effect of following our inferences should be on our audiences, and we can sense when they have missed our intent.

We especially know how to feed back a communications failure onto our own generation strategies so that we will make different choices the next time we need to get across a similar idea. We should make our machines able to do the same. The problem of how best to match a system's input and output language abilities is likely to turn out to be a red herring as well, one that will go away naturally as soon as our understanding systems become as syntactically and lexically competent as our generators.[4]

The problem is that presently if the generator produces a more sophisticated construction than the understander can parse or uses a word that it does not know, then the human user, mimicking what the generator has done, will be frustrated when he turns out not to be understood. If this were the only difficulty, then it could be solved by straightforward software engineering: consistency tools would force one to drop items from the generator's repertoire that the understander did not know. Unfortunately the problem goes deeper than that. The mismatch is not the issue, since people's abilities do not match either: we all can understand markedly more than we would ever say. The real problem for a non-research interface is—direct queries for literal information aside—that machine understanding abilities are so far below the human level that any facile, inference-motivating output from the generator is going to suggest to the user that the system will understand things that it cannot.

Because of this, I personally would never include language input in a non-research interface today. Interactive graphics and menu facilities do not suffer from the ambiguity and scope of inferencing problems faced by language, and give a realistic picture of what a system is actually able to comprehend. Interfaces based on a "graphics in, graphics and speech out" paradigm have not been given enough study by the language and communications research community, and are likely to be a much better match to the deliberative and intentional abilities of the programs we can experiment with today.

Controling Decision-making

There are volumes to be said on how one could or should control for syntactic and lexical choice—this is the primary question that any computational theory of generation answers. Rather than attempt to summarize my position in the little space that remains, let me point out two issues that I believe distinguish much of the work presently going on; for a larger discussion of these see McDonald, Pustejovsky, and Vaughan (1987). The first issue is whether one attempts to make psychological claims with the form and operation of the generator. This is the more demanding road to take. It may also turn out to be the only one that provides for continuous extension and elaboration. Language, like vision, may be so tied up with the nature of the human mind and its computational properties that no design that goes against those properties will ever be more than a special purpose hack. Making claims with a computational process requires one to take exceptional discipline in designing the operations and representations it will use. Much of the explanatory load will be taken on by the restrictions on the mechanism's behavior, and these can be easily diluted by the kinds of programming conveniences that make a generator easier to engineer.

Adopting a psychological point of view can thus retard efforts to make a generator more competent. The second issue is how much generation knowledge is to be found in the non-linguistic, "underlying program" in whose service the generator is operating. The more that we take to be there, the greater the burder we place on our knowledge-based system colleagues to make sure that it is included; our theories, however, may have very good reasons for requiring it. This knowledge might be the direct encoding of rhetorically relevant structural relations: How deeply do we believe that the notions of "compare and contrast" are to be found in the mind or should be found in a program? It might be of lexical identities: Are the conceptual primitives of the underlying program fine-grained and closely matched to real words, or large-grained and abstract? It might also be in the modularity of the underlying system's information: Is it propositional and easily mapped onto kernel clauses and noun phrases, or does it have some drastically different organization?

Generation research today has the lion's share of the important computational linguistics problems. As more and more people work in it, it will quickly become the cutting edge, forcing extensions on understanding and knowledge representation if they are to match it as a source of insight into the nature of language and thought in the human mind. There is no appropriate goal for generation research short of matching human performance, part of which entails understanding the limits on that performance. We don't really know how good people are at using language; our experiments with mechanical speakers may someday tell us.

Notes

1. Presently they don't—generation has more. Generation demands knowledge of the conventions and heuristics of language use, but understanding systems today do not attempt to recover any such assessments

of why speakers say what they do in the particular manner that they do. They don't have to—the programs they are presently working for wouldn't appreciate the information if they did.

2. My own candidate for the neutral, shared encoding would be a catalogue of all the minimal elementary surface structure trees of the language, plus the rules that govern how they can be combined, e.g., a Tree Adjoining Grammar. Paired with each tree fragment would be a mapping function associating it with the situations in which its use was appropriate for the individual speaker. Besides my own use of TAGs (McDonald & Pustejovsky, 1985), this framework is a reasonable description of at least the PHRAN and PHRED systems at Berkeley (Jacobs, 1985), and Doug Appelt's (1985) use of functional unification grammar.

3. Since programs wouldn't talk to us if they didn't need to communicate, saying things to us that we don't understand would just be failing to achieve their own goals. Perhaps they might choose to talk this way to each other (though why should they, since given any commonality in their internal designs, telepathy would be much simpler and more satisfying), but if we give them any sensitivity to their audience's reactions (and how could communication be effective without it) they will quickly realize that we're missing the point of most of what they're saying to us and change their techniques.

4. It is trivial to specify a linguistically complex phrase and have a generator utter it by rote. Such canned or template-based text is often the best route to take in a practical interface. If the programmer is sure that the situation warrants the phrase, then it can safely be used, even though there may be no explicit model within the system from which the phrase could have been deliberately composed.

Chapter 9.3

BIDIRECTIONAL GRAMMARS AND THE DESIGN OF NATURAL LANGUAGE GENERATION SYSTEMS

Douglas E. Appelt

Bidirectional Grammars for Generation

Intuitively considered, a grammar is bidirectional if it can be used by processes of approximately equal computational complexity to parse and generate sentences of a language. Because we, as computational linguists, are concerned with the meaning of the sentences we process, a bidirectional grammar must specify a correspondence between sentences and meaning representations, and this correspondence must be represented in a manner that allows one to be computed from the other. Most research in computational linguistics has focused on one or the other of the two sides of the problem, with the result that relatively little attention has been given to the issues raised by the incorporation of a single grammar into a system for tasks of both comprehension and generation.

Clearly, if it were possible to have truly bidirectional grammars in which both parsing and generation processes were efficient, there would be some compelling reasons for adopting them. First, Occam's razor suggests that, if language behavior can be explained by hypothesizing only one linguistic representation, such an explanation is clearly preferable to two that are applicable in complementary circumstances. Also, from the practical standpoint of designing systems that will carry on sophisticated dialogues with their users, a single unified formalism for specifying the syntax and semantics of the language is likely to result in a simpler, more robust implementation. The problems of maintaining consistency between comprehension and generation components when one of them changes have been eliminated. The lexicon is also simpler because its entries need be made but once, and there is no problem of maintaining consistency between different lexical entries for understanding and generation.

It is obvious that not all grammars are bidirectional. The most fundamental requirement of any bidirectional grammar is that it be represented declaratively. If any information is represented procedurally, it must of necessity be represented differently for parsing and generation processes, resulting in an asymmetry between the two. Any change in the grammar would have to be made in two places to maintain the equivalence between the syntactic and semantic analyses given to sentences by each process. A grammar like DIAGRAM (Robinson, 1982) is an example of a grammar for which the encoding of linguistic information is primarily procedural; it is inconceivable how it could be used for generation.

Also, reversibility requires that the grammar define a one-to-one mapping from surface strings to some meaning representation. Presumably this representation would consist of a logical form specifying the predicate argument structure of the sentence, together with a set of functional features that distinguish sentences according to their pragmatic or functional role. For example, active and passive sentences have the same logical form, but different functional features.

The PATR-II formalism (Shieber, 1986), which is based on the unification of feature structures, has properties that make a bidirectional grammar possible. This formalism has been demonstrated to be very useful in encoding linguistic information and accommodates a wide variety of linguistic theories (Shieber, 1986, Uszkoreit, 1986). The PATR-II formalism has many elegant formal properties, including a denotational semantics (Pereira, 1984), but the one most important for bidirectionality is that the unification operation is associative and commutative. This implies that the result of unifying feature structures is independent of the order in which they are unified. This characteristic allows one to write grammar rules that satisfy the two properties cited above, without incorporating into the structure of the rules themselves any assumptions about the process that will employ these rules. Shieber (in progress) has developed a generation system based on PATR-II grammar rules. The grammar is bidirectional; given a logical form that a parser would have produced had it been given the sentence to parse, the generator will produce the same sentence. All features of the analysis are identical in both cases. If the combination of logical form and functional features is insufficient to determine a unique sentence, the generator can produce a set of sentences whose meanings unify with the specification.

Implications of Bidirectionality for System Design

Adopting a bidirectional grammar for a language-understanding and -generation system implies certain constraints on the system's design. Because the grammar for such a system must consist of declarative rules to be interpreted, it must provide exactly the same information to both parsing and generation processes. This implies that at least the lowest level of these processes must be symmetric.

The role the grammar plays in most understanding systems is to define a mapping from surface utterances to a logical form that abstracts predicate-argument structure and quantifier scoping from the sentence. This logical form provides a basis from which inferences are drawn, both to resolve anaphora and to determine the speaker's intentions behind the utterance. The symmetry requirement specifies that the generation process must produce a logical form (together with functional features) that determines the utterance to be produced. Figure 1 illustrates this basic design.

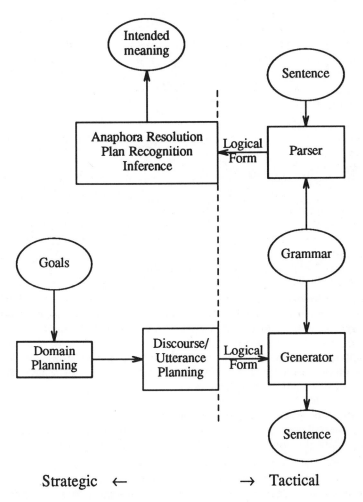

Figure 1: Organization of a Bidirectional System

In most understanding systems there is an easily identifiable boundary between the parsing/morphological component and the part of the system that draws inferences from the resulting logical form. The former is the only component that is concerned directly with the form and content of the grammatical rules, while the latter is the only one that is called upon to do general reasoning. It has been argued that intermediate fragments should undergo semantic and pragmatic analysis as an aid in resolving ambiguities such as prepositional-phrase attachment, as well as for inferring the intentions behind ill-formed input. At present, however, syntactic analysis has been sufficiently cheaper than semantic and pragmatic analysis to nullify any advantage that might be gained from integration of parsing and general inference. In any case, the inference procedures, while perhaps requiring access to certain features of the syntactic and semantic analysis, need not be concerned with the rules themselves. This modularity is clearly beneficial. The grammar, parser, and morphological analyzer, being a more or less self-contained unit, are portable among different applications, domains, and knowledge representation languages.

Because it is so plausible to assume there is a clearly defined "division of labor" among modules in the understanding part of the system, it is natural to wonder whether a similar modularization could exist on the generation side. Such a division of labor has been referred to as a distinction between strategy and tactics (McKeown, 1985; Thompson, 1977), which can be very roughly characterized as a distinction between "deciding what to say" and "deciding how to say it." This distinction has been adopted in some form in nearly every language generation system built to date (Appelt, 1985b and Danlos, 1984 are among the few to publish objections) although, as might be expected, different researchers have drawn the boundary in different ways.

In a bidirectional system, the obvious choice for a strategic/tactical modularization is at the point indicated in Figure 1. The strategic component of the system is the part that produces a logical form plus a set of functional features, while the tactical component realizes the strategic specification as an utterance. The implication of drawing the line as suggested is that there are such significant differences on either side of the line between the respective processes and the information they need to access that it makes sense to modularize the system in this manner. By symmetry with understanding, such a modularization is reasonable if, as in understanding, the strategic component need not be concerned with the specific details of grammar rules and, moreover, the tactical component does not have to perform general reasoning.

The Problem Posed by Strategic/Tactical Modularization

Shieber (personal communication) has observed a serious problem that arises as a result of the disparate treatment of logical forms by the strategic and tactical modules, which I shall refer to as the problem of logical-form equivalence. As far as the strategic component is concerned, logical forms are constructed because of their meaning. This does not mean that the strategic process is as simple as figuring out what propositions the hearer needs to know, then using those propositions as logical forms for utterances. In the KAMP system (Appelt, 1985b), for example, high-level actions were planned to satisfy requirements about the mental state of the hearer, but those specifications were refined into surface speech acts. The propositional content of the surface speech act serves as the logical form of the utterance finally produced. A good deal of reasoning is involved in the expansion of a plan to perform illocutionary acts into a plan incorporating particular surface speech acts. In fact, there is no one-to-one correspondence between illocutionary acts and the surface speech acts that realize them.

If detailed knowledge of grammar rules is to be avoided by the strategic component, the logical forms of surface speech acts must be planned because of their meaning. Any equivalent logical form is as good as the one actually chosen as long as it means the same thing. However, to a tactical generation component (as well as a parser), the logical form is an object that is important primarily because its syntax is related to an utterance in a certain way. Just as the logical form doesn't actually mean anything to a parser, it doesn't mean anything to the tactical generation component in this typical bidirectional system.

To see why this is a problem, consider a task from a domain of circuit repairs in which the speaker (the system) wants to inform the hearer that a particular resistor has a resistance of 500 ohms. The strategic planner may decide that its goal would be satisfied if it uttered a declarative sentence with the propositional content

Equation 1: {Resistance-of}({R1}, {ohm}(500)).

If the grammar is constructed properly, this logical form might result in the production of the sentence "The resistance of R1 is 500 ohms." However, it is unlikely that this statement would be specified by a general grammar of English as the logical form for the utterance, because its constituents bear no simple relationship to the constituents of any sentence. It is much more likely that the following statement would be the desired logical form:

Equation 2: ⍳ x {Resistance-of}({R1}, x) (x = {ohm}(500)).

Logical form (Eqn. 2) is more suitable as a representation of the intended utterance than (Eqn. 1) because there is a more natural mapping from constituents of the logical form to constituents of the sentence. It introduces the equality predicate, corresponding to the verb be, and the subject and predicate noun phrases correspond directly to arguments to the equality predicate.

But here is the problem: how can a procedure that cares only about the meaning of the logical form decide to produce Equation 2 rather than Equation 1? Or how is it to avoid producing Equation 3?

Equation 3: ⍳ x {Resistance-of}({R1}, x) ({ohm}(500) = x).

Commutativity of equality guarantees the logical equivalence of Equation 2 and Equation 3, but Equation 3 is likely to produce the sentence "Five hundred ohms is the resistance of R1." If the functional features state that the resistance is the topic of the sentence, then that plus Equation 3 constitutes an inconsistent specification; consequently no output will be produced at all.

Because the syntax of the logical form is significant, as well as its meaning, knowledge of what constitutes a legitimate logical form must be incorporated into the module that produces logical forms. Because the determination of which of several possible equivalent variations of a logical form actually corresponds to an utterance depends on the details of the grammar, the surface speech act planner must have detailed knowledge of the grammar— thus rendering meaningless the symmetric strategic/tactical modularization suggested above. The only other alternative would be to have the tactical generation component produce logically equivalent variations on the logical form until one is found that succeeds. There are two problems with this approach: (1) there are a great many possibilities for generating equivalent expressions, and (2) it may be possible to propose logical forms that, while logically equivalent to the intended utterance, are quite inappropriate. For example, the sentence "The resistance of R1 is 500 ohms and Bruce Springsteen is the Boss or Bruce Springsteen is not the Boss" is not ruled out in principle.

Obviously, a number of language generation systems have been developed that do not seem to suffer from this problem, so there must be a way out. If you examine a collection of better known generation systems (e.g., KAMP: Appelt, 1985b; TEXT: McKeown, 1985; MUMBLE: McDonald, 1980; NIGEL/PENMAN: Mann, 1983) you will see that, in spite of vast differences in general approach, coverage, application domain, grammar representation, and system interface, there is one very striking similarity: none of the grammars employed by these systems has an explicitly represented formal semantics. In theory, KAMP (to choose the example with which the author is most familiar) plans a surface speech act whose propositional content is intended as the logical form of the utterance produced. This is really in the nature of a white lie: the actual situation is that the logical form of the utterance is something logically equivalent to propostional content of the surface speech act. There is a procedure that uses the propositional content of the surface speech act as a specification to create an initial feature structure for the unification grammar. Knowledge about the way feature structures relate to the logical form (i.e., the semantics of the grammar) is embedded in this procedure. Although the details differ in each case, an analogous story can be told for each of the generation systems under consideration. There is no problem of logical-form equivalence because the logical form of the utterance plays no direct role in the generation process for any of these systems.

Of course, this procedural embedding of semantics is unsuitable for bidirectional systems. Naturally, none of the authors of the generation systems have made any positive claims about the suitability of their grammars for understanding. In fact, MUMBLE (McDonald, 1986), unlike the others, does not even represent its grammar as a set of rules that one can consider in isolation from the rest of the generation system. For those systems with explicit grammars, it may be possible to integrate an explicit formal semantics into the grammar and use it for understanding, but as long as a different procedurally embedded semantics is being used for generation, the grammar cannot be considered bidirectional.

At this time it is not clear what would be the best solution to the problem of logical-form equivalence for bidirectional systems, but there are several approaches that may prove fruitful. One approach is to allow the tactical component to substitute equivalent logical forms whenever it is necessary to produce a sentence, but to restrict the types of inferences that can be drawn. For example, if we assume that a PATR-II grammar is used by the parser and generator, allowing the unification algorithm to assume that equality and logical connectives in logical forms are associative and commutative is one way of making it possible for a limited class of inferences to be drawn during the tactical generation process. Whatever solution is ultimately adopted, it is our belief that the advantages inherent in bidirectional systems are sufficient to warrant a close examination of the problems entailed in a bidirectional design.

Acknowledgments:

This research was sponsored by the Nippon Telegraph and Telephone Corporation under a contract with SRI International. The author is grateful for comments by Phil Cohen on an earlier draft of this article.

REFERENCES,

SUBJECT INDEX,

and

AUTHOR INDEX

REFERENCES

Abelson, R. (1981). "Constraint, construal, and cognitive science." In the *Proceedings of the Third Annual Cognitive Science Conference* pp.1-9. Berkeley, California.

Allen, J.L., & Perrault, C.R. (1980). "Analyzing intention in utterances." *Artificial Intelligence*, (15), pp. 143-178.

Alshawi, H. (1986). *Processing dictionary definitions with phrasal pattern hierarchies.* Computer Laboratory, University of Cambridge.

Alshawi, H., Moore, R.C., Moran, D.B., & Pulman S.G. (1987). *Research Programme in Natural Language Processing.* Annual Report, SRI International Cambridge Computer Science Research Centre.

Amsler, R.A. (1980). *The Structure of the Merriam-Webster Pocket Dictionary.* Doctoral dissertation, TR-164, University of Texas, Austin.

Amsler, R. (1983). *Experimental research on knowledge representation for lexical disambiguation of full-text sources.* Research proposal for the NSSRI International, Menlo Park, California.

Appelt, D. (1985a). *Planning English Sentences.* Cambridge University Press.

Appelt, D. (1985b). "Some pragmatic issues in the planning of definite and indefinite noun phrases." In *Proceedings of the 23rd Annual Meeting of the Association for Computational Linguistics.*

Appelt, D. (1986). "Toward a plan-based theory of referring actions." In *Proceedings of the 3rd International Workshop on Language Generation.* Nijmegen, The Netherlands, August 19-23, 1986.

Atkins, B.T., Kegl, J., & Levin, B. (in press) "Explicit and Implicit Information in Dictionaries." In *Proceedings of the Conference on Advances in Lexicology.* Center for the New Oxford English Dictionary, Waterloo, Canada.

Backus J. (1978). "Can Programming Be Liberated from the von Neumann style? A Functional Style and Its Algebra of Programs." (1977 ACM Turing Award Lecture). *Communications of the ACM*, 21(8), pp. 613-641.

Barwise, K.J. (1986). *Noun phrases, generalized quantifiers and anaphora.* Center for the Study of Language and Information, Report 86-52, Stanford, California.

Bates, E., & MacWhinney, B. (1987). "Competition, variation and language learning: What is not universal in language acquisition." In B. MacWhinney (Ed.), *Mechanisms of language acquisition*. Lawrence Erlbaum Associates, Hillsdale, New Jersey.

Bell, A. (1986). *A parser and grammar for use in speech synthesis*. Cambridge University, M. Phil. Thesis.

Berlin, B., & Kay, P. (1969). *Basic color terms: Their universality and evolution*. University of California Press, Berkeley and Los Angeles.

Birnbaum, L. (1987), *Let's Put The AI Back In NLP*. Yale University, Department of Computer Science, New Haven, Connecticut.

Boguraev, B. (1986). "Machine-readable dictionaries and research in computational linguistics." In *Proceedings of a Workshop on Automating the Lexicon*. Grosseto, Italy.

Boyd, R. (1979). "Metaphor and theory change: What is 'metaphor' a metaphor for?''. In A. Ortony (Ed.), *Metaphor and thought*. Cambridge University Press, New York.

Bresnan, J. (Ed.). (1982). *The Mental Representation of Grammatical Relations*. MIT Press, Cambridge, Massachusetts.

Brown, J.S., & VanLehn, K. (1980). "Repair Theory: A Generative Theory of Bugs in Procedural Skills." *Cognitive Science*, 4, pp. 379-426.

Burstein, M.H. (1983). "Concept formation by incremental analogical reasoning and debugging." In *Proceedings of the 1983 International Machine Learning Workshop*. University of Illinois, Montecello.

Calzolari, N. (1984). "Detecting patterns in a lexical database." In *Proceedings of the Tenth International Congress on Computational Linguistics*, pp. 170-173. Stanford, California.

Carbonell, J. (1981). *Metaphor: An Inescapable Phenomenon in Natural Language Comprehension*. Technical Report, Computer Science Department, Carnegie-Mellon University. Pittsburg, Pennsylvania.

Carbonell, J.G. (1983), "Learning by analogy: Formulating and generalizing plans from past experience." In R.S. Michalski, J. Carbonell, & T. Mitchell (Eds.), *Machine Learning*. Tioga Publishing Company, Palo Alto, California.

Carnap, R. (1947). *Meaning and Necessity*. University of Chicago Press, Chicago, Illinois.

Carroll, J.M. (1985). "Review of Mental Models." In *Contemporary Psychology*, Volume 30, No. 9, p. 694.

Carroll, J.M. (1985). *What's in a Name?: An Essay in the Psychology of Reference*. W.H. Freeman and Company, New York.

Carver, D.J. et al., (Eds.) *Collins English Learner's Dictionary*. Collins, Ltd., London.

Chodorow, M., Byrd, R., & Heidorn, G. (1985). "Extracting semantic hierarchies from a large on-line dictionary". In *Proceedings of the 23rd Annual Meeting of the Association for Computational Linguistics*, pp. 299-304. Chicago, Illinois.

Chomsky, N. (1951). *Morphophonemics of Modern Hebrew*. MA thesis, University of Pennsylvania, Philadelphia. Published by Garland, New York, in 1979.

Chomsky, N. (1983). *Noam Chomsky on the Generative Enterprise* [in conversation with Riny Huybregts and Henk van Riemsdijk]. Foris, Dordrecht.

Chauvin, Y. (1986). "Hypermnesia, back-propagation, categorization, and semantics." In *Preprints of the Connectionist Models Summer School, Carnegie-Mellon University*, Pittsburgh, Pennsylvania.

Clark, E. (1973). "Non-Linguistic Strategies and the Acquisition of Word Meaning." *Cognition*, Vol. 2, pp. 161-182.

Clark, H. (1973). "Space, Time, Semantics and the Child." In T.E. Moore, (Ed.), *Cognitive Development and the Acquisition of Language*. Academic Press, New York.

Clark, H.H., & Clark, E.V. (1977). *Psychology and Language*. Harcourt, Brace, Jovanovich, New York.

Cohen, P.R. (1978).
On Knowing What to Say: Planning Speech Acts. Ph.D. thesis, University of Toronto.

Cohen, P.R. (1981). "The need for identification as a planned action." In *Proceedings of the Seventh International Joint Conference on Artificial Intelligence*, pp. 31-36.

Cohen, P.R. (1984). "Referring as requesting." In *Proceedings of the Tenth International Conference on Computational Linguistics*, pp. 207-211.

Cohen, P.R. (1984). "The Pragmatics of Referring and the Modality of Communication." *Computational Linguistics*, 10(2), pp. 97-146.

Cohen, P.R. and Perrault, C.R. (1979). "Elements of a plan-based theory of speech acts." *Cognitive Science*, 3, pp. 117-212.

Collins English Learner's Dictionary. (1974). (Carver, D.J, Wallace, M.J., Cameron, J., Eds.). Collins, London.

Collins Dictionary of the English Language. (1986). (P. Hanks, Ed.). Collins, London.

Cottrell, G.W. (1985). *A connectionist approach to word sense disambiguation*. (PhD thesis) Available as University of Rochester Computer Science Department TR-154.

Cottrell, G., Munro, P., & Zipser D. (1987). "Image compression by back propagation: A demonstration of extensional programming." In *Review of Cognitive Science*, N. Sharkey (Ed.). Ablex (in press). Also University of California at San Diego Institute of Cognitive Science, Technical Report 8702.

Cottrell, G.W., & Small, S.L. (1983). "A connectionist scheme for modelling word sense disambiguation." *Cognition and Brain Theory*, Vol. 6, pp. 89-120.

Dahl, D.A. (1987). "Determiners, Entities, and Contexts." In this volume.

Dahl, D.A. (1984a). "The Rise of Shared Knowledge." *Penn Review of Linguistics*, Vol. 8, pp. 1-14.

Dahl, D.A. (1984b). *Recognizing Specific Attributives.* Presented at the 59th Annual Meeting of the Linguistic Society of America, Baltimore, Maryland.

Dahl, D.A. (1986). *Focusing and Reference Resolution in PUNDIT.* Presented at AAAI, Philadelphia, Pennsylvania.

Danlos, L. (1984). "Conceptual and linguistic decisions in generation." In *Proceedings of the Tenth International Conference on Computational Linguistics*, pp. 501-504.

Davitz, J.R. (1969). *The language of emotion.* Academic Press, New York.

De Rivera, J. (1977). *A structural theory of the emotions.* International Universities Press, New York.

Derthick, M. (1986). *A connectionist knowledge representation system.* Thesis proposal, Carnegie-Mellon University, Department of Computer Science, Pittsburgh, Pennsylvania.

De Kleer, J., & Brown, J.S. (1985). "A Qualitative Physics Based on Confluences." In J.R. Hobbs & R.C. Moore (Eds.), *Formal Theories of the Commonsense World*, pp. 109-184. Ablex Publishing Corp.

Dijkstra, E. (1986). Public lecture at New Mexico State University, Las Cruces, New Mexico.

Dinneen, D.A. (1962). *A left-to-right generative grammar of French.* Unpublished Ph.D. dissertation, MIT.

Donnellan, K. (1971). "Reference and Definite Descriptions." In D.D. Steinberg & L.A. Jakobovits (Ed.), *Semantics.* Cambridge University Press, Cambridge.

Dunin-Keplicz, B. (1984). "Default reasoning in anaphora resolution." *Proceedings of the European AI Conference.*

Elman, J.L. & Zipser, D. (1986). *Discovering the structure of speech.* Paper presented at the 112th meeting of the Acoustical Society of America. Anaheim, California.

Fabry, R.S (1963). *Sentence generation and parsing with a single grammar.* Unpublished M.A. dissertation, MIT, Cambridge, Massachusetts.

Fahlman, S.E. (1979). *NETL: A System For Representing and Using Real-World Knowledge.* MIT Press, Cambridge, Massachusetts.

Falkenhainer, B., Forbus, K.D., & Gentner, D. (1986). "The structure-mapping engine." In *Proceedings of the American Association for Artificial Intelligence,* Philadelphia, Pennsylvania. Also (in press), *Artificial Intelligence.*

Fargues, J., Landau, M-C., Dugourd, D., & Catach, L. (1986). "Conceptual Graphs for Semantics and Knowledge Processing." *IBM Journal of Research and Development,* Vol. 30(1), pp. 70-79.

Feldman, J.A., & Ballard, D.H. (1982). "Connectionist models and their properties." *Cognitive Science,* Vol. 6(3), pp. 205-254.

Fine, K. (1978). "Model Theory for Modal Logic: Part I." *Journal of Philosophical Logic 7, pp. 125-156.*

Fine, K. (1978). "Model Theory for Modal Logic: Part II." *Journal of Philosophical Logic 7, pp. 277-306.*

Fine, K. (1978). "Model Theory for Modal Logic: Part III." *Journal of Philosophical Logic 7, pp. 293-307.*

Fodor, J. (1982). *The Modularity of Mind.* MIT Press, Cambridge, Massachusetts.

Frijda, N. (1986). *The emotions.* Cambridge University Press, New York.

Gazdar, G., Klein, E., Pullum, G., & Sag, I. (1985). *Generalized Phrase Structure Grammar.* Basil Blackwell, Oxford.

Gentner, D. (1982). "Are scientific analogies metaphors?" In D. Miall (Ed.), *Metaphor: Problems and perspectives.* Harvester press, Brighton, England.

Gentner, D. (1980). *The Structure of Analogical Models in Science.* BBN Report No. 4451, Bolt Beranek and Newman Inc., Cambridge, Massachusetts.

Gentner, D. (1982). "Are scientific analogies metaphors?" In D. Miall, (Ed.). *Metaphor: Problems and Perspectives.* Harvester Press, Hassocks, England.

Gentner, D. (1983). "Structure-mapping: A theoretical framework for analogy." *Cognitive Science,* 7(2), pp. 155-170.

Gentner, D., & Clement, C. (in press). "Evidence for relational selectivity in interpreting analogy and metaphor." To appear in G.H. Bower, (Ed). *The Psychology of Learning and Motiviation: Advances in Research and Theory,* Vol. 22. Academic Press, New York.

Gentner, D., Falkenhainer, B. and Skorstad, J. (1988). "Viewing Metaphor as Analogy: The Good, The Bad and The Ugly." In Helman, D.H. (Ed.), *Analogical Reasoning: Perspectives of Artificial Intelligence, Cognitive Science and Philosophy*, pp. 171-177. D. Reidel Publishing, Dordrecht, the Netherlands.

Golden, R. (1986). "Representing causal schemata in connectionist systems." In *Proceedings of the Eighth Annual Conference of the Cognitive Science Society*, pp. 13-22. Amherst, Massachusetts.

Goodman, B.A. (1984). *Communication and Miscommunication.* Ph.D. Thesis, University of Illinois, Urbana, IL. Also Report No. 5681, BBN Laboratories Inc., Cambridge, Massachusetts.

Goodman, B.A. (1985). "Repairing Reference Identification Failures by Relaxation." In *Proceedings of the 23rd Annual Meeting of the Association for Computational Linguistics*, pp. 204-217.

Goodman, B.A. (1987). "Reference and Reference Failures." In this volume.

Goodman, B.A. (1986). "Reference Identification and Reference Identification Failures." *Computational Linguistics*, 12(4), pp. 273-305.

Grossberg, S. (1987). "Competitive Learning: From Interactive Activation to Adaptive Resonance." *Cognitive Science*, 11(1).

Grosz, B.J. (1980). "Focusing and description in natural language dialogues." In Joshi, A., Sag, I., and Webber, B. (Eds). *Elements of Discourse Understanding,,* pp. 85-105. Cambridge University Press, Cambridge, England.

Grosz, B.J. (1977). *The Representation and Use of Focus in Dialogue Understanding.* Ph.D. Thesis, University of California, Berkeley, California. Also, Technical Note 151, Stanford Research Institute, Menlo Park, California.

Grosz, B.J., Joshi, A.K., & Weinstein, S. (1983). "Providing a unified account of definite noun phrases in discourse." *Proceedings of the Conference of the Association of Computational Linguistics.*

Grosz, B.J., & Sidner, C.L. (1985). "Discourse structure and the proper treatment of interruptions." In *Proceedings of the Ninth International Joint Conference on Artificial Intelligence*, pp. 832-839.

Gruber, J. (1976). *Lexical Structures in Syntax and Semantics.* North-Holland, Amsterdam.

Hale, K., & Laughren, M. (1983). "Preface to Dictionary Entries of Verbs." Unpublished manuscript, MIT, Cambridge, Massachusetts.

Hale, K., & Keyser, S.J. (1986). "A View from the Middle." *Lexicon Working Papers 10*, Center for Cognitive Science, MIT, Cambridge, MA.

Hanks, S., & McDermott, D. (1986). "Default reasoning, nonmonotonic logics, and the frame problem." *Proceedings of the Conference of the American Association of Artificial Intelligence.*

Hawkins, J.A. (1978). *Definiteness and Indefiniteness.* Humanities Press, Atlantic Highlands, New Jersey.

Hawkins, J.A. (1984). "A Note on Referent Identifiability and Co-Presence." *Journal of Pragmatics.*

Heidrich, C.M. (1975). "Should generative semantics be related to intensional logic?" In Keenan (Ed.), *The Formal Semantics of Natural Language,* Cambridge University Press, Cambridge.

Heim, I. R. (1982). *The Semantics of Definite and Indefinite Noun Phrases.* Ph.D. dissertation, University of Massachusetts, Amherst.

Hendler, J. (1986). *Integrating Marker-passing and Problem Solving.* Ph.D. thesis, Brown University, Providence, Rhode Island.

Henkin, L. (1950). "Completeness In the Theory of Types." *Journal of Symbolic Logic,* Vol. 15, [1], pp. 81-91.

Hewitt, C. (1972). *Description and theoretical analysis of PLANNER.* Ph.D. thesis, Massachusetts Institute of Technology, Department of Mathematics, Cambridge, Massachusetts.

Hillis, D. (1985). *The Connection Machine.* MIT Press, Cambridge, Massachusetts.

Hinton, G. E. (1981). "Implementing semantic networks in parallel hardware." In G.E. Hinton & J.A. Anderson (Eds.), *Parallel models of associative memory,* pp. 161-188. Lawrence Erlbaum Associates, Hillsdale, New Jersey.

Hinton, G. (1986). "Learning distributed representations of concepts." In *Proceedings of the Eighth Annual Conference of the Cognitive Science Society,* pp. 1-12. Amherst, Massachusetts.

Hinton, G.E., McClelland, J.L., & Rumelhart, D.E. (1986). "Distributed Representations." In D.E. Rumelhart, J.L. McClelland, & the PDP research group (Eds.), *Parallel distributed processing: Explorations in the microstructure of recognition. Volume I.* Bradford Books, Cambridge, Massachusetts.

Hinton, G., & Anderson, J., (Eds.) (1981). *Parallel Models of Associative Memory.* Lawrence Erlbaum Associates, Hillsdale, New Jersey.

Hjelmslev, L. (1935) "La Categorie du Cas." *Acta Jutlandica,* Vol. 7, pp.i-xiii, 1-184.

Hobbs, J.R. (1979). Metaphor, Schemata, and Selective Inference. Technical Note 204, SRI International, Menlo Park, California.

Hobbs, J.R., & Moore, R.C. (Eds.) (1985). *Formal theories of the common-sense world.* Ablex, Norwood, New Jersey.

Hobbs, J.R., Croft, W., Davies, T., Edwards, D., & Laws, K. (1986). "Commonsense Metaphysics and Lexical Semantics." *Proceedings of the 24th Annual Meeting of the Association for Computational Linguistics,* pp. 231-240.

Holyoak, K. (1985). "The pragmatics of analogical transfer." In G.H. Bower (Ed.), *The Psychology of Learning and Motiviation: Advances in Research and Theory,* Vol. 19. Academic Press, New York.

Hornby, A.S., & Cowie, A.P. (Eds.). (1974, first edition 1948). *Oxford Advanced Learner's Dictionary of Current English.* Oxford University Press, Oxford, England.

Jackendoff, R. (1983). *Semantics and Cognition.* MIT Press, Cambridge, Massachusetts.

Jacobs, P. (1985). *PHRED: A generator for natural language interfaces.* Report No. TR-85/198, Computer Science Department, Berkeley, California.

Johnson, R.E. (1970). "Recall of prose as a function of the structural importance of the linguistic unit." *Journal of Verbal Learning and Verbal Behavior,* 29, 12-20.

Johnson-Laird, P.N. (1983). *Mental Models: Towards a Cognitive Science of Language, Inference, and Consciousness.* Harvard University Press, Cambridge, Massachusetts.

Jordan, M. I. (1986). *Serial order: A parallel distributed processing approach.* ICS Report No. 8604, University of California, San Diego, Institute for Cognitive Science.

Joshi, A.K. (1985). "Tree Adjoining Grammars: How much context sensitivity is required to provide reasonable structural descriptions." In D. Dowty, L. Karttunen, & A. Zwicky (Eds.), *Natural Language Processing.* Cambridge University Press, Cambridge.

Joshi, A.K., Webber, B.L., & Weischedel, R.M. (1986). *Some aspects of default reasoning in interactive discourse.* University of Pennsylvania Technical Note, MS-CIS-86-27, Philadelphia.

Joshi, A.K. (1978). "A Note on Partial Match of Descriptions: Can One Simultaneously Question (Retrieve) and Inform (Update)?" *Theoretical Issues in Natural Language Processing-2,* pp. 184-186. Urbana, Illinois.

Kamp, H. (1981). "A theory of truth and semantic representation." In J. Groenendijk et al. (Eds.), *Formal Methods in the Study of Language.* Mathematics Center, Amsterdam.

Kaplan, R., & Bresnan, J. (1982). "Lexical functional grammar: A formal system for grammatical representation." In J. Bresnan (Ed.), *The mental representation of grammatical relations.* MIT press, Cambridge, Massachusetts.

Kasher, A. (1985). "Philosophy and discourse analysis." In *Handbook of Discourse Analysis,* Vol. 1, Chapter 9, pp. 231-248. Academic Press, New York.

Kasher, A. (1977). "What is a theory of use?" *Journal of Pragmatics,* 1, pp. 105-120.

Kawamoto, A. II. (1985). *Dynamic processes in the (re)solution of lexical ambiguity.* Unpublished doctoral dissertation, Brown University, Providence, Rhode Island.

Kay, M. (1979). "Functional Grammar." In C. Chiarello et al. (Eds.), *Proceedings of 5th annual meeting of the Berkeley Linguistics Society,* pp. 142-158. University of California, Berkeley.

Kautz, H.K., & Allen, J.F. (1986). "Generalized plan recognition." In *Proceedings of the Conference of the American Association of Artificial Intelligence.*

Kroch, A. (1987). "Limits on the Human Sentence Generator." In proceedings of TINLAP-3: Theoretical Issues in Natural Language Processing 3 — Position Papers. New Mexico State University, 7-9 January, 1987. ACL Proceedings series, Association for Computational Linguistics, Morristown, NJ.

Kronfeld, A. (1986). "Donnellan's distinction and a computational model of reference." In *Proceedings of the 24th Annual Meeting of the Association for Computational Linguistics,* pp. 186-191.

Kronfeld, A. (1987). "Goals of Referring Acts." In this volume.

Kronfeld, A. (1985). "Reference and Denotation: The Descriptive Model." Technical Note 368, Artificial Intelligence Center, SRI International, October 1985.

Kronfeld, A. (1981). The Referential Attributive Distinction and the Conceptual-Descriptive Theory of Reference. Ph.D. thesis, University of California at Berkeley.

Lakoff, G. (1987). *Women, Fire and Dangerous Things.* University of Chicago Press, Chicago.

Lakoff, G., & Johnson, M. (1980). *Metaphors We Live By,* University of Chicago Press, Chicago.

Lenat, D., Prakash, M., & Shepherd, M. (1986). "CYC: Using common sense knowledge to overcome brittleness and knowledge acquisition bottlenecks." *AI Magazine*, 6(4), pp. 65-92.

Lesk, M. (1986). *Automatic sense disambiguation: how to tell a pine cone from an ice cream cone.* Bell Communications Research, Morristown, New Jersey.

Levin, B. (1983). *On the Nature of Ergativity.* Unpublished doctoral dissertation, MIT, Cambridge, Massachusetts.

Lewis, D. (1972). "General Semantics." In Davidson & Harman (Eds.), *Semantics of Natural Language.* Reidel, Dordrecht.

Lifschitz, V. (1986). "Pointwise circumscription." In *Proceedings of the Conference of the American Association of Artificial Intelligence.*

Longman Dictionary of Contemporary English. (1978). (Proctor, P. Ed.). Longman, London.

Luria, M.C. (1986). "How to Identify Potential Plan Failures." In *Proceedings of the Third Annual Workshop on Conceptual Information Processing.* Philadelphia, Pennsylvania.

MacWhinney, B.J. (1987). "The competition model." In B. MacWhinney, (Ed.), *Mechanisms of language acquisition.* Lawrence Erlbaum Associates, Hillsdale, New Jersey.

Mann, W.C. (1983). "An overview of the PENMAN text generation system." In *Proceedings of the Conference of the American Association for Artificial Intelligence*, pp. 261-265.

Marcus, M. P. (1980). *A theory of syntactic recognition for natural language.* MIT Press, Cambridge, Massachusetts.

Marcus, M., Hindle, D., and Fleck, M. (1983). "D-theory: Talking about Talking about Trees." In *Proceedings of the 21st Conference of the Association for Computational Linguistics,* Cambridge, Massachusetts, pp. 129-136.

Marslen-Wilson, W., & Tyler, L.K. (1980). "The temporal structure of spoken language understanding." *Cognition,* (8), pp. 1-72.

Masterman, M., Needham, R.M., Sparck Jones, K., & Mayoh, B. (1957). "*AGRICOLA INCURVO TERRAM DIMOVIT ARATRO*": *First stage translation into English with the aid of Roget's Thesaurus.* Report No. ML92, Cambridge Language Research Unit, Cambridge.

Mayfield, J. (1986). "When to Keep Thinking." In the *Proceedings of the Third Annual Workshop on Conceptual Information Processing.* Philadelphia, Pennsylvania.

McClelland, J.L. (in press). "How we use what we know in reading: An interactive activation approach." In M. Coltheart (Ed.), *Attention and performance XII: The psychology of reading.* Lawrence Erlbaum Associates, Hillsdale, New Jersey.

McClelland, J.L., & Kawamoto, A. (1986). "Mechanisms of Sentence Processing: Assigning Roles to Constituents." In Rumelhart & McClelland (Eds.), *Parallel Distributed Processing: Explorations in the Microstructures of Cognition*, Vol. 2. Bradford Books, Cambridge, Massachusetts.

McClelland, J.L., Rumelhart, D.E., and the PDP Research Group. (1986). *Parallel Distributed Processing: Explorations in the Microstructure of Cognition.* MIT Pr., Cambridge, Massachusetts.

McDonald, D.D. (1980). *Natural Language Generation as a Process of Decision Making under Constraint.* Ph.D. thesis, MIT, Cambridge, Massachusetts.

McDonald, D.D. (1986). *Natural Language Generation: Complexities and Techniques.* Counselor Project Technical Memo 14, University of Massachusetts, Amherst, Massachusetts.

McDonald, D., & Pustejovsky, J. (1985). "TAGs as a Grammatical Formalism for Generation." *Proceedings of the Conference of the Association for Computational Lignuistics,* Chicago, pp. 94-103.

McDonald, D., Pustejovsky, J., & Vaughan, M. (1987). "Factors Contributing to Efficiency in Natural Language Generation." In Kempen (Ed.), *Papers from the Third International Workshop on Language Generation,* The Netherlands, Martinus Nijhoff Press (Kluwer).

McKeown, K. (1985). *Text Generation.* Cambridge University Press, Cambridge.

McKinsey, J.C.C., and Tarski, A. (1946). "On Closed Elements in Closure Algebra," *Annals of Mathematics,* 47, pp. 122-162.

McKinsey, J.C.C., and Tarski, A. (1948). "Some Theorems about the Sentential Calculi of Lewis and Heyting," *Journal of Symbolic Logic* 13(1), pp. 1-15.

McKinsey, J.C.C., and Tarski, A. (1944). "The Algebra of Topology," Annals of Mathematics 45, pp. 141-191.

Mercer, R., & Reiter, R. (1982). *The representation of defaults using defaults.* University of British Columbia Tech. Report.

Miller, G.A., Gelanter, E. & Pribram, K. (1954). *Plans and the Structure of Behavior.* Holt, Rinehart, and Winston, New York.

Miller, G.A. (1985). "Dictionaries of the Mind." *Proceedings of the 23th Annual Meeting of the Association for Computational Linguistics,* pp. 305-314. Chicago.

Minsky, M.L. (1980). "K-lines: a theory of memory." *Cognitive Science,* (4), pp.117-133.

Minsky, M.L. (1986). *The Society of Mind.* Simon and Schuster, New York.

Montague, R. (1974). Formal Philosophy: Selected papers of Richard Montague, (Richmond H. Thomason, Ed.). Yale University Pr., New Haven.

Nagy, W. (1974). *Figurative Patterns and Redundancy in the Lexicon*. Ph.D. dissertation, University of California at San Diego.

Newell, A. (1980). "Physical Symbol Systems." *Cognitive Science*, 4(4), pp. 135-183.

Nii, H.P. (1986). "Blackboard Systems Part Two: Blackboard Application Systems." *AI Magazine*, 7(3), pp. 82-106.

Nilsson, N.J. (1983). "Artificial Intelligence Prepares for 2001." *AI Magazine*, 4(4), pp. 7-14.

Norman, D. (1983). "Some Observations on Mental Models." In D. Gentner & A. L. Stevens (Eds.), *Mental Models*, pp. 7-14. Lawrence Erlbaum Associates, Hillsdale, New Jersey.

Ortony, A. (Ed.). (1979). *Metaphor and thought*. Cambridge University Press, New York.

Ortony, A. (1975), "Why metaphors are necessary and not just nice." *Educational Theory*, 25, pp. 45-53.

Ortony, A., Clore, G.L. & Collins, A. (1988). *The cognitive structure of emotions*. Cambridge University Press, New York.

Ortony, A., & Fainsilber, L. (1987). *The Role Of Metaphors In Descriptions Of Emotions*. University of Illinois, Urbana-Champaign.

Oxford Advanced Learner's Dictionary of Current English. (1974). (A.S. Hornby, Ed.). Oxford University Pr., London.

Oxford Universal English Dictionary on Historical Principles. (1936). (W. Little and H.W. Fowler, Ed.). Clarendon Pr., Oxford.

Palmer, M.S., Dahl, D.A., Passonneau-Schiffman, R., Hirschman, L. Linebarger, M., & Dowding, J. (1986). "Recovering Implicit Information." In *Proceedings of the Conference of the Association for Computational Linguistics*, Columbia University, New York.

Pentland, A.P., & Fischler, M.A. (1983). "A more rational view of logic or, up against the wall, logic imperialists!" *AI Magazine*, 4(4), pp. 15-18.

Pereira, F., & Warren, D. (1980). "Definite Clause Grammars for Language Analysis." *Artificial Intelligence*, 13, pp. 231-278.

Pereira, F.C.N., & Shieber, S.M. (1984). "The semantics of grammar formalisms seen as computer languages." In *Proceedings of the Tenth International Conference on Computational Linguistics*, pp. 123-129, Stanford University, Stanford, California.

Perrault, C.R., (in preparation). *An application of default logic to speech act theory*.

Plantinga, E. (1986). "Who Decides What Metaphors Mean?" In *Proceedings of the Conference on Computing and the Humanities—Today's Research, Tomorrow's Teaching*, pp. 194-204. Toronto, Ontario, Canada.

Potts, T. (1975). "Model theory and linguistics." In E. Keenan (Ed.), *Formal Semantics of Natural Language*. Cambridge University Press, Cambridge, England.

Prince, E.F. (1981). "Toward a Taxonomy of Given-New Information." In P. Cole (Ed.), *Radical Pragmatics*. Academic Press, New York.

Proctor, P. (Ed.). (1978). *Longman Dictionary of Contemporary English*. Longman, London.

Pylyshyn, Z.W. (1980). "Computation and cognition: Issues in the foundations of cognitive science." *The Behavioral and Brain Sciences*, 3, pp. 111-169.

Quillian, M.R. (1968). "Semantic memory." In M. Minsky (Ed.), *Semantic information processing*. MIT Press, Cambridge, Massachusetts.

Reddy, M. (1979). "The Conduit Metaphor—A Case of Frame Conflict in our Language About Language." In A. Ortony (Ed.), *Metaphor and Thought*. Cambridge University Press, Cambridge.

Regoczei, S., & Plantinga, E. (1986). "Ontology and Inventory: A Foundation for a Knowledge Acquisition Methodology." In *Proceedings of the Workshop on Knowledge Acquisition*, Banff, Alberta, Canada.

Reiter, R. (1980). "A Logic for default reasoning." *Artificial Intelligence*, 13.

Ritchie, G.D. (1986). "The computational complexity of sentence derivation in functional unification grammar." In *Proceedings of the 11th International Conference on Computational Linguistics*, pp. 584-586, Bonn.

Robinson, J. (1982). "DIAGRAM: a grammar for dialogues." *Communications of the ACM*, 25(1), pp. 27-47.

Rosch, E., & Mervis, C. (1975). "Family resemblances: Studies in the internal structure of categories." *Cognitive Psychology*, 7, pp. 573-605.

Rumelhart, D.E., & McClelland, J.L. and the PDP Research Group (Eds.). (1986). *Parallel Distributed Processing: Explorations in the microstructure of cognition*, Volumes 1 and 2. MIT Press, Cambridge, Massachusetts.

Rumelhart, D.E., Hinton, G.E., & Williams, R.J. (1986). "Learning internal representations by error propagation." In D.E. Rumelhart, J.L. McClelland, and the PDP research group (Eds.), *Parallel Distributed Processing, Vol. I*. MIT Press, Cambridge, Massachusetts.

Rumelhart, D.E., Smolensky, P.E., McClelland, J.L., & Hinton, G.E. (1986). "Schemata and sequential thought processes in PDP models." In D. E.

Rumelhart & J.L. McClelland, (Eds.), *Parallel Distributed Processing: Explorations in the microstructure of cognition*, Vol. 2. Bradford, Cambridge, Massachusetts.

Sabot, G. (1986). *Bulk Processing of Text on a Massively Parallel Computer*. Technical Report 86-2, Thinking Machines Corporation, Cambridge, Massachusetts.

Satterthwait, A. C. (1962). *Parallel sentence-construction grammars of Arabic and English*. Unpublished doctoral dissertation, Harvard University, Cambridge, Massachusetts.

Schiffer, S. (1987). Remnants of Meaning. MIT Press, Cambridge, MA.

Searle, J.R. (1983). *Intentionality: an Essay in the Philosophy of Mind*. Cambridge University Press, Cambridge, England.

Seidenberg, M.S., Tanenhaus, M.K., & Leiman, J.M. (1980). *The time course of lexical ambiguity resolution in context*. Technical Report 164, Center for the Study of Reading, University of Illinois, Urbana.

Sejnowski, T.J., & Rosenberg, C.R. (1986). *NETtalk: A Parallel Network that Learns to Read Aloud*. Technical Report JHU/EECS-86-01, Electrical Engineering and Computer Science, The Johns Hopkins University, Baltimore.

Selman, B., & Hirst, G. (1985). "A rule-based connectionist parsing system." In *Proceedings of the Conference of the Cognitive Science Society*, pp. 212-221, Irvine, California.

Sharkey, N.E., Sutcliffe, R.F.E., & Wobcke, W.R. (1986). "Mixing binary and continuous connection schemes for knowledge access." In *Proceedings of the National Conference on Artificial Intelligence*, pp. 262-266. Philadelphia.

Shastri, L., & Feldman J.A. (1985). "Evidential reasoning in semantic networks: A formal theory." In *Proceedings of the International Joint Cconference on Artificial Intelligence*, pp. 465-474. Los Angeles.

Shieber, S.M. (1984). "The design of a computer language for linguistic information." In *Proceedings of COLING84*, pp. 362-366.

Shieber, S.M. (1985). "Criteria for designing computer facilities for linguistic analysis." *Linguistics*, 23, pp. 189-211.

Shieber, S.M. (1985). "Using restrictions to extend parsing algorithms for complex-feature-based formalisms." In *Proceedings of the Conference of the Association for Computational Linguistics*. University of Chicago, Chicago.

Shieber, S. (1986). *An Introduction to Unification-Based Approaches to Grammar*. Lecture Note Series Vol. 4, Center For the Study of Language and Information, Stanford, California.

Shieber, S. (1986). "A simple reconstruction of GPSG." In *Proceedings of the Eleventh International Conference on Computational Linguistics*, pp. 211-215.

Shieber, S.M. (1987). "Separating Linguistic Analyses from Linguistic Theories." In P. Whitelock et al. (Eds.), *Linguistic Theory and Computer Applications*, pp. 1-36. Academic Press, London.

Shieber, S.M. (1987). *An Introduction to Unification-Based Approaches to Grammar*. University of Chicago Press, Chicago, Illinois.

Shoham, Y. (1986). "Chronological ignorance." In *Proceedings of the Conference of the American Association of Artifical Intelligence*.

Sidner, C. L. (1979). *Towards a Computational Theory of Definite Anaphora Comprehension in English Discourse*. MIT-AI TR-537, Cambridge, Massachusetts.

Small, S. (1980). *Word expert parsing: A theory of distributed word-based natural language understanding*. Technical Report 954, Department of Computer Science, University of Maryland, College Park.

Smith, E.E., & Medin, D. (1981). *Categories and Concepts*. Harvard University Press, Cambridge, Massachusetts.

Schmolze, J. (1987). *Physics for Robots*, BBN Technical Report No. 6222, Bolt, Beranek and Newman Inc., Cambridge, Massachusetts.

Sowa, J. (1984). *Conceptual Structures: Information Processing in Mind and Machine*. Addison-Wesley, Reading, Massachusetts.

St. John, M.F. (1986). *Reconstructive memory for sentences*. Working paper, Department of Psychology, Carnegie-Mellon University, Pittsburgh, Pennsylvania.

Stanfill, C., & Waltz, D. (1986). *Memory-based reasoning*. Technical Report No. 86-7, Thinking Machines Corp, Cambridge, Massachusetts.

Stanfill, C., & Waltz, D.L. (1986). "Toward memory-based reasoning." *Communications of the ACM*, 29(12), pp. 1213-1228.

Steiner, G. (1975). *After Babel: Aspects of Translation*. Oxford University Press, New York.

Tarski, A. (1956). "Foundations of the Geometry of Solids," reprinted in 1956 in *Logic, Semantics, and Metamathematics*, Oxford University Press, Oxford.

Tarski, A. (1938, repr. 1956). "Sentential Calculus and Topology." In *Logic, Semantics, Metamathematics*, Oxford University Press, pp. 421-459. Reprinted from "Der Aussagenkalkül und die topologie" (German translation of original Polish), *Fundamenta mathematicae* 31(1938), pp. 103-134.

Thesaurus of English Words and Phrases: Roget's International Thesaurus. (1977). Harper and Row, NY.

Thompson. H. (1977). "Strategy and tactics: A model for language production." In *Papers from the Thirteenth Regional Meeting,* Chicago Linguistics Society.

Touretzky, D.S., & Hinton, G.E. (1985). "Symbols Among Neurons: Details of a Connectionist Inference Architecture." In *Proceedings of International Joint Conference on Artificial Intelligence,* pp. 238-243. Los Angeles, California.

Touretzky, D.S. (1986). "BoltzCons: Reconciling connectionism with the recursive nature of stacks and trees." In *Proceedings of the Eighth Annual Conference of the Cognitive Science Society,* pp. 522-530. Amherst, Massachusetts.

Uszkoreit, H. (1986). "Categorial unification grammars." In *Proceedings of the International Conference on Computational Linguistics,* Bonn, pp. 187-194.

Vijay-Shanker, K., Weir, D., & Joshi, A.K. (1986). "Tree adjoining and head wrapping." In *Proceedings of the International Conference on Computational Linguistics,* Bonn.

Vosniadou, S. & Ortony, A. (Eds.). (1989). *Similarity and analogical reasoning.* New York: Cambridge University Press.

Walker, Donald E. (forthcoming). "Introduction." In Donald E. Walker, Antonio Zampolli, and Nicoletta Calzolari (Eds.), *Automating the Lexicon: Research and Practice in a Multilingual Environment.* To be published by Cambridge University Press.

Walker, D.E., & Amsler, R.A. (1986). "The Use of Machine-Readable Dictionaries in Sublanguage Analysis." In R. Grishman & R. Kittredge (Eds.), *Analyzing Language in Restricted Domains: Sublanguage Description and Processing,* pp. 69-83. Lawrence Erlbaum Associates, Hillsdale, New Jersey.

Waltz, D.L., & Pollack, J.B. (1985). "Massively parallel parsing: a strongly interactive model of natural language interpretation." *Cognitive Science,* 9(1), pp. 51-74.

Webber, B.L. (1978). "Description formation and discourse model synthesis." In *Proceedings of the Second Tinlap Conference,* University of Illinois, Urbana-Champaign, pp. 42-50.

Webber, B.L. (1987). "Event reference." In this volume.

Webber, B.L. (1983). "So what can we talk about now?" In Brady & Berwick (Eds.), *Computational Models of Discourse.* MIT Press, Cambridge, Massachusetts.

Webster's Seventh New Collegiate Dictionary. 1965. G. and C. Merriam Co., NY.

Weintraub, D.K. (1970). *The syntax of some English relative clauses.* Unpublished Ph.D. dissertation, University of Chicago, Chicago, Illinois.

Wilensky, R. (1983). *Planning and Understanding: A Computational Approach to Human Reasoning.* Addison Wesley, New York.

Wilensky, R., Mayfield, J., Chin, D., Luria, M., Martin, J., and Wu, D. (1988). "The Berkeley Unix Consultant Project". *Computational Linguistics,* 14, pp. 4-.

Wilks, Y. (1971). "Decidability and Natural Language." *Mind.*

Wilks, Y. (1974). "One small head: Models and theories in linguistics." *Foundations of Language 11:77-95.*

Wilks, Y. (1976). "Parsing English II." In Charniak & Wilks (Eds.), *Computational Semantics,* pp. 155-184. North-Holland, Amsterdam.

Wilks, Y. (1977). "Good and bad arguments about semantic primitives." *Communication and Cognition,* 10, pp. 181-221.

Wilks, Y. (1984). "Is Frege's principle trivial or false?" In *Proceedings of the Annual Conference of the Linguistics Association of Great Britain,,* University of Essex, England.

Winograd, T. (1985). "Moving the semantic fulcrum." *Linguistics & Philosophy.*

Woods, W. (1981). "Procedural semantics as a theory of meaning." In Joshi, A., Webber, B., and Sag, I. (Eds.), *Elements of discourse understanding.* Cambridge University Press, Cambridge, England.

Yngve, V.H. (1958). "A programming language for mechanical translation." *Mechanical Translation,* 5, pp. 25-41.

Yngve, V.H. (1967). "MT at MIT 1965." In A.D. Booth (Ed.), *Machine Translation,* pp. 452-523. North-Holland, Amsterdam.

SUBJECT INDEX

Action subsumption: 151; theory of action: 150 (See also Knowledge)

Analogy: as alternative to situation description for describing emotion, 179; as similarities of object description and/or relational structures, 172 ff.

Artificial Intelligence (AI): xiii, 3, 115, 119 ff., 133, 187, 191; as part of Cognitive Science, 118.

Associationist: xviii, 31, 47, 56 ff. (See also Knowledge); activation patterns, 57, 59, 61-62, 64-5, 67-70, 71, 73, 75-76, 78-80, 81-83, 86, 93, 95 ff., 102, 160; associative memory, 101, 161; link weight and content, 59, 61, 65, 67, 75; nets as non-static data structures, 89; node as co-occurrence in schema, 61; node as concept or conceptual relation, 185; node as module, 60; node as object, 75; node as word-sense, 60, 64-65; semantic and inheritance nets, xvi, 166 ff.; systemic networks, 33, 102; vs. connectionist, 58. (See also Completeness, Inheritance, Metaphor types)

Augmented Transition Network (ATN): 29, 47, 56, 119.

Automation: office, 5; reading, 8; taxonomy, 9.

Autonomy of syntax: as definitional vs. functional, 120; resultant exclusion of semantics, 120.

Belief, mutual: (See Knowledge, shared).

Bi-directionality: of analysis and production of strings by unification methods, 39; due to declarative nature, 38.

COMIT: 29-31 (See also Turing equivalence of COMIT and PATR, Unification vs. merger rules, Rewrite rules).

Case roles: 78, 92, 136; as arguments or features, 98, 103; as input to connectionist word-sense disambiguation, 67; as predicate-argument structure of type: thematic (source, goal, theme), 23, deep case or "semantic" (agent, patient), 23, 80, surface (subject, object), 23, 80; assignment by successive unifications, 43; connectionist reasoning and frames, 87; distributed in connectionist nets, 77, 83, 94; examples, 24-26, 66, 76, 79, 103; Fillmore type case grammars, 33, 43; interact with verb class, 26; predicate-argument changes: shown by [variable/instantiated] features on syntactic constituent, 33 (See also Case roles, transitivity alternation); transitivity alternation, 26, 45.

connectionist method, 103 (See also Microfeatures); events, abstraction, individualization and axiomatizability of natural world/language, 142.

Head Driven Phrase Structure Grammar (HPSG): 31, 37.

Head Grammar (HG): 37, 38.

Heuristics: 56-57.

Higher order logics: 141 ff., 145; completeness of Henkin's w-order logic, 124.

Individuating set: (See Constraints, identification (reference/individuation)).

Inference patterns: 144, 175, 201 (See also Associationist, activation patterns; Relations, higher order); vs. language constraints, 195. (See Constraints, matchup)

Inferences in modelling discourse motivation: 107, 109, 120, 136, 195, 200; metaphor for vividness, 181; rule known but not applied, in speech acts, 159. (See also Knowledge; Metaphor types)

Information flow: from situation vs. from text.

Information retrieval: 5.

Information science: 3, 68.

Inheritance: 9, 94; semantic hierarchy, 21, 74-75, 76, 166-168.

Innate: (See Cognitive)

Interfaces: natural language, 2, 7, 62; workstations, 4.

KL-ONE: strict type hierarchy, 9.

KL-TWO: propositional x typal, 9.

KLONE: xviii.

KRYPTON: propositional x typal, 9.

Knowledge Acquisition Bottleneck: 7, 95. (See also Knowledge, acquisition; Knowledge, learning)

Knowledge Representation (KR): 155, 177. (See Knowledge, Constraints, KRL, Situation semantics, Plans/Intentions of speaker, etc.)

Knowledge Representation Language (KRL): strict type hierarchy, 9.

Knowledge bases: for communication vs. events prediction, 20.

Knowledge: about events, 89, 149, 151; acquisition from text, 11, 154 ff., 196 ; applied to semantic interpretation, 126, 127, 134, 141, 173, 178 (See also Formal logic semantics); as a metaphysics for formal semantics, 147; commonsense 3, 8, 16, 26, 74, 126, 130, 134; commonsense vs. specialized, 8, 139, 142; encoded in net, 93, 103, 137; events, abstraction, individualization and axiomatizability of natural world/language, 142; experiential, 26, 56, 61, 88, 93, 178; formalized commonsense, 20,

AUTHOR INDEX